SHIFTING CLIMATES, SHIFTING PEOPLE

SHIFTING CLIMATES, SHIFTING PEOPLE

Edited by Miguel A. De La Torre

the pilgrim press

The Pilgrim Press, 1300 East 9th Street
Cleveland, Ohio 44114
thepilgrimpress.com

© 2022 Miguel A. De La Torre

Published 2022.

Scripture quotations, unless otherwise noted, are from the New Revised Standard Version of the Bible, © 1989 by the Division of Christian Education of the National Council of Churches of Christ in the United States of America. Used by permission. Changes have been made for inclusivity. Figure 1, chapter 1 by Monica Curca of Climate Refugee Stories, used by permission, all rights reserved. Figure 2, chapter 10 by Faafetai Aiava, used by permission, all rights reserved.

Printed on acid-free paper.

Library of Congress Cataloging-in-Publication Data on file.
LCCN: 2022935372

ISBN 978-0-8298-0012-8 (paper)
ISBN 978-0-8298-0013-5 (ebook)

Printed in The United States of America.

 *Dedicated to* DESMOND GRAY

Contents

INTRODUCTION

Miguel A. De La Torre

DURING A SEASON OF DEATH, as the different variants of the coronavirus wreak havoc throughout the globe, new life emerged. As the editing of this manuscript was being finalized during the month of November 2021, I was blessed with my first grandchild—Desmond Grey. He was born healthy and as good-looking as his *abuelo*. Dezi, for me, represents a new generation, ensuring my family bloodline will continue in the future. As joyful and hopeful as this moment might be, I remain concerned about the world that will welcome my progeny. What is this future that Dezi and his generation will inherit? We all love our grandchildren (and children). And like all who love their offspring, I too dream of a brighter future for my descendants, of passing on to them a world that is better than the one I found.

No doubt Dezi will get to witness the dawn of the twenty-second century. Will all that breathes life then flourish because of the investments we make now to heal our planet? Or will this blue marble upon which we find ourselves be unhabitable? Will our avariciousness for earth's resources, callousness toward sustainability, and unsympathetic attitude about the costs we are postponing for future generations to pay condemn them? Will Dezi, when he becomes an adult with children and grandchildren of his own, praise us who are adults today for having the foresight of minimizing, if not reversing, some of the consequences of environmental degradation? Or will he and his generation rise up and bear witness against our self-centeredness and short-sightedness?

I confess fear for what this world might look like when Dezi gets to be my age. The hunger for profits by some, and the embrace of ignorance by others, have contributed to a deadly milieu pushing humanity past the point of no return—if that point hasn't already been crossed. It is to Dezi—and all those who will grow old under the shadow of this generation's refusal to create a cleaner, healthier, and safer world—that not only do I dedicate this book, but more importantly, my life and energy to contribute toward environmental healing.

Exactly one month before Dezi entered the world, I organized an international conference on the intersection of environmental racism and immigration. As a political refugee who was relegated to live in the rat and roach infested slums of this nation, which even back then were the epicenter of environmental racism, this issue touches my skin. Today, environmental degradation is no longer contained in areas where only people of color live. Instead, it is spilling over to the vanilla suburbs where those of European descent escaped. A warming planet knows no boundaries. The severe storms it creates are not restricted to human-constructed international borders or redlined neighborhoods. The degradation of the environment touches us all: those occupying the center of former colonizers and those who remain among the colonized; those who are rich and those who are poor; those who are white and those who have been relegated to the underside of whiteness.

And while all are and will be impacted, those whose lands have been economically devasted due to the colonial venture are experiencing the full force of the changing climate while others, falsely believing their whiteness will keep them safe, advance the notion that climate change is a hoax. What happens to the world's poor whose lands and lives are devasted by the effects of climate change? What happens when the soil that provided sustenance no longer can yield food? When rebuilding homes and livelihoods becomes a vain enterprise? What impact does the shifting climate have on populations whose lands are being ruined? Few want to be migrants, especially migrants forced to leave because of the consequences of environmental degradation. No one wants to leave the land that witnessed their birth, especially when the land in which they seek refuge is unwelcoming and hostile.

But what if you have no choice but to leave? To stay could mean death. To leave could also mean death. The hopelessness of such a choice propels many toward action. What does it mean to be at the mercy of the consequences of environmental degradation? What does it mean if survival necessitates leaving all that is familiar, all that defines your identity? What impact do these shifting people have on overstrained world resources? Titled "Displacement Climes: Shifting Climates—Shifting People," the Iliff School of Theology provided the necessary funding and resources for a conference that virtually gathered scholars from around the world to enter into dialogue on how climate change, intensified storms, rising sea levels, and severe droughts disproportionately impact the poor of the earth, those who are predominantly not from the Eurocentric colonizing center. Special attention was given to the role and impact colonialism has had and continues to have on the struggles against environmental racism. That conference laid the groundwork for this book.

All too often when a discussion emerges concerning environmental justice, the voices of those on the margins who are most impacted are ignored. The world's disenfranchised are all too often dismissed to the role of object of the conversation. What does it mean to center their voices and explore environmental degradation from the perspective of those on the global margins? The scholarship contained in this book focuses on the voices of those most impacted and those allies who stand with them in solidarity. For this reason, both the virtual conference and this book explored how the intersection of climate change and migration have negatively impacted regions throughout the world like Palestine, Nigeria, the Caribbean, the Himalayas, Tonga, Fiji, Indonesia, India, the US borderlands, and Puerto Rico, and communities like the Dalit community, the African and Latinx communities in the United States, and the Indigenous peoples of North America.

As the organizer of the conference and editor of this book, I want to express my gratitude to several individuals who made this venture possible.

The Iliff School of Theology, and its president, Tom Wolfe, deserve recognition for working behind the scenes to acquire the resources to make the conference a reality. Also, as someone who is technologically inept, I relied on Michael McMillan to organize the virtual conference, which went off without a hitch. Of course, I remain grateful to Rachel Hackenberg of The Pilgrim Press, who immediately saw the importance of this book and the contribution it will make to the environmentalist discourse, and to Adam Bresnahan at The Pilgrim Press, for his hard work and dedication in helping get this manuscript ready for publication; this book is better because of his editing skills. Finally, I want to lift up Dezi, to whom this book is dedicated, praying that his grandchildren will one day live in a safe and flourishing environment because of the collective actions we seek to take today.

A Climate of Refugee-Ness? Vulnerabilities, Violence, and Voices from around the World

Tina Shull, Saumaun Heiat, Tanaya Dutta Gupta,
Emma Crow-Willard, and Christine Wheatley

INTRODUCTION *by Tina Shull*

Climate Refugee Stories is a multimedia public education and archiving project that documents stories of people around the world displaced by the impacts of climate change and a global hardening of borders, broadly defined.[1] Accompanied by a #ClimateMigrationSyllabus, K–12 curriculum, and other supplemental materials, the stories we share are meant to engage students, non-governmental organizations, and affected communities in questions about who climate refugees are, the historical origins of climate change and its disparate impacts, and how communities are responding to a convergence of crises, including the COVID-19 pandemic.

A confluence of events in 2016–2017 gave rise to the project. One was an increasing number of asylum seekers traveling in caravans to the US-Mexico border, who, after being placed in US immigration jails, explained that environmental issues and climate impacts were among the reasons that they had decided to migrate. Another was the fear and eco-grief expressed by my students at University of California Irvine during a time of rising xenophobia, climate denialism, and refugee refusal under the Trump administration. *Climate Refugee Stories* originated as a student-led response to these intersections—a shared desire to bring history to bear on current events and show solidarity with climate migrants in the United States and around the world, many of whom are Indigenous and/or impacted by racial capitalism, settler colonialism, and industries of extraction. We are now a small, global team of interdisciplinary scholars, practitioners, students, im/migrants and refugees, artists, educators, and storytellers.

Guided by those whose voices we feature, this is a project by and for climate refugees who share experiences of displacement and survival on their own terms. We believe those who are closest to the problem are closest to the solution, and so, in line with emerging praxis in critical refugee studies, we employ a participatory action research (PAR) approach to center storytellers as stakeholders with direct knowledge and expertise. In doing so, our aim is to shift focus away from suffering, trauma, and eco-grief—although those elements are surely present in our work—to what happens next: community-building, survival, and resilience.

Who are climate refugees? We acknowledge that the term *climate refugee* is problematic. It currently has no legal standing and is difficult to define. On the one hand, it expands the definition of refugee and acknowledges that political, economic, and environmental factors often work together to cause displacement. On the other hand, many resist the label because it implies an adaptive (as opposed to reparative) response to climate change, or because it reduces a person or a group's power in public perception.[2] As project contributor Tanaya Dutta Gupta writes:

> When we think of violence, and people fleeing violence, we think of refugees. But what about internal migrants who, without crossing international borders, are nevertheless crossed by violent border-like effects and bordering processes, exacerbated by climate and other crises? Perhaps moving beyond debates around labels like "climate refugees" as a category of concern, to recognize *climate*

refugee-ness as an emergent condition of concern can take us a step towards addressing such questions.[3]

In this chapter, project collaborators discuss their experiences of gathering stories from Bangladesh, India, Puerto Rico, and Ghana, as well as the challenges and opportunities we have encountered.

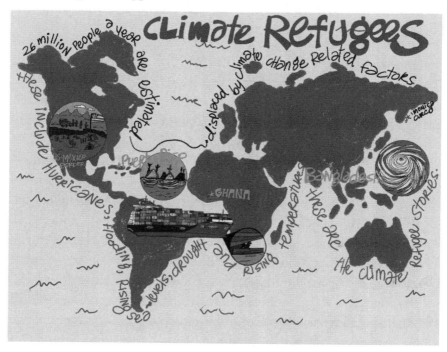

Figure 1. Artwork by Monica Curca featuring a world map with locations of stories included in the *Climate Refugee Stories* project. Curca is founder of the organization Active Labs.

COX'S BAZAR AND DHAKA, BANGLADESH *by Saumaun Heiat*

Climate migration in Bangladesh largely encompasses people from the country's coastal areas, which, because they are low lying, are being significantly affected by rising sea levels. The resulting soil erosion, decrease in arable farmland, and higher water salinity impact agrarian livelihoods dependent on farming. Additionally, the warming of the Bay of Bengal creates conditions for more frequent cyclonic events, causing large disruptions to coastal livelihoods.

Coinciding with my work with the International Organization for Migration (IOM) in 2017 on the Rohingya Crisis in Bangladesh, I collaborated with *Climate Refugee Stories* to obtain first-hand narratives from persons affected by climate and environmental changes within Bangladesh, with support from my former professor Tina Shull at the University of California, Irvine. During her course "Climate Refugees," she and a group of students developed the idea to create a media project featuring stories of climate displacement. This project took me to the Bhola slum in Dhaka's Mirpur neighborhood. The slum is named for a coastal region on the shores of the Bay of Bengal, where rising sea levels have led to the drastic salination of once-fertile farmland. The subsequent loss of livelihoods has caused many of coastal Bhola's inhabitants to migrate inward into Bangladesh.[4]

With the help of my translator Ripon—a former IOM colleague—I recorded personal narratives from the inhabitants of the densely packed and makeshift slum. They all had a recurring theme of livelihoods lost to soil erosion, rising water levels, and the increased salt content of the water. These testimonies run parallel to the concerns within the Rohingya refugee camps in Cox's Bazar—both Bhola and Cox's Bazar border the Bay of Bengal. The makeshift camps are prone to environmental hazards, such as flooding and landslides from the strong cyclones and heavy rainfall of Bangladesh's monsoon season. These temporary homes within the camps, constructed out of tarps and bamboo, were meant to last only for months, not to withstand the annual monsoon cycle. It is only a matter of time before these political refugees become environmental refugees in this new context.

Comparing the stories the Rohingya told about being political refugees and those the Bhola slum community told about being environmental refugees reveals similarities and differences both in their personal narratives and their thoughts about their own futures.[5] The Rohingya, at that time only recently arrived at Cox's Bazaar, recounted escaping violence, familial separation, and loss of property and assets, all of which caused grave psychosocial trauma. In contrast, the members of the Bhola community we interviewed seemed more willing to adapt and accept their new urban environment, even though their narratives of losing their agrarian livelihoods also evidenced trauma. Regarding their future prospects, the newly arrived Rohingya were overall more optimistic about eventually being able to return to their homes in Rakhine State, but they were also wary about the reintegration process, which today is looking increasingly bleak. The Bhola slum community, on the other hand, voiced more acceptance of the reality of how climate change has caused irreversible change to their homes and livelihoods, resulting in individuals being more resigned to their fate as urban dwellers in Dhaka who must adapt to a new livelihood.

BENGAL DELTA REGION OF BANGLADESH AND INDIA
by Tanaya Dutta Gupta

Sitting inside a room in one of the largest slums in Dhaka, her voice breaking with effort to keep tears at bay, forty-year-old Nafisa (pseudonym) shared her experience of migrating from rural Bangladesh:

> We used to live on the banks of the Payra River, near its confluence with the sea . . . My house fell outside the embankment, near the river. When the river started breaking, my home was wiped away, that is when we came to Dhaka . . . When this slum burnt in 2004, we again became destitute . . . I went back to our village with my small children. In 2007 during cyclone Sidr, the water came, and in only five minutes . . . seven members of my family, including my parents, were washed away by the water . . . everything became a graveyard, where would I go? Nowhere else to go, so I came again to Dhaka with my children.

Nafisa's ordeal is not an isolated experience. It conveys how, for people moving within Bangladesh and India, migration is not a linear move from rural to urban areas. Rather, it consists of circular trajectories that may not follow a fixed seasonal rhythm and are erratic and uncertain, often occurring in uneven intervals.

What role might climate play in making people from this region variably mobile and immobile? And how might the circular (im)mobility of people moving within their own countries be related to experiences of insecurity and violence? Using borders as an analytical tool, I propose moving beyond what I call the "people crossing borders" framework that has dominated migration theories and call for developing a deeper critical understanding of how borders cross people, which then places certain groups on the "wrong" side of history, territory, and policy.[6]

Divided yet connected by the India-Bangladesh border, the Bengal Delta, also depicted as a "climate borderland," is characterized by shared ecology, culture, colonial history, and climate impacts.[7] Climate impacts in this fragile ecoregion could be experienced through loss of homes and livelihoods due to intensifying cyclones, storm surges, and saltwater inundation of agricultural lands. Many are left with no option but to migrate to cities like Dhaka, while at the same time "keeping one foot in the village" through social ties and remittances in order to maintain safety nets and a pathway to return, especially during a crisis.

In fieldwork I conducted in Bangladesh and India in 2020, I sought to examine how migrants—specifically, internal circular migrants from this region moving within Bangladesh and India—could experience violent border-like effects without having physically crossed an international border. In Bangladesh, I interacted with a wide range of actors, including migrants in Dhaka's slums, inhabitants in rural polder areas, as well as organizations working on research, policy, humanitarian aid, and development in the region. My fieldwork in Bangladesh was abruptly truncated due to the advent of the COVID-19 pandemic and the closure of the India-Bangladesh border. I arrived in India just before the countrywide lockdown began.

This lockdown, as a national policy response to COVID-19, disproportionately affected internal migrant workers, who found themselves stranded in urban centers without adequate food, shelter, and income support. I spoke over the phone with migrants who returned to their villages in the Indian Sundarbans, navigating checkpoints and barriers in their perilous journeys across impermeable state boundaries. They were further confronted by the disastrous effects of Cyclone Amphan, which made landfall in coastal areas of Bangladesh and eastern India on May 20, 2020. The intersecting impacts of COVID-19 and Cyclone Amphan created a peculiar juxtaposition of mobility and immobility for these returning migrants, trapping them in a precarious situation of serious food and livelihood insecurity without the ability to plan for the future.[8]

"There is water in every direction, and we are floating in the middle." Abir's words describing a cyclone-damaged village during a global pandemic echo an outcome of the structural violence that continues to shape human security and survival for such "floating" people in this era of shifting climates.

PUERTO RICO *by Emma Crow-Willard*

In May of 2019, I headed to Puerto Rico for the second time. I had been there for one week in August of 2018 to explore what stories needed to be told that hadn't. Post-Hurricane Maria, I naively thought, not having been to Puerto Rico: "Shouldn't everyone leave? It's in the path of hurricanes that are just going to get worse *and* it's susceptible to rising sea levels." But when I arrived, I realized just how big the main island is (Puerto Rico is actually multiple islands). It is an island of mountains, with its highest point reaching 4,390 feet. Most of the island would not be impacted by rising sea levels. A really bad hurricane only occurs once every twenty years or so, and the cost of living cannot be beat—it's far cheaper than any of the states. Plus, it's got the only tropical rainforest in the United States National Forest System, beautiful weather and beaches, fresh mangoes falling from the trees, and everyone is so friendly. It kind of made me want to live there, too. [9]

However, Puerto Rico has major problems stemming from its history as a colonized nation, which proved especially catastrophic when disaster hit. Rather than go into that history here, I recommend Jesse Martinez and Marc D. Joffe's book *Origins of the Puerto Rico Fiscal Crisis* and Amelia Cheatham's book *Puerto Rico: A U.S. Territory in Crisis*.[10] Here, I instead share some of the stories I heard. First, a few brief notes on why this background reading is important. The United States' policies have caused Puerto Rico to become debt-dependent, which has led to an economic crisis and massive migration from the island. This migration has a cyclical effect of inciting more migration from the island, because it reduces the numbers of workers, taxpayers, and, notably, well-educated young professionals, thus reducing funds for public services such as education, maintaining the electrical grid, etc., all of which ultimately reduces the quality of life.

Victor, a PhD student from Aguada studying at the University of Puerto Rico, Mayaguez, decided to transfer to Arizona State University when, after Hurricane Maria, his program basically disappeared. He said (translated): "It is important to realize that the Hurricane (Maria) wasn't the precise problem. It's a political problem, an economic problem." There is a great deal of distrust of the government on the island. Immediately after Hurricane Maria, the entire island's power was knocked out because of poor management of the centralized grid. Yet many residents were still charged for power use during the time they were not supplied electricity, said two University of Puerto Rico professors I interviewed.

Luis, a nursing student in Puerto Rico, graduated just before the hurricane and was forced to leave the island to find work. He now works as a nurse in Colorado, where he chose to move because he had family there. Based on many of the interviews I conducted, job security is very hard to find on the island, because most positions are only offered as one-year contract jobs as opposed to salaried positions. Most people who do migrate move somewhere where they have friends or relatives. There are varying perspectives in Puerto Rico on migration, just like there are varying perspectives on whether Puerto Rico should become a state, or an independent country (of note: no one I spoke with thought Puerto Rico was good in its current political limbo—neither a state nor independent). Some believe if you leave, you are privileged, because you can afford to leave. Others believe if you stay you are privileged because you can afford to stay. Today, the majority of Puerto Ricans now live on the US mainland, predominantly in New York, Florida, Pennsylvania, and New Jersey.

GHANA *by Christine Wheatley*

Located in West Africa, Ghana has a 330-mile-long coast on the Atlantic Ocean. Ghana's coast makes up about seven percent of the country's total land area and is home to over five million people, many of whom depend on the fishing industry. Yet, it has become more difficult for local fishermen and women to make a living in recent years. First, Ghana's waters have become severely overfished, largely due to illegal fishing by mostly Chinese-owned industrial fishing vessels, which enter shallow waters where local fishers get their stocks.[11] Furthermore, in places like Keta on the eastern coast, rising sea levels have exacerbated the perennial storm surges and tidal waves, making it too dangerous for small and non-motorized fishing boats to enter. Coupled with a general lack of jobs—as reflected in the country's high rates of un- and under-employment, especially among youth—this has contributed to high rates of emigration.[12] As undocumented migrants from the coast seek better opportunities elsewhere, they often make dangerous journeys as stow-aways on cargo ships bound for Europe, the United States, and Canada.[13] Stowaways are often caught on board and subsequently deported back to Ghana.[14]

Rising sea levels represent another driver of emigration, as well as internal displacement, as coastal residents lose their homes to the sea. This is what we learned while producing the Ghana film for *Climate Refugee Stories*, documenting stories of return migrants, individuals, and commu-nities fighting erosion and flooding and experiencing displacement as a result of climate-related stressors along Ghana's coasts, including island communities on and near the Volta River, Ghana's main river system. Overall, we found that over the last thirty years, many communities have lost vast lands to the sea, which has broken down and washed away hun-dreds of homes or buried them in sand. This has left residents with no choice but to relocate inland, though many do not have the resources to do so. Furthermore, return migrants face challenges with economic rein-corporation as they struggle to find work and housing.

Such challenges of reincorporation were revealed to us by return migrants like Michael and Jonathan, both of whom are from Takoradi, a town on the west coast that is home to the country's second largest port. Both were stowaways on cargo ships—bound for Senegal and Greece, respectively—and both were discovered on board and deported. As Michael, a fisherman, told us:

> This is my third time of being caught and thrown back [to Ghana] after being a stowaway. This time around I decided not to go back again. I decided to stay home to do something for myself but it has not been easy. What we do, we are fishermen, we normally go fish-ing but these days it's hard to get a catch. Things are very hard... We just go patrol the sea and don't get any fish and burn our fuel which results in debt.

Jonathan has similarly struggled since returning to Takoradi. As he reported to us: "I don't have a job . . . this morning, when I woke up not having anything to eat, I went to the beach to look for firewood to be sold before I could get something to eat. I'll get 4 cedi [$0.75 USD] for that."

Michael and Jonathan admitted that due to economic hardship upon return, they considered attempting another stowaway journey—despite the dangers they have faced. Michael said that on his most recent trip, he and other stowaways were beaten badly by the ship's crew members after a stowaway fell gravely ill. He also spoke of the risk of being thrown overboard by the crew. Michael explained:

> As I sit here right now, I'm scouting for any of the ships that I could use to stowaway because things are just so hard right now in Ghana. And it is the reason why most of the youth are gathered at the port right now, to get an opportunity to stowaway . . . For stowaway, it's not about where you want to go. Anywhere abroad is abroad.

Jonathan told us:

> I don't see myself belonging to the community anymore. Every part of the community seems to have been occupied. I don't see myself as part of the community because I don't own any property in the community. I would want to [stowaway again]. There are so many countries on my mind but any country out there that looks like I could get something to do, I will go.

Further down the coast, in and around the town of Keta, we collected stories from people who have been displaced by huge tidal waves that have washed away their homes. Tidal waves have been a perennial occurrence along Ghana's east coast for decades. However, the devastation has increased dramatically in recent years due to rising sea levels and illegal sand mining—often committed by some of the same people who have lost their fishing livelihoods, desperate for an alternative source of income—that has eroded the coastline, rendering their homes more vulnerable to the sea.[15] In fact, the areas around Keta—including the communities we visited in July 2021 shortly after hundreds of residents were displaced by tidal waves—were once again hit hard in mid-November 2021, as a tidal surge swept through more than five hundred houses, rendering at least 4,000—and possibly as many as 7,000—residents homeless.[16]

We spoke to people like Joseph, Amele, and Abina, who were displaced after losing their homes to tidal waves. They now live in temporary thatch houses made from coconut palms in a makeshift camp built perilously close to the sea on private land without consent from landowners. As Joseph and others reported to us, the landowners are waiting to be compensated by the government. Like other displaced residents, Joseph, Amele, and Abina do not have the resources to relocate and rebuild further inland. Joseph, a man in his thirties with a wife and young children, told us:

> I never expected the sea waves to come close to us as they did. We thought we had more time . . . We've been asked to relocate to another land which is inland but the space is not big enough to accommodate all of us. The new place given to us is similar to this place and we're afraid that the tidal waves will also occur there.

Similarly, Amele, also in her thirties with a husband and young children, reported to us:

> I do not have a job. When the fishermen go to the sea, I try to help them get a little bit of catch but since the sea started rising, the tidal waves and everything, they no longer go fishing anymore [because it is too dangerous]. It's been very hard for me and my kids . . . We would want to relocate but we do not have the money. That is why we are stuck here.

And Abina, in her sixties, reported to us:

> I just heard that one of my relatives has been swept away by the sea. That's why I'm crying . . . I would like to relocate but I do not have the resources. Where I sit right now, I'm sick. Without holding a stick, I cannot even walk. Without the means, I cannot contemplate relocating without any help.

We also collected stories from people living on Azizakpe Island, located on the east coast approximately thirty miles west of Keta, where the Volta River opens into the sea. Azizakpe is also experiencing devastating flooding due to rising sea levels. We had the opportunity to interview the island's sub-chief, who reported to us:

> [When islanders' houses are washed away by the sea], some with no families or anywhere to go get stranded. The people who have family on the other islands or on the mainland, they were given assistance by these family members. The problem is, if you [relocate] to the mainland and you don't have land, you don't have a house, you get stranded there . . . Even if you rent a house inland, the type of job you do there, it's not what you're an expert in, so you can't survive well. What are you going to eat, how are you going to survive?

The Ghana film also features the work of New-Age Environmental Development of Africa (NED Africa), a Ghana-based social enterprise and charity organization where I serve as the executive director that is dedicated to addressing climate change in cooperation with local communities. NED Africa aims to support internally displaced persons and return migrants by providing sustainable livelihoods through the establishment of new green industries in Ghana, such as biogas.

Recognizing that many of the individuals we spoke to who face displacement and economic hardship would prefer to stay in Ghana, NED Africa is working to create opportunities for them to live well within the country. Most residents of Azizakpe Island live on fishing, shrimping, pig rearing, and oil processing from the island's abundant coconut trees. Working with a group of women residents, NED Africa is helping establish a women's cooperative to process and sell organic extra virgin coconut oil using a commercial processor that meets the standards for export. We'll also use coconut husks and pig manure to produce biogas for boat fuel and electricity.

Conclusion

What might we learn from climate refugee stories? By illuminating experiences of climate refugee-ness along borders—including in the gaps between policy and reality in various parts of the world—we prompt audiences to interrogate the historical, political, economic, and environmental causes of global inequality and displacement, and identify ways in which climate refugees are already resilient. How do we, in turn, recognize and build resilience in our own communities?

For us, work like that of NED Africa represents one manifestation of climate justice: that the people most directly affected by climate change are not only heard, but also given opportunities to benefit from mitigation and adaptation efforts. That is, solutions to climate change must be developed with climate refugees leading the way.

NOTES

1. *Climate Refugee Stories*, https://climaterefugeestories.com.

2. Here, we find the University of California Critical Refugee Studies Collective's definition of *refugee* useful: "Human beings forcibly displaced within or outside of their land of origin as a result of persecution, conflict, war, conquest, settler/colonialism, militarism, occupation, empire, and environmental and climate-related disasters, regardless of their legal status. Refugees can be self-identified and are often unrecognized within the limited definitions proffered by international and state laws." See The Critical Refugee Studies Collective, Critical Vocabularies, https://critical refugeestudies.com/resources/critical-vocabularies.

3. "Who are Climate Refugees?," *Climate Refugee Stories*, https://www.climate refugeestories.com/stories/climate-refugees-post/.

4. Sonya Ayeb-Karlsson, Dominic Kniveton, and Terry Cannon, "Trapped in the Prison of the Mind: Notions of Climate-induced (Im)mobility Decision-Making and Wellbeing from an Urban Informal Settlement in Bangladesh," *Humanities and Social Sciences Communications* 6, no. 62 (2020): 2.

5. Karen E. McNamara, Laura Olson, and Md. Ashiquir Rahman, "Insecure Hope: The Challenges Faced by Urban Slum Dwellers in Bhola Slum, Bangladesh," *Migration and Development* 5, no. 1 (2015): 1–15.

6. Douglas S. Massey, Arango Joaquín, Hugo Graeme, Kouaouci Ali, Pellegrino Adela, and J. Edward Taylor, "Theories of International Migration: A Review and Appraisal," *Population Development Review* 19, no. 3 (1993): 431–66; Gloria Anzaldúa, *Borderlands/La Frontera: The New Mestiza* (San Francisco: Spinsters/Aunt Lute Books, 1987).

7. Jason Cons, "Staging Climate Security: Resilience and Heterodystopia in the Bangladesh Borderlands," *Cultural Anthropology* 33, no. 2 (2018): 271–74.

8. Tanaya Dutta Gupta, Amrita Chakraborty, and Anamitra Anurag Danda, "Confronting Cascading Disasters, Building Resilience: Lessons from the Indian

Sundarbans," Observer Research Foundation Occasional Papers, no. 297 (New Delhi: Observer Research Foundation, January 29, 2021), 3.

9. "El Yunque National Forest," USDA Forest Service, https://www.fs.usda .gov/elyunque.

10. Marc D. Joffe and Jesse Martinez, *Origins of the Puerto Rico Fiscal Crisis* (Washington, DC: Mercatus Research, George Mason University, 2016); Amelia Cheatham, *Puerto Rico: A US Territory in Crisis* (Washington, DC: Council on Foreign Relations, 2020).

11. Environmental Justice Foundation, *A Human Rights Lens on the Impacts of Industrial Illegal Fishing and Overfishing on the Socio-Economic Rights of Small-Scale Fishing Communities in Ghana* (London: Environmental Justice Foundation, 2021), 25.

12. Aaron O'Neill, "Unemployment Rate in Ghana 2020," *Statista*, June 30, 2021, https://www.statista.com/statistics/808481/unemployment-rate-in-ghana/; Ernest Aryeetey, Priscilla Twumasi Baffour, and Festus Ebo Turkson, "Addressing Youth Unemployment in Ghana by Supporting the Agro-Processing and Tourism Sectors," The Brookings Institution, June 29, 2021, https://www.brookings.edu/blog/africa-in-focus/2021/06/29/addressing-youth-unemployment-in-ghana-by-supporting-the-agro-processing-and-tourism-sectors/; International Organization for Migration, *Migration in Ghana: A Country Profile 2019* (Geneva: IOM, 2020), 17.

13. *Recruitment Costs Pilot Survey Report—Ghana: Measuring SDG Indicator* (10.7.1) (Accra: Ghana Statistical Service, 2020), 14; Stephen Kotochie, "Life for Sale? The Adventures of Stowaways in Ghana," *The Vaulz News*, January 5, 2021; OluTimehin Adegbeye, "Lessons on Freedom of Movement from a Stowaway," *The Correspondent*, December 20, 2019.

14. Alexander Nyarko Yeboah, "Ghana Immigration Service Disembarks Four Ghanaian Stowaways," *Ghana News Agency*, October 30, 2020.

15. Fred Duhoe, "Sand Winning Banned at Keta Beaches Over Recent Tidal Waves," *Citi Newsroom*, November 10, 2021.

16. "Almost 4,000 People Displaced by Tidal Surge in Ghana," *Agence France-Presse*, November 10, 2021; "V/R Tidal Wave: Over 7000 people rendered homeless – MP," *GhanaWeb*, November 10, 2021, https://www.ghanaweb.com/GhanaHomePage /NewsArchive/V-R-tidal-wave-Over-7000-people-rendered-homeless-MP-1398871.

2

How the Eurochristian Invasion of Turtle Island Created Our Environmental Crises

tink tinker (wazhazhe/Osage Nation)

ABOUT A YEAR AGO, I noticed a news article about an australian tourist who had bought a $19,000 alligator skin purse in italy.[1] Upon re-entry into australia, her new purse was confiscated by border control agents as contraband merchandise because she had failed to file the proper paperwork for importing alligator skin. At that moment, I recalled my own experience with australian border control about a decade ago and experienced a momentary shiver. A constant travel companion was accompanying me on that trip, an Eagle Wing who had already been with me to four other continents. She always helped me focus my thinking and always kept me safe on these innumerable excursions away from home. For some reason, the customs form they handed us on the plane intimidated me more than previous forms for other countries, threatening me unduly if I failed to claim any "animal parts" I was bringing into the country. At first, I thought they might mean my feet or my ears, but then I remembered my Eagle Wing relative and thought, oh, no. So, I dutifully explained my situation on the form, using both sides, before we landed in melbourne so that the customs officials would know that I knew what I was doing.

When I finally deplaned and approached the customs counter, I handed over my form and waited. Finally, the officer, a young man, asked to see the wing. So, I unzipped her case and cautioned him, "you can look, but please don't touch her." After hemming and hawing, he punted, and escalated to his supervisor, an equally young woman. She too was very respectful not to touch, but like the young man she was baffled as to what to do. Finally, after escalating to a couple of other supervisors I was remanded to the chief supervisor on duty, who took me off to a quiet (and much darker) corner of the customs area—leaving this Indian fearing for the worst. A cop interrogating an Indian in a dark corner is never a hopeful moment, but he too was very respectful and equally perplexed. Finally, he looked up and asked, "Might, er you Night-ive?" "Yes, sir," I said, "an American Indian," adding the name of my Native People. He half smiled and replied waving me through into australia, "Get outa' heah!" And I was none too quick to make that move, gathering up my relative and my bags.

Through the ordeal, I had been thinking that I might have to reboard the plane to return to the u.s., leaving the conference in want of a keynote speaker. I certainly was not going to abandon my close relative for the sake of going to a conference—no matter how far we had traveled. This news item from last year, however, put the reality clearly into dramatic focus in a different way. Colonialism is much more powerful than even I had imagined. They could have chosen to not even give me the choice to get back on the airplane with my relative. They actually could have confiscated her as contraband property and destroyed her forthwith! They were enmeshed in a very different worldview, the eurochristian worldview.[2] They could not have begun to understand that she did not belong to me, that she is not my property. Their imagination could not possibly have conceived that she has her own personhood, and as a person was accompanying me. The personhood that she experienced when she was alive in this world is still fully present in this wing, and that person lives with me, and travels with me wherever I go. When I eat, she is one of the relatives for whom I set a little of my food aside in order to maintain the close relationship. Indeed, that is why I invite her to accompany me. It is not a matter of having a cool Indian show-and-tell—beads and feathers, as it were.

Today across Turtle Island, the universal cry of Indigenous Peoples is "LandBack!" Like my Eagle Wing, one should not think that Native folk are asking for the return of property. To non-Natives, I know that sounds counter-intuitive because property is the basic negotiable form of Land for eurochristians. But for Natives it is about relationship and not about property. Let's go back historically and trace an important colonialist contrivance that immediately changed north america. You see, from columbus in the caribbean to the episcopalians in jamestown to the puritans in plymouth and boston further north, the first order of business of these invaders was to convert the Land, our Grandmother, into private property.[3] Along with reducing Grandmother to property came the eurochristian notion that the whole of the cosmos is present only to serve human pleasure and need. So, once the cognitive ideal of property was in place, extraction became the next order of business, leading to human dependence on fossil fuels, mining, and monocrop agriculture. This immigration and its imposition of a new worldview with its own idealized cognitive models has left our world in what my *wazhazhe* ancestors called *ganitha*, a world out of balance, in chaos, out of order.

Thus, as an American Indian I realized I have a different concern for immigration, racism, and climate change than most of my colleagues writing for this volume. Many of these essays will analyze how environmental issues generated by the increasing globalization of capital has compelled the immigration of people from the South into the North as they escape the conditions created by exploitive northern "investments" and extractive projects. My concern, however, is for the invasive immigration, dare I say invasion, that begins in 1492 with its powerful new technologies of destruction that changed the landscape so radically and seemingly irrevocably from the beginning, so that today it threatens the very viability of human life on the planet. I want to press an analysis of that most destructive immigration and its continuing consequences yet today: Consequences for the Land herself; consequences for Water; consequences for the people who live here, including the Native Peoples who were so violently shoved aside and murdered, and whose relationship with the Land was brutally transfigured by its utter objectification: the conversion of the Land to a new abstract category called property.

I want to press my analysis that the brute force of our environmental Devastation, the enormity of our climate emergency, is rooted in this abstract thing called private property and that the damage starts from the beginning of the eurochristian invasion. If we're going to stop the degradation and bring this climate emergency to some sort of good resolution, then we have got to deal with this thing called private property, real estate, and the rule of law that so privileges property because that is the originating source of the worldview that has created the modern situation of climate emergency we are experiencing today. To purposefully misquote the martinican writer aimé césaire, the conversion of the land, Grandmother, into property, was the original eurochristian *thingification* of our Grandmother, the commodification of the Earth. Césaire, of course, was talking about the thingification of humans.[4] When we talk about the consequences of the current crisis for humans, American Indians want to ensure that we include the thingification consequences for all peoples, including all the nonhuman people of this Earth, particularly the Land herself.

The Land, our Grandmother, was commodified—turned into a thing with abstract currency value that could be bought and sold just as human beings were bought and sold as natural resources in order to create wealth for the eurochristian, for the few. Here we should remember that in 1650 there were more Indian bodies being shipped out of charleston south carolina than there were african bodies being shipped in.[5] The thingification of the Land, however, changed the very relationships of the Native Peoples who were still here. First, of course, Natives were displaced from their own Land in order to generate this thing called private property for the invaders. The Genocide of Indian Massacres and the loss of populations to eurochristian disease and slavery is well-known. The bigger threat came, however, with the further need to generate profits to pay for the invasion itself and then to generate wealth for the invaders. So, the needs of extraction industries to exploit Native "natural resources" led the corporate assault on Native Land. Mineral wealth like gold and silver were the earliest targets, targets that continued into the colonialists' penetration into colorado and california in the nineteenth century and even still today in Shoshone Land now called nevada. Fuels, like coal and oil and gas, became another target. But today the extractive industry threat is around more sublime elements like zinc, copper, molybdenum, and lithium, even as fossil fuels continue to dominate their share of the extractive industries conversation. The waste footprint on Native Lands has been and will continue to be huge, as will the new Genocidal devastation to Native populations.[6]

By naming consequences for people who live here, I mean to include all people and not just humans. I mean to include people that eurochristian culture regularly reduce to property or, to pick another powerful eurochristian abstraction, natural resources. So, think here of the thingification of the Grandmothers—Corn, Beans, and Squash—which American Indians relied on for much of their sustenance. And now the relationship of these relatives have been forcibly severed and they are grown in huge industrial agribusiness farms, turned into hybrid morphs of themselves. Even as Natives try to grow their traditional Corn, Beans, and Squash relatives, they are liable to become cross-contaminated with monsanto corporation seed stock. That not only means that new seed from the new harvest will now be hybrid and not the old "heritage" seed, but that monsanto corporation can sue Native farmers for the "cost" of the seed, since they hold the legal patent for the hybrid that Native corn has suddenly become.

As property leads to extraction and then industrial extraction, the soil and the water are also tainted, so that it is harder every day for Native People to rebuild or maintain those relationships. But we should note that in the twenty-first century there are those who are making that effort. Native farmers are rescuing heritage seeds and planting in their old ways— on Reservations and even in urban centers. They continue to harvest today foods that retain their excellence of taste and nutritional value—even if they fail to meet the harvest quantities of industrial agriculture accomplished with its huge machines and chemical additives.[7]

As we think of factory farming today, remember the animal people raised recklessly for human food consumption with no regard for the personhood of the animals: chicken farms, cattle feedlots, massive corporate pork slaughterhouses. Think of tree people who have been and are still being clear-cut. Think of old growth cedar forests up north; of the Native People who still live with those cedars and how this totally upends their lives—just to provide human people with more stuff—at whatever cost to the Land, to the tree nation, and to the Native Peoples who live in those places.

Remember, too, the mineral people dug up to satisfy human greed for more and greater mobility, technology, and human comfort. Yes, we are trying responsibly to replace fossil fuels with electric vehicles but are doing so by destroying "thacker pass" and severely impacting the land of Piute and Shoshone peoples, not to speak of impacting the other-than-human peoples in northeastern nevada—basically to satisfy joe biden's campaign promise to make america lithium independent, and so we can have battery-operated vehicles. While this is intended to make america lithium independent, it should be noted that the company, lithium nevada (aka lithium americas), is actually owned by a canadian mining company. So, we are dealing here not only with environmental justice issues, but with international business, international politics, and u.s. foreign policy.[8] And most importantly, as a *new york times* article posits, "electric cars and renewable energy may not be as green as they appear."[9]

Among the mineral people being exploited by the extractive industry is line 3 in minnesota, which is cutting through pristine wetlands and threatening those wetlands with both immediate construction and the nearly certain potential of severe crude oil leakage in the not-too-distant future. In the moment, line 3 is using up precious groundwater by the billions of gallons. The dakota access pipeline (dapl) already won its immediate political battle against Native protest to recklessly tunnel crude oil under lake oahe, the missouri river, the fresh water source for Standing Rock Reservation, Cheyenne River Reservation, and other Indian reservations on the river and other humans who live all the way down the missouri and mississippi rivers.[10]

Today it is also important to notice the resolution copper project at "oak flats" in arizona, a proposed copper mine that can, as its website insidiously says, "supply the world with the copper it needs to support ongoing technological and environmental innovation."[11] The answer we are told is anthropocentric industrial extraction. In order to do that, resolution copper proposes to tunnel a web of underground mines beneath a mountain sacred to the San Carlos Apache. They will need to tunnel so extensively—in order to remove an estimated 120 billion dollars worth of copper ore—that when they are done the entire mine will collapse in on itself, leaving a dangerous, unstable crater where a mountain used to be. We should note here that resolution copper is a company wholly owned by the largest mining corporation in the world, an australian company called "rio tinto zinc," who managed to destroy a 46,000-year-old Aboriginal sacred site in western australia just a couple of years ago, something they absurdly presumed they resolved with a formal apology.[12]

Needless to say, all of these extractive industries—oil, lithium, copper, coal, others—are being protested vigorously by both Native Peoples and their environmentalist allies. Yet, as Diné lawyer michelle cook says, "Indigenous Peoples in the u.s. are still today unable to say 'no' to development and extraction projects that occur within their traditional ancestral territories they use and occupy." She goes on to say we need to pressure decision-makers and financial institutions "to make real their human rights rhetoric and protect the human rights and cultural survival of Native Peoples."[13]

Yet even that call to action should remind us that we are caught in a complex web that would seem to bend us again towards miguel de la torre's theology of hopelessness.[14] After all, in this scenario of calling on decision-makers and financial institutions to ensure the human rights of Natives, who is it actually that we need to call on? Who is it that is powerful enough to "grant" Native People their "rights?" In this late colonial world, quite frankly, it is the conqueror's courts and legislatures that we need to approach in order to beg them to grant us rights. But they have little interest in ensuring Native rights, because it will so limit their own need to extract for profit. After all, it was in oppressing the Natives of the Land that the Land was converted to property and was thus made available for eurochristian extractive industry.

Moreover, it is the legal discourse of property rights that is invariably summoned to make every serious Native protest futile. As we saw in the dapl/Standing Rock protests of 2016–17, even though the Land in question was "unceded Treaty Land," the legal discourse was clouded enough that the state of north dakota could use property rights in order to arm a small sheriff's department with heavy military weaponry so that they could simply muscle the pipeline project through to completion. And that was the case even when Indian resistance was avowedly and persistently non-violent, peaceful.

Once property rights are invoked, they get attached somehow to Human Rights because it's human beings that have property rights and not trees, not Buffalo, not Eagles or Squirrels.[15] Yet when property rights are invoked, the person who "owns" property can say I demand my freedom to do with my property whatever I will, even if that destroys the property value of people who live next to me.

Of course, the legal discourse gets thicker than that because in its infinite wisdom, eurochristian legal discourse has granted personhood not to trees, not to the rivers, nor to mountains but to these abstract entities called corporations: lithium america, resolution copper, enbridge pipeline company, rio tinto zinc, the largest mining corporation in the world (which actually owns resolution copper).

Once these corporations exert their property rights, it's not a matter of an acre next to my acre or forty acres next to my forty acres. It is a matter of millions of acres owned by these corporations that they have the right to do whatever they want with. Sure, they have to do these environmental impact statements and whatnot. But they have all the powerful political connections and tons of money in order to pay for those things so that the result always turns out in their favor in order to allow them to do whatever it is they want to do with our Grandmother. Of course, by converting the Land to property, they made a move that denies or erases or attempts to erase native peoples' relationship with the Earth as a person, as Grandmother. My goal here is to initiate a shift away from the presumed normativity of property rights to a restored sense of relationship with the Earth as Grandmother and of human responsibility for maintaining harmony and balance in all that we do.

Pundits may respond, "Didn't you Native peoples gather wood for your fireplaces? Didn't you gather willow trees for home construction? Didn't you gather medicines like Cedar and Sage?" And indeed, Indian folk hunted and killed our close relatives for food: Buffalo, salmon, deer, and the like. And we did plant and harvest the Three Grandmothers: Corn, Beans, and Squash, in order to sustain our lives. Pundits will continue,

"Are we not all similar after all, equally culpable for extracting the Earth's resources?" Of course, the stark difference is in the word, "relationship." Relationship calls upon each of us (and the social whole of all of us) to interact with utmost respect. That is, respect for the Earth, for Water, for trees and for every other-than-human person—as well as for each other.

Every Indian Community paid close attention to what they took from their relatives, and how they took it, and how much they took. Their relationships were based on reciprocity and respect rather than an anthropocentric hierarchy. There were Ceremonies for every gift an Indian person took from the world around her. If I need a new stem for my pipe, I'm going to look for a particular kind of tree. Then I will talk to the trees, especially the one from whom I want to take a particular branch. And I would talk to all the trees around that particular one. I would sing a song, and certainly offer a gift back to the tree in return for the branch I need for my pipe. That is how I would show respect for my tree relative.

Likewise, before engaging in a community Buffalo hunt, the whole Community might perform a long and arduous ceremony, which, in the case of the Osages, might take up to thirteen days. And in my own Nation one of the twenty-four Clans was dedicated to maintaining the relationship between the Buffalo people and our community. In order to do that important work, this clan abstained from eating flesh of the Buffalo, since their relationship with the Buffalo People was so close. Buffalo meat was the main protein that sustained the other twenty-three Clans, and the hides and other parts of the Buffalo were used in all sorts of household activities.

I have a twelve-year-old daughter who is a member of the *tohka towa^{n}to^n*, Buffalo clan. When she moved into my house as a toddler, I promised her that I would join her in abstaining from eating buffalo meat in our home or whenever I'm with her. That was a major concession because buffalo meat is far superior, both in taste and in nutrition, to the cow meat that most people in north america eat with such reckless abandon. To this day it is a favorite food of most American Indians—along with other natural american foods like deer or moose, and corn, beans, and squash, and most of the foods other americans call "wild," like (wild) rice, onions, turnips, spinach, etc.

So let me close by saying that private property, the eurochristian notion of private property, is not a natural or universal state of affairs. It is an invented way of being, much like making corporations persons. It is a legal and theological imaginary, but it has worked persistently and efficiently to dispossess American Indian peoples of their relationship with the land. And, we can add, it has worked equally to alienate eurochristian folk from the very land that they have so coveted as property.

Across the Indian country today there's a persistent cry for LandBack. And what you need to know about LandBack is this: LandBack is not about returning property to Native Peoples. Rather, LandBack is about restoring relationship: the relationship between humans and the Earth Mother. LandBack is about doing away with private property and "real estate" and extractive industry so that we can actually relate to Grandmother and bring balance back into our world. LandBack includes restoring the Native worldview, restoring our cultures, and all that entails, including our languages. LandBack is what Native folk are calling for across Turtle Island regardless of real estate and statist boundaries. LandBack includes relationships with Water and Sky, Air and Land.

Nestlé corporation, "energy transfer corporation" with its dakota access pipeline, and especially today enbridge corporation with its "line 3" in minnesota have all signaled that they intend to treat water now as just another commodity. They all have property-ized and thingified water for a profit.[16] Our Grandfather *wazhazhe*, Water, like the Land, is now for sale in the marketplace—bought by the plastic bottle or by the acre-foot. And some now argue that Water could be the spark that fuels the next worldwide war.

By saying LandBack, Native folk are insisting we want our relationships back—with Land, with Water, with the Air around us, all that. Y'all can have the property, that is everything the hardcore capitalist class can load up on the next plane and take with them. Just leave our relatives here, please, all of them. There is much more to it than that, of course. Relationship is a very complex notion in and of itself, but maybe this could begin an important conversation between us and prove productive in bringing an end to this climate crisis in a good way, in restoring the Earth, our Grandmother, in a good way. Indian Peoples know that this is a way to ensure that our Grandmother can sustain human life into the distant future. That's my desire for all of us and my goal for my eurochristian relatives. Join us in this business of LandBack, the proclamation of Indian people that they want their important relationship returned to them.

NOTES

1. My idiosyncratic capitalization is intentional and serves the purpose of unsettling the usual hierarchies of being in the eurochristian (especially, english-speaking) world.

2. See my article on worldview and the color code: "what are we going to do with White people?" *the new polis*, december 17, 2019, https://thenewpolis.com/2019/12/17/what-are-we-going-to-do-with-white-people-tink-tinker-wazhazhe-osage-nation/. I argue here for the use of "eurochristian" instead of the color coded "White" person/people.

3. See anthony j. hall, *earth into property: colonization, decolonization, and capitalism* (montreal: mcgill-queen's university press, 2010).

4. Aimé césaire, *discourse on colonialism*, trans. by joan pinkham (new york: monthly review press, 1972 [1955]).

5. See andrés reséndez, *the other slavery: the uncovered story of Indian enslavement in america* (boston: houghton mifflin harcourt, 2016).

6. See winona laduke (White Earth Anishinaabe), "uranium mining, Native resistance, and the greener path," *orion magazine* 28, no. 1 (january/feburary 2009).

7. For example, note the work of shannon francis (Hopi/Navajo) and her "spirit of the Sun" organization (https://www.spiritofthesun.org/).

8. Maya l. kapoor, "nevada lithium mine kicks off new era of western extraction," *high country news*, february 18, 2021.

9. Ivan penn and eric lipton, "the lithium gold rush: inside the race to power electric vehicles," *new york times*, may 6, 2021.

10. Nick estes (Lakota), *our history is the future: Standing Rock versus the dakota access pipeline, and the long tradition of indigenous resistance* (new york: verso, 2019).

11. See resolution copper website: https://www.resolutioncopper.com/.

12. "Mining firm rio tinto sorry for destroying Aboriginal caves," *bbc*, may 31, 2020, https://www.bbc.com/news/world-australia-52869502.

13. "In exhibition at brown, Wampanoag Artist draws on tradition to celebrate Indigenous rights," news from brown, october 7, 2021, https://www.brown.edu/news/2021-10-07/wampum.

14. miguel a. de la torre, *embracing hopelessness* (minneapolis: fortress press, 2017).

15. Of course, there is the hyper-liberal move in legal discourse to grant "rights" to "nature." I protest. Who is so powerful and ego-centered to grant rights to anyone other than themselves? Our relationship to one another (including tree people and rivers) ought to be rooted in relationship and not in some abstract discourse about rights. That discourse is important only in providing new sources of revenue for lawyers and employment for academics whose expertise is in sorting out abstract categories of cognition.

16. For a good analysis of Water, both in the Native worldview and in the commodification worldview of the colonizer, see: loring abeyta, "Worldviews, Water, and justice—sustainability in a time of scarcity," in *gonna trouble the Water: ecojustice, Water, and environmental racism*, ed. miguel a. de la torre (cleveland: the pilgrim press, 2021), 15–23.

Blockade and Climate Change Vulnerability: The Environmental Realities of Gaza after Fifteen Years under Siege

Abeer Butmeh and Memona Hossain

CURRENTLY, MORE THAN TWO MILLION PALESTINIANS inhabit the Gaza Strip under Israeli occupation and siege.[1] This has major impacts on land, water, air, deforestation, and wildlife.[2] The livelihoods of Palestinian agricultural communities have been transformed by a combination of seizure of land and water, military attacks, and climatic shifts. Palestinian farmers face severe challenges because of these impacts. This chapter explores the climate change and land degradation realities in Palestine and what they mean for a land that is under siege. The chapter then examines how Palestinian people have learned to cope with these realities, what resilience looks like, and how Palestinians are engaging in climate change discourse. Finally, the chapter closes with recommendations on how the global community can engage to dismantle the systemic oppression of Palestinian people and Palestinian lands. In Palestine, we must understand that all environmental commitments are particular because they are intrinsically linked with human rights, sovereignty, fairness, justice, control over resources, and access to decision-making. Human conflict is also earth-based. In Gaza, the earth and humans are both vulnerable to the impacts of climate change in complicated ways.

CONTEXTUALIZING GAZA, PAST AND PRESENT

Geographically, Palestine sits along the Jordan Valley, and Gaza is located on the western part of Palestine on the Mediterranean Sea. It is an area of fertile land that was once considered the "breadbasket" of Palestine. The valley is an integral part of the main migration route for many birds around the world, connecting Europe, Asia, and Africa.[3] In 1948, during the Nakba, 750,000 Palestinians[4] were uprooted from their homeland,[5] creating the Jewish state of Israel.[6] After this event, over 500 towns and villages along with a whole country and its people disappeared from international maps and dictionaries.[7] About ninety percent of Palestinians were driven out through means of psychological warfare and/or military pressure, many at gunpoint.[8] In June 2007, Israel intensified their closure of the Gaza Strip in Palestine, imposing a crippling land, air, and sea blockade[9] that trapped two million Palestinians in "the world's largest open prison in human history."[10] The Gaza blockade is a denial of basic human rights in contravention of international law and amounts to collective punishment.[11] In 2021, UN Secretary General António Guterres said "if there is a hell on earth, it is the lives of children in Gaza."[12]

A UN report states that fifteen years of blockade by Israel has caused 16.7 billion US dollars in economic damage.[13] Israel controls what goes in and out of the Gaza Strip. Half of Palestinians in Gaza live in poverty, eighty percent depend on some form of humanitarian aid, sixty-eight percent are food insecure, and sixty-nine percent of the youth are unemployed.[14] The lack of vital resources such as water and electricity together with the deterioration of the environment make Gaza uninhabitable.[15] Academics and international health professionals have stated that: "Guided by our moral values and professional obligations, the international community must act now to end structural violence by confronting the historical and political forces entrenching a cyclical, violent, and mutable reality for Palestinians."[16]

CLIMATE INJUSTICE

Climate change is political. While the earth doesn't divide itself across geopolitical borders, humans do, and this division has disproportionate impacts. Countries in situations of armed conflict are disproportionately affected by climate variability extremes.[17] In 2020, the International Committee of the Red Cross released a report on the combined impact of armed conflict and climate change:

- Sixty percent of the twenty countries considered to be most vulnerable to climate change are affected by armed conflict.
- Fourteen of the thirty-four countries in food crisis experienced the double burden of conflict and climate shocks in 2017.
- Areas where climate shocks and conflict interact to drive food crises have high to very high prevalence rates of acute malnutrition in children under the age of five.[18]

More than sixty percent of the land in the West Bank and more than eighty-five percent of water resources are controlled by the Israeli occupation, which makes it impossible for Palestinians to cope with climate change.[19] Gaza's coastal aquifer, which is its only natural source of drinking water, has collapsed and is significantly contaminated.[20] With more than ninety-six percent of water in the coastal aquifer no longer safe for human consumption, the water crisis in Gaza is a humanitarian catastrophe; this is exacerbated by the fact that damage to the aquifer will soon become irreversible.[21] Israeli restrictions on imports of basic construction materials prevent repair of the aquifer.[22] The Israeli occupation harms Palestinian agriculture by confiscating land and controlling water.[23] "Approximately half of Gaza's population receives water for domestic use for only eight hours every four days . . . Limited water causes a decline in both water consumption and hygiene standards."[24] Additionally, Israel fully controls electricity and fuel in Gaza. Between 2016 and 2017, 186 health, water, sanitation, and solid waste collection facilities were closed because of power and fuel shortages.[25]

IMPACTS ON THE LAND

About eighty percent of the untreated wastewater in Gaza flows into the sea, and twenty percent seeps into the groundwater aquifer.[26] Muhammad

Saleem, from the Al-Sheikh Redwan neighborhood in northern Gaza, said the water was too polluted and "all my plants dried up and died because of high water salinity and high chloride ... If the plants have died because of this water, what will it do with people's bodies?" he asks.[27]

Sewage discharge from Israel into the Gazan Sea has caused its wastewater levels to be more than twice the globally recommended levels,[28] causing seventy-five percent of Gaza's beaches to be unsuitable for swimming and recreation.[29] Water contamination causes twenty-six percent of all illnesses in Gaza and more than twelve percent of child deaths.[30] Access to the beaches is one of the very few activities available to children and families in Gaza under siege. Mohammed al-Sayis, a five-year-old boy, swimming in Gaza's beach with his family to escape the heat in 2017, died from the toxic effects of sewage contamination,[31] while others reported illness during the same period.[32]

In addition to this, fisheries, which serve as a significant source of income and food consumption for Gazans, witnessed during the first quarter of 2021 damages to 3,000 freshwater fish farms, which represents fifty percent of the total capacity of fish farms in Gaza.[33] Increasing carbon dioxide within the atmosphere leads to acidification of the seawater, which dissolves the shells of some marine animals, reduces their rate of survival, and affects fish behavior.[34]

For fifty-one days in 2014, the Gaza Strip was subject to a brutal Israeli assault called Operation Protective Edge. During the attack, the Israeli Defense Forces (IDF) dropped 21,000 tons of explosives on the strip, which seriously damaged the soil and thus reduced agricultural productivity.[35] Moreover, it led to the internal displacement of more than 108,000 people.[36] Intense bombing caused air pollution with smoke, chemicals, and polluted particles.[37] Israel uses many types of bombs and missiles, including prohibited weapons such as cluster bombs, white phosphorus shells, which are extremely toxic and violate the laws of war, and depleted-uranium explosives, which cause cancers and fetal malformations.[38] In May 2021, a two-day period of indiscriminate bombing within a concentrated residential area displaced 42,000 Palestinians and severely damaged 285 housing units, rendering them uninhabitable.[39] Israeli artillery targeted the Khudair group complex, the largest storehouse of agricultural supplies in Gaza, causing hundreds of tons of pesticides, fertilizers, and agricultural materials such as plastic, nylon, and water pipes to be released into the air.[40] Toxic gases emitted by burned pesticides are hundreds of times more toxic and dangerous to humans and the environment than the inherent toxicity of pesticides during their normal use.[41]

A sixteen-month study investigating Israeli aircraft spraying herbicide over the Gaza Strip[42] reported that "since 2014, the clearing and bulldozing of agricultural and residential lands by Israeli military close to the eastern border of Gaza has been complemented by unannounced aerial spraying of crop-killing herbicides."[43] This ongoing practice destroys entire swaths of formerly arable land along the border fence, but also crops and farmlands hundreds of meters deep into Palestinian territory, resulting in the loss of livelihoods for Gazan farmers."[44] The report states that pesticide spraying is killing crops and causing "unpredictable and uncontrollable damage." The spray is reaching more than 300 meters (980 feet) into Gaza, which leads the researchers to estimate that it has damaged about 4,936,000 square meters of agricultural land.[45] Additionally, heavy metal contamination of the lands bombed during the attacks of 2008, 2012, 2014, and 2021 continues to cause soil contamination and loss in soil fertility.[46]

Water quality will further deteriorate due to heavy metals and radioactive contamination from the 2014 attack.[47] Experts suspect that heavy metals like cadmium, copper, and lead contaminating the soil will percolate slowly to the aquifer, adding pollutants and posing serious health risks, including cancer.[48] "Most heavy metals persist in the environment for long periods of time causing chronic uptake by living organisms and accumulate in animal bodies and plants."[49] Research shows that the long-term effects of heavy metals in weaponry can last decades, and retrospective studies show a progressive increase in birth defects since the 2006 Gaza attacks.[50]

RESILIENCE THROUGH LAND CONNECTEDNESS

The Palestinian connection to the land is a powerful symbol of rootedness, making clear the injustice of displacement.[51] This "rootedness" is characterized by its unselfconscious quality, opposed to the concept of "sense of place," which signifies distance between self and place.[52] In the Palestinian frame of mind, there is no distancing of the self and the land as two separate entities, but rather a seeing of the self as "in and of" the land. Along with the concept of rootedness, there is the role that memories play in Palestinian identity. In the words of Nur Masalha, the Palestinian writer and academic who served as the director of the Centre for Religion and History at St. Mary's University, UK: "The rupture of 1948 and the 'ethnic cleansing' of the Nakba are central to both the Palestinian society of today and Palestinian social history and collective identity."[53] Together, these two components of rootedness and memories inform the way Palestinian identity is inherently one of resilience. Here, we will look at three specific examples of how such land connected resilience is manifested. First, through the way narratives of planting and farming are passed on through generations; second, through the way Palestinians are connected to the olive tree; and third, how Palestinian earth and soil itself serve as a means of deep human connection.

PLANTING AND CULTIVATION NARRATIVES

Devin Atallah, an assistant professor of psychology at the University of Massachusetts, Boston, studies decolonizing narratives and has researched communities in Palestine, exploring how "Palestinian families cultivate positive adaptation across [seven] generations"[54] of settler colonialism and intergenerational trauma. Resilience is passed across generations through narratives about practices like planting methods. These narratives can take multiple forms, including teaching the actual practice or storytelling.[55] He identifies three specific narrative topics: (a) skills and knowledge for *muqawama*/resistance; (b) roots for *awda*/return; and (c) morals, beliefs, and values for *sumoud*/perseverance, which are all metaphorically connected to planting methods.[56] In the form of land-based cultivation practices, storytelling, and memories of Palestinian land prior to settler colonialism, resilience is developed and inherited through generations.

CONNECTIONS TO THE OLIVE TREE

Palestine has some of the world's oldest olive trees, some of which have been there for 4,000 years.[57] Olive trees are ancient trees that establish a sense of continuity between Palestinians and the land, in shared history and bearing witness to shared realities. Some families, in passing down land over several generations, have also passed down olive trees for several generations.[58] The olive harvest season bears a socio-cultural meaning that has brought families together for generations.[59] Economically, olives are a main source of income for around 80,000 Palestinian families.[60] Beyond shared experiences and historical continuity, the characteristic of olive trees as drought-resistant trees that are able to grow and bear fruit under poor soil conditions are metaphorically and literally connected as shared characteristics of Palestinian resistance.[61] Rehab Nazzal, a Palestinian-born multidisciplinary artist and academic based in Canada, writes about her own experiences of growing up in Palestine, which she calls "the land of olives."[62] Nazzal writes that for Palestinians, olive trees "signify life's continuity beyond human mortality . . . Palestinians regard olive trees as their children, care for them with love until they mature and become independent, but never abandon them."[63] Nazzal also writes about how, along with Palestinian uprooting, olive trees have been uprooted in drastic numbers over seven generations. Olive trees inherently bear the Palestinian resilience and resistance to settler-colonialism narrative, and each year, during harvest season, Palestinian families are often prevented from returning to their homelands (from refugee camps) to harvest their own olives.

CONNECTION TO THE EARTH OF PALESTINE

Tarek Bakri is a Palestinian-born researcher based in Jerusalem who receives old photographs and drawings from Palestinians, or their descendants, uprooted during the Nakba.[64] He tries to locate the places of people's homes[65] and often arranges for them to see their homes, at least for a short one-time visit.[66] Tarek worked with Halima Khaddash, who was displaced from the village of Beit Nabala[67] and then lived in the Al-Jalazon refugee camp in Ramallah, a city in the West Bank.[68] In 2016, Tarek arranged for Halima, at the age of eighty-four, to return to her home after seventy-eight years.[69] A video recording shows how Halima returned with a few friends and immediately recognized the ruins of where her home used to be, while a well and olive trees remained.[70] Khaddash gets a burst of sudden energy as she becomes elated visiting the seaside in Jaffa.[71]

When Halima visited her home, she "took some soil from her home village, placed it in a bag and brought it away with her. When she got back to Al-Jalazon refugee camp in the occupied West Bank—where she now lives—Halima planted some mint in the soil."[72] "I want to grow mint in them, so every time I drink tea I can have some mint from home," Halima said.[73] Bakri says that not a single person comes from abroad without bringing a plastic bag to fill with soil to take back with them. "Some have taken soil to put on a parent's or grandparent's grave, some just want it in their home," he explains.[74] It is not simply a nostalgic memory, but a deeply visceral "agro-gastronomic attempt to keep the connection alive where even if a Palestinian cannot return permanently to the land," carrying some soil back can at least play part in connecting "the land to its rightful cultivator."[75]

In his dissertation, Atallah presents his research on how "processes of resilience are developed amongst Palestinian refugee families living under Israeli occupation for multiple generations."[76] Atallah organizes his findings in a representation metaphorically through a tree, which he explains is "inspired by cultural emphases on agriculture and interconnectedness between family life cycles, land, and dignity expressed by participants."[77] He emphasizes the rich cultural significance of the Palestinian family value of *cultivation*, or the encouragement of growth from seed to land, dignity, and self-determination.[78] Such forms of resilience guide Palestinians to not only sustain themselves amidst the occupation's devastating impact on human and natural life, but simultaneously to become active participants and contributors within the global climate change discourse.

PALESTINIAN CLIMATE ACTION

Amidst occupation, blockade, and climate change, Palestine has been actively contributing to global climate action. Palestine signed onto the Paris Agreement in 2016 and developed a climate adaptation strategy. In climate research, vulnerability is the propensity of people or systems to be harmed by hazards or stresses,[79] determined by "their exposures to hazard[s], their sensitivity to the exposures, and their capacities to resist, cope with, exploit, recover from and adapt to the effects."[80] Gaza is identified as having one of the highest levels of climate vulnerability in the world.[81] The strategy identifies research-building initiatives and disaster risk reduction policies and practices, amongst other initiatives.[82] Finally, Palestinians have introduced alternative energy practices such as solar energy as well as smart adaptation strategies within their daily practices.

Palestine is a member of the Climate Vulnerable Forum, which includes forty-eight developing countries highly vulnerable to climate change.[83] As part of the Paris Agreement, Palestine has set nationally determined contributions—climate-change mitigation benchmarks established to "reduce emissions and adapt to the impacts of climate change."[84] Palestine is currently working on passing climate change legislation, says Nedal Katbeh-Bader, climate change advisor at the Palestinian Environmental Quality Authority.[85] While PENGON was not able to participate at COP26, some of its network organizations carried the main message: "No climate justice under occupation." Palestinians have made significant achievements in environmental work, yet Palestine still struggles for sovereignty and the right to manage their own natural resources.

RECOMMENDATIONS

In April 2021, Human Rights Watch issued the report *A Threshold Crossed: Israeli Authorities and the Crimes of Apartheid and Persecution*. The report concludes that Israel must:

> Dismantle all forms of systematic oppression and discrimination that privilege Jewish Israelis at the expense of Palestinians and otherwise systematically violate Palestinian rights in order to ensure the dominance of Jewish Israelis, and end the persecution of Palestinians, including by ending discriminatory policies and practices in such realms as citizenship and nationality processes, protection of civil rights, freedom of movement, allocation of land and resources, access to water, electricity, and other services, and granting of building permits.[86]

The following are recommendations for the local Palestinian and international community:

1. The Palestinian Authority should encourage sustainable agriculture and agroecology, and work towards a cooperative economy that can achieve more resilience and sustainability.

2. The Palestinian Authority and other national and international organizations should work to coordinate the collection, analysis, and sharing of climate-related information.

3. The international community should put pressure on Israel to stop its illegal practices and policies against Palestinians and their properties, and to put an end to the expansion of settlements.

4. Israel should adhere to complete sovereignty of the Palestinian state over the natural resources including the Dead Sea and the Jordan River.

5. The most important recommendation is for the international community to focus on interventions to end the illegal occupation of Palestine.

CONCLUSION

Marginalized narratives need to be a part of the climate change discourse. The narratives of the lived visceral experiences that Palestinian people have with the land continue to live, despite conflict, and the Palestinian land continues to produce natural resources like olives. Resilience is the shared narrative of Palestinian people and the land and there is much to be learned about resilience through this narrative. However, the vulnerabilities of Palestinian land caused by climate change and armed conflict must be stopped.

Adaptation to climate change will not be possible for Palestinians without genuine realization of the collective right to self-determination and permanent sovereignty over their natural resources. Israel continues unabatedly to illegally expropriate Palestinian resources, which severely hampers the right to development and efforts to adapt to the consequences of climate change in Palestine. While the world responds to climate change, sixty-eight percent of Palestinians in Gaza are food insecure. It is time for this siege to be unconditionally lifted and for the two million people and all living elements of the land in Gaza to be allowed to live with dignity.

NOTES

1. United Nations County Team in the Occupied Palestinian Territory, *Gaza in 2020: A Liveable Place?* (Jerusalem: Office of the United Nations Special Coordinator for the Middle East Peace Process – UNSCO, 2012), 2.

2. Irus Braverman, "Environmental Justice in the Occupied Palestinian West Bank," The Baldy Center for Law and Policy at the University at Buffalo, https://www.buffalo.edu/baldycenter/events/conferences/west-bank.html.

3. See Wildlife Palestine, "Conserve Species, Habitats and Sites Program – Wildlife Palestine," 2021, http://www.wildlife-pal.org/en/category/43/1/Conserve-species,-habitats-and-sites.

4. See Nur Masalha, *The Palestine Nakba: Decolonising History, Narrating the Subaltern, Reclaiming Memory* (London: Zed Books, 2012).

5. Ahmad H. Sa'di and Lila Abu-Lughod, *Nakba Palestine, 1948, and the Claims of Memory* (New York: Columbia University Press, 2007), 8.

6. Cynthia G. Franklin, "Against Erasures: Why Life-Writing Scholars Should Address the Nakba," *a/b: Auto/Biography Studies* 32, no. 2 (2017): 311–14.

7. Masalha, *The Palestine Nakba*, 3.

8. Nur Masalha, "60 Years after Nakba: Historical Truth; Collective Memory; Ethical Obligations," *Kyoto Bulletin of Islamic Area Studies Area* 3, no. 1 (July 2009): 37.

9. David Mills, Bram Wispelwey, Rania Muhareb, and Mads Gilbert, "Structural Violence in the Era of a New Pandemic: The Case of the Gaza Strip," *The Lancet*, March 27, 2020.

10. Roald Høvring, "Gaza: The World's Largest Open-Air Prison," *Norwegian Refugee Council*, April 26, 2018.

11. United Nations, *Territory, Humanitarian Situation in the Gaza Strip Fast Facts – OCHA Factsheet* (Jerusalem: Office for the Coordination of Humanitarian Affairs Occupied Palestinian, October 2011).

12. United Nations Plenary – Seventy-fifth Session, "Guterres: Gaza Children Living in 'Hell on Earth' Secretary-General Tells General Assembly, as Calls for End to Violence Crescendo, News of Israel-Hamas Ceasefire Breaks," United Nations Press Release, May 20, 2021, https://www.un.org/press/en/2021/ga12325.doc.htm.

13. United Nations Economic Development, "UN Report Finds Gaza Suffered $16.7 Billion Loss from Siege and Occupation," *United Nations News*, November 25, 2020, https://news.un.org/en/story/2020/11/1078532.

14. Butmeh Abeer, "We Call for a Just Recovery for Gaza and an Immediate End to Israel's Illegal Occupation," *Friends of the Earth Asia Pacific*, October 5, 2021, https://foeasiapacific.org/2021/10/05/we-call-for-a-just-recovery-for-gaza-and-an-immediate-end-to-israels-illegal-occupation/?utm_source=rss&utm_medium

=rss&utm_campaign=we-call-for-a-just-recovery-for-gaza-and-an-immediate-end-to-israels-illegal-occupation.

15. Ibid.

16. David Mills, Mads Gilbert, and Bram Wispelwey, "Gaza's Great March of Return: Humanitarian Emergency and the Silence of International Health Professionals," *BMJ Global Health* 4, no. 3 (May 11, 2019): 4.

17. International Committee of the Red Cross, *When Rain Turns to Dust: Understanding and Responding to the Combined Impact of Armed Conflicts and the Climate and Environment Crisis on People's Lives* (Geneva: International Committee of the Red Cross, 2020), 8.

18. Ibid., 10–11.

19. Abeer Butmeh, "Palestine Is a Climate Justice Issue," *Al Jazeera*, November 28, 2019.

20. "Water in Gaza: Scarce, Polluted and Mostly Unfit for Use," B'Tselem – The Israeli Information Center for Human Rights in the Occupied Territories, August 17, 2020, https://www.btselem.org/gaza_strip/20200818_gaza_water_scarce_polluted _mostly_unfit_for_use.

21. Ibid.

22. Zena Agha, "Israel's Problematic Role in Perpetuating Water Insecurity for Palestine," *Atlantic Council*, June 28, 2019.

23. Susanna Reskallah, "Food Insecurity in Palestine: A Future for Farmers," *Wilson Center*, August 30, 2021.

24. Shira Efron, Melinda Moore, Rouslan I. Karimov, Ilana Blum, and Jordan R. Fischbach, *The Public Health Impacts of Gaza's Water Crisis: Analysis and Policy Options* (Santa Monica: RAND Corporation, 2018), 3.

25. Ibid., 87.

26. World Bank, "Securing Water for Development in West Bank and Gaza" (Washington, DC: World Bank Publications, 2018), 14–15.

27. Maram Humaid, "Gaza's Undrinkable Water 'Slowly Poisoning' Palestinians," *Al Jazeera*, October 12, 2021, https://www.aljazeera.com/news/2021/10/12/gaza-undrinkable-water-slowly-poisoning-people.

28. Efron et al., *The Public Health Impacts of Gaza's Water Crisis*, 93.

29. OXFAM International, "Seawater Pollution Raises Concerns of Waterborne Diseases and Environmental Hazards in the Gaza Strip," *United Nations Office for the Coordination of Humanitarian Affairs*, August 9, 2018.

30. Efron et al., *The Public Health Impacts of Gaza's Water Crisis*, 1.

31. "Palestinian Boy Dies after Ingesting Poison at Gaza's Increasingly Polluted Beaches," *Independent*, August 28, 2017, https://www.independent.co.uk/news/world /middle-east/gaza-pollution-kills-five-year-old-boy-electricty-sewage-water-crisis-israel-hamas-palestinian-authority-a7916326.html.

32. Efron et al., *The Public Health Impacts of Gaza's Water Crisis*, 1.

33. Palestinian Environmental NGOs Network, "Palestine: A Case of Climate Change" (Ramallah, Palestine: PENGON, 2021), 1.

34. Ibid.

35. Khalidi Rashid, "The Dahiya Doctrine, Proportionality, and War Crimes," *Journal of Palestine Studies* 44, no. 1 (2014): 5–13; State of Palestine, "The National Early Recovery and Reconstruction Plan for Gaza," International Conference in Support of the Reconstruction of Gaza, October 2014, https://reliefweb.int/report/occupied-palestinian-territory/national-early-recovery-and-reconstruction-plan-gaza.

36. Safi Saleh Ahmad, *2014 War on Gaza Strip: Participatory Environmental Impact Assessment* (Ramallah, Palestine: Palestinian Environmental NGO's Network through Maan Development Center & Funded by Heinrich-Böll-Stiftung, 2015), 15.

37. Ibid.

38. Marc Garlasco, Fred Abrahams, Bill van Esveld, Fares Akram, and Darryl Li, *Rain of Fire: Israel's Unlawful Use of White Phosphorus in Gaza* (New York: Human Rights Watch, 2009), 61.

39. "Israeli Occupying Forces Perpetrate Widespread and Systematic Attacks Against the Civilian Palestinian Population in the Gaza Strip, the International Criminal Must Prioritise Investigation," *Al-Haq*, May 17, 2021, https://www.alhaq.org/advocacy/18381.html.

40. Ibid.

41. Mervat Ouf, "Israeli Bombs Ignite Pesticide Stores, Spew Dangerous Chemicals in Gaza," *Al-Monitor*, June 14, 2021, https://www.al-monitor.com/originals/2021/06/israeli-bombs-ignite-pesticide-stores-spew-dangerous-chemicals-gaza.

42. Miriam Berger, "Israeli Spraying of Herbicide near Gaza Harming Palestinian Crops," *The Guardian*, July 19, 2019, https://www.theguardian.com/world/2019/jul/19/israeli-spraying-of-herbicide-near-gaza-harming-palestinian-crops.

43. Ibid.

44. Forensic Architecture, "Herbicidal Warfare in Gaza," *University of London*, July 19, 2019: https://forensic-architecture.org/investigation/herbicidal-warfare-in-gaza.

45. Ibid.

46. Nabil al Baraquoni, Samir R. Qouta, Mervi Vänskä, Safwat Y. Diab, Raija-Leena Punamäki, and Paola Manduca, "It Takes Time to Unravel the Ecology of War in Gaza, Palestine: Long-Term Changes in Maternal, Newborn and Toddlers' Heavy Metal Loads, and Infant and Toddler Developmental Milestones in the Aftermath of the 2014 Military Attacks," *International Journal of Environmental Research and Public Health* 17, no. 18 (September 14, 2020): 6698.

47. Ahmad, *2014 War on Gaza Strip*, 17–18.

48. Ibid., 29, 32.

49. Paola Manduca, Nabil Al Baraquni, and Stefano Parodi, "Long Term Risks to Neonatal Health from Exposure to War – 9 Years Long Survey of Reproductive Health and Contamination by Weapon-Delivered Heavy Metals in Gaza, Palestine," *International Journal of Environmental Research and Public Health* 17, no. 7 (April 8, 2020): 2538.

50. Ibid.

51. "Palestinian Relationships with and Rootedness to the Land," Museum of the Palestinian People Website, 2017, https://mpp-dc.org/gallery/palestine-relationship-with-rootedness-to-the-land/.

52. Roger Heacock, "Palestinians: The Land and the Law, An Inverse Relationship," *Journal of International Affairs* 57, no. 2 (2004): 151.

53. Nur Masalha, "Remembering the Palestinian Nakba: Commemoration, Oral History and Narratives of Memory," *Holy Land Studies, A Multidisciplinary Journal* 7, no. 2 (2008): 123.

54. Devin G. Atallah, "A Community-Based Qualitative Study of Inter-generational Resilience with Palestinian Refugee Families Facing Structural Violence and Historical Trauma," *Transcultural Psychiatry* vol. 54, no. 3 (2017): 357.

55. Ibid., 373.

56. Ibid.

57. Ibid.

58. Ibid.

59. Ibid.

60. Ibid.

61. Palestinian Initiative for the Promotion of Global Dialogue and Democracy (MIFTAH), "Fact Sheet: Olive Trees – More Than Just a Tree in Palestine – Occupied Palestinian Territory," United Nations Office for the Coordination of Humanitarian Affairs, November 21, 2012.

62. Rehab Nazzal, "Reflections: The Olive Tree and the Palestinian Struggle against Settler-Colonialism," *Canada and Beyond* 8, no. 1 (2019): 86–93, 89.

63. Ibid.

64. Bahira Amin, "The Power of Palestinian Return, If Only for an Afternoon," *Scene Arabia*, May 15, 2020.

65. Ibid.

66. Ibid.

67. Tarek Bakri, "This Sea Belongs to Halima," uploaded October 2, 2016, YouTube video, https://www.youtube.com/watch?v=NeWVfEtRfnQ.

68. Ibid.

69. Ibid.

70. Ibid.

71. Amjad Ayman Yaghi, "Giving Palestinians a Glimpse of Home," *The Electronic Intifada*, January 14, 2021, https://electronicintifada.net/content/giving-palestinians-glimpse-home/32111.

72. Ibid.

73. Amin, "The Power of Palestinian Return."

74. Ibid.

75. Ibid.

76. Atallah, "A Community-Based Qualitative Study," 357.

77. Ibid., 365.

78. Ibid.

79. Michael Mason, Mark Zeitoun, and Ziad Mimi, "Compounding Vulnerability: Impacts of Climate Change on Palestinians in Gaza and the West Bank," *Journal of Palestine Studies* 41, no. 3 (January 2012): 38.

80. Neil Leary, et al., "For Whom the Bell Tolls: Vulnerabilities in a Changing Climate," in *Climate Change and Vulnerability*, ed. Cecilia Conde, Jyoti Kulkarni, Neil Leary, Anthony Nyong, and Juan Pulhin (London, UK: Earthscan, 2008), 4.

81. Richard Smithers, Mike Harrison, Ziam Mimi, Khaled Hardan, Sadiq Abdelall, and Atif Hasan, *National Adaptation Plan to Climate Change* (Ramallah, Palestine: Environment Quality Authory, 2016), 15.

82. Ibid., 47.

83. Najla Abdellatif, "Palestine Leading International Climate Negotiations," Heinrich-Böll-Stiftung: Palestine and Jordan, January 13, 2020, https://ps.boell.org/en/2020/01/13/palestine-leading-international-climate-negotiations.

84. Ibid.; United Nations, "Nationally Determined Contributions," https://unfccc.int/process-and-meetings/the-paris-agreement/nationally-determined-contributions-ndcs/nationally-determined-contributions-ndcs.

85. Ibid.

86. Omar Shakir and Eric Goldstein, "A Threshold Crossed: Israeli Authorities and the Crimes of Apartheid and Persecution" (New York: Human Rights Watch, 2021), 205.

The (Non)Existence of Uprooted Bodies:
The Limits of Authorized Imaginations and Languages in Assisting Bodies on the Move Due to Environmental Causes

César "CJ" Baldelomar

GROWING UP IN HIALEAH, a city in southern Florida's Miami-Dade County, I recall almost daily news accounts of Cuban "refugees" arriving onshore, especially in the wake of the 1995 "wet foot, dry foot" policy that permitted Cubans who landed on United States soil to stay and qualify for expedited legal permanent residency a year later. The prevailing rhetoric within my community and on the news presented these sea voyagers as deserving of special protection because of the dire communist situation in Cuba under Fidel Castro. Meanwhile, Haitians who undertook a similarly perilous but longer journey through treacherous Atlantic waters were not so lucky upon reaching US land. Immigration authorities rounded them up to promptly deport them, despite Haiti's longstanding political, social, and economic instability. Even as a child, I began to understand that some lives mattered more than others in the eyes of the state and the community. I felt a sense of injustice stirring within, but I did not yet have the conceptual or rhetorical understanding of necropolitics or of biopower, which are both tied to notions of territoriality, sovereignty, and citizenship.

In my teaching and scholarship, I seek to engage in thought experiments that begin to complexify conversations over seemingly quotidian topics and events. In this vein, as a heuristic and pedagogical commitment, I seek to demystify rhetoric that has become encased in almost sacrosanct auras, preventing imaginations from dreaming otherwise. Some words, such as liberation and hope, ring so hollow and yet enjoy the utmost persuasion in the rhetorical economy. Some concepts, such as the legal fiction of migrant versus refugee, enjoy epistemological privilege within narratives designed to confine "thinking otherwise" to the category of the abnormal, the degenerate, the criminal, the insane, or the pathogen. And to raise the specter of nihilism in light of the meaninglessness and hopelessness spawned by mass senseless and arbitrary death, pain, and suffering is to risk derision or censure.

As a Latinx scholar, audiences usually expect me to "fight for justice" within approved channels (politics, education, liberation theology) and to disclose every aspect of my own identity,[1] as if such chatter is possible.[2] This essay is a thought experiment that hopes to begin fragmenting rhetoric and concepts that, though well-intentioned, buffer the self from engagement with the brutal (and perhaps hopeless) nature of living in a fundamentally unfair and violent world. Maybe this is justice talk too— but from a different angle and with less expectations or faith in collective human agency.

ENTERING THE THOUGHT EXPERIMENT

This essay challenges the simplistic chimeras of liberation talk prevalent within political and legal action and fueled by a politics of hope. According to Afro-pessimists like Calvin Warren, "the politics of hope posits that one *must* have a politics to have hope; politics is the natural habitat of hope itself."[3] Politics is the only arena, the sole scene of instruction where hope plays out and utopian dreams take flight in a never-ending cycle that obfuscates alternative forms of resistance within the continual history, or loop, of domination upon domination. To quote Warren once again, "the pursuit [of a not-yet social order] marks a cruel attachment to the means of subjugation and the continued widening of the gap between historical reality and fantastical ideal."[4] Indeed, the notion of progress (especially in the context of social justice) depends on fantasies of liberation as a one-time event (a utopia) rather than as the continual practice of freedom that starts within by consistently undoing perceived fixed boundaries.[5]

Rather than presenting standard facts and statistics on environmental causes for displacement or rehashing legal narratives and political pleas for justice, this essay seeks to dislodge and fracture contemporary justice and liberation rhetoric about uprooted bodies. By dislodging imaginations beholden to idolatrous concepts (such as justice and hope), one can perhaps begin to envision what never was. This essay urges careful attention to the words we use, to the speeches we enact and reactivate, especially when referring to people teetering on the edge of hopelessness, such as those on the move because of environmental concerns. Bodies on the move represent a dual threat at the macro and micro levels, from the geopolitical down to the personal. The "uprooted" present existential and physical threats to the cherished ideal of sovereignty (and the security it provides to its rooted bodies, known as citizens). They also put into question the very notion of personal identity, which stems largely from nationalistic and patriotic narratives that situate individuals in a spatial and temporal nation-building fiction. The displaced simultaneously exist and do not exist, which raises several uncomfortable questions about human worth and the bankrupt rhetoric of equality.

Frank Wilderson III argues that "human life is dependent on Black death for existence and for its conceptual coherence. There is no world without Blacks, yet there are no Blacks who are in the world."[6] Just as human life (understood as a Eurocentric legal-religious construct) depends on Black people for its existence and continuation, so do sovereignty and territoriality (in essence, borders) depend on uprooted bodies on the move for their conceptual clarity. Citizenship (and its attendant privileges and rights) requires the exclusion of an "Other"—and the strategic timid inclusion of still "Others"—for it to become legally and culturally operative. What easier Other to target for out-right exclusion than the migrant crossing a border to escape environmental degradation, who represents the archetype of those on the move for allegedly non-emergency purposes?

International law and justice related to people on the move operate on a series of binaries that essentialize the experiences of these uprooted bodies. In particular, the binary of refugee and migrant still dictates who receiving states see as deserving of protection. The refugee and migration system upholds sovereignty, territoriality, and citizenship as constitutive of a sacred political and social order that must be defended at all costs—not least from the threat of thinking otherwise.

Before analyzing the categories spawned by the modern refugee regime, whose origins are as recent as the second decade of the twentieth century, it is essential to raise a couple of questions that often leave fellow interlocutors confused and even angry: Do all humans matter equally within our contemporary nationalistic legal and global economic systems? Is every hominid really human within the current colonial arrangement, with origins in 1492 but with its development during the "long sixteenth" century?[7]

ON "(NON)HUMAN" LIVES

Of course, by instinct, most in theological, pastoral, or justice-oriented and advocacy circles will answer those two questions with a resounding yes, if after some whispers of disapproval at the questions themselves. I raise these questions not as trite provocations but as key to envisioning multiple possibilities for selves through theological and civic education and (re)imagination. Let me slightly reframe the questions: What does it mean to be considered human or not in a world demarcated by differences within the coloniality matrix? More specifically, what does it mean to be human in a world dominated by capital, war, technologies, and the subjugation of nature, a world that was imposed five centuries ago on Indigenous peoples and spread through discovery, industrialization, capitalism, Christianity, and even scientific socialism, but that now operates as normative (and is understood as eternal) via globalization on *all* bodies?[8] With a limited field of vision, can collective populations ever see the relativity of all knowledges, values, and morals that have and continue to order Western-liberal societies and their conceptions of sovereignty, citizenship, and even the human?

The human is understood as a universal subject with equal rights, dignity, and privileges—a nice rhetorical sentiment supported by religious and political speeches of the common good and human rights, respectively. But this sentiment remains realistic only in the rhetorical realm. In practice, evidence that humans are assigned different values in capitalism are ubiquitous, from insurance companies calculating the monetary worth of the dead based on a person's net worth, earning power potential, age, and education, to the fact that some humans are held in cages simply for trying to cross a border that others cross with impunity, even after overstaying their visas. A missing young white woman garners more national attention than a missing trans person or a Salvadoran or Haitian child who crossed the border and is missing. Similarly, criminals, the "insane," those with certain diseases and disabilities, and the elderly (especially the non-wealthy elderly) are deemed less worthy as humans and as citizens (or as potential citizens). Recall here the "public charge" category in existing US immigration law as a way to gauge human worth based on potential economic production and consumption power.[9]

Certain bodies, then, appear as defective, as less desirable ("ugly") and so more disposable and less deserving of rights and protections.[10] Exclusion of all sorts of bodies legitimizes the inclusion of other bodies into a normative framework that bestows personhood (via citizenship) upon certain subjects. To be considered a subject—with rights and privileges, including the ability to create knowledge—others have to become objects subject to all kinds of violence, from the epistemological to the physical, often under the veneer of legal protections and state paternalism. The loop of history around coalescing arrangements of power and social organization requires both mechanisms of violence and of protections against those very forms of violence.

Michel Foucault writes, "Humanity does not gradually progress from combat to combat until it arrives at universal reciprocity, where the rule of law finally replaces warfare; humanity installs each of its violences in a system of rules and thus proceeds from domination to domination."[11] Those able to understand and interpret the rules are then able to bend and even pervert them until the next interpreter comes along with another will or purpose for modifying the rules, perhaps even creating new ones in the process. In essence, "the development of humanity is a series of interpretations."[12] Out of these interpretations emerge "truth regimes" that structure reality.

In the US, broadly speaking, the current truth regimes are American exceptionalism abroad and white supremacy domestically. As the world's police, the US forces its will on less stable sovereignties in the name of democracy, decency, and human rights.[13] It even engages in endless wars under the banner of freedom and rule of law, promoting Western liberal ideals as the only paradigm for social organization.[14] Regarding domestic "truth," Cristina Beltrán opines that "American conceptions of equality, freedom, and democracy have historically been constituted through white supremacy. In other words, the experience of democracy, equality, and freedom cannot be fully detached from the political project of whiteness in the United States."[15]

Whiteness is a protean category though. While certainly speaking to privileges and rights attached to phenotype, whiteness should actually be replaced by or at least understood alongside the term "normalized"— a sort of coalescing of grammars of normalizing powers that function to safeguard what Burton Mack calls a narrative logic: "the collective agreements about the way the world works [which] are lodged in the world of imagination and storied as having taken place in other times."[16] These agreements then settle "into place as a register of mental agreements about the way life should be lived."[17] Protecting these collective agreements entails committing to a center of truth with hard and fixed borders. Enter policing (by all) of bodies (tangible and intangible) within and outside those borders in order to preserve some arbitrary and imaginary way of life for identities that seem similarly fixed and grounded within the circle of truth.

Bodies on the move, especially due to seemingly non-essential reasons, represent both a threat and an opportunity: a threat to national and personal identities and stability but an opportunity to tighten the borders around such identities through authorized violence. After all, as Warren states, "corporal fracture engenders ontological coherence."[18] Or in the words of Reinhold Niebuhr, "all human life is involved in the sin of seeking security at the expense of other life."[19]

LEGAL FICTIONS AND UPROOTED BODIES

International law is part and parcel of the coloniality matrix. It has its origins in traditional European humanist and Enlightenment philosophy and its mission serves "to justify the belief that the non-European world was not sovereign, because those people had not earned the right to sovereignty."[20] According to Swiss jurist Emmerich de Vattel, legal title to land depended on signs of "civilization," such as densely settled terrain replete with buildings and agricultural technologies. The doctrines of *terra nullius* and discovery, as well as the landmark US Supreme Court Decision *Johnson v. McIntosh*, were essentially a genealogical product of Vattel's legal imagination. Mythmaking through imagination can have real-life consequences.

Arguably, only a cadre of thinkers undertake the related tasks of interpretation and knowledge creation and transmission while the rest accept it as given, as natural, as the way things are. These others then police themselves and others to guard against threats to porous personal, social, and political borders. "Power is no longer substantially identified with an individual who possesses or exercises it by right of birth," Foucault claims. "It becomes a machinery that no one owns."[21] All contribute to this machinery, albeit at different levels.

Those able to create knowledge—that is, categories and conceptual frames of reference that structure reality and so inform characters—are usually citizens of a sovereign state. And not just any citizen but those with the highest forms of privilege because of whatever arbitrary marker of superiority they are trying to protect with their so-called knowledge. It is a rigged power game. A platform emerges only for ideas, even ones that appear contrarian, that ensure the survival of the current truth regimes in power.

The refugee regime is part of the international legal rights "truth" regime. Rebecca Hamlin notes that "the refugee concept is deeply linked to questions of sovereignty and territoriality, neither of which was an organizing principle of the world until the modern period."[22] Walter Mignolo and other decolonial scholars trace the genesis of modernity to the colonial conquest of 1492, when Euro-Christian imaginations had to integrate into their narrative logics peoples previously unaccounted for in Euro-Christian origin myths. Nation-building, following the end of empires, necessitated making sense of these colonial encounters among distinct epistemologies, ontologies, and spiritualities. It required the "persecution of minorities, and caused people to flee across newly crystallizing international borders," Hamlin observes. "Displaced people were then understood to be the products of either the state's failure to protect their citizens, or the citizen's failure to fit within the state."[23] Blame had to accrue somewhere, either in an ineffective state or in defective individuals or groups—all under the aegis of sovereignty and the then-emerging identities rooted in a particular territory. So emerged the doctrine of sovereignty, with its "ultimate expression largely [residing] in the power and capacity to dictate who is able to live and who must die."[24]

Talk of refugees before the twentieth century is anachronistic. A refugee is someone seeking access to a sovereign state. But the modern concept of sovereignty did not exist prior to the 1648 Peace of Westphalia, and it did not crystallize in its modern form until after the end of empires. Nonetheless, stories of the Huguenots and Puritans as refugees remain unchallenged. The story usually goes like this: both groups were escaping persecution in their homelands; they fled and found refuge in new lands—lands ripe with opportunities for new lives, new homes, new economic arrangements. Yet, in the case of the Huguenots, sovereignty was still relatively weak in France. And European law did not recognize Indigenous lands as sovereign, so the Puritans were certainly not refugees. These stories, essentially myths, are told to accentuate the entrepreneurial spirit of these "refugees" even after they suffered persecution in their own lands. By implication, states grant contemporary refugees protection only when persecuted politically (now usually by a communist regime, or if Christian, by Islamic states) and when able to contribute economically to the state.

Terms used for people on the move included exiles, strangers, emigrants, and "distressed Protestants." It wasn't until the 1951 Refugee Convention and its 1967 Protocol that the term "refugee" was defined and gained international traction. Article 1(a)(2) delimits who can be considered a refugee:

As a result of events occurring before 1 January 1951 and owing to well-founded fear of being persecuted for reasons of race, religion, nationality, membership of a particular social group or political opinion, is outside the country of his nationality and is unable or, owing to such fear, is unwilling to avail himself of the protection of that country; or who, not having a nationality and being outside the country of his former habitual residence as a result of such events, is unable or, owing to such fear, is unwilling to return to it.[25]

The 1967 Protocol removed the clause of "as a result of events occurring before 1 January 1951" from the definition. A couple of observations are in order. First, the drafters clearly had in mind only those displaced by the aftermath of the Second World War. Second, as deeply contextual documents with limited fields of reference, the convention and its protocol are mute regarding environmental factors of displacement. The entire international refugee regime, then, stems from concerns of Europeans fleeing the aftermath of state-led violations and abuses of human rights. The regime thus depends on clear causes for leaving a territory, usually related to political instability. These causes then become markers to legally label, neatly categorize, and clearly understand bodies that are on the move for often very distinct reasons.

Under the current international law and refugee law regime, those displaced because of environmental factors are migrants, not refugees. The terms matter. International and domestic laws provide refugees (which is a protected legal status) with certain rights and protections; migrants (an umbrella term) receive almost none.[26] The dichotomy between refugee and migrant has resulted in a legal fiction that, on the one hand, views refugees as deserving of protection because they have been forced to leave their home countries by political factors. Migrants, on the other hand, leave voluntarily for purely economic reasons. Since, according to the legal fiction, migrant lives are not in any immediate threat, they are undeserving of legal protection under international and domestic rights regimes. The suffering of refugees takes precedence over that of migrants, who are portrayed in the media as opportunistic border crossers. Refugee lives immediately differ in worth from migrant ones, as citizens of receiving states are usually more supportive of refugees than of migrants. Essentially, this legal regime makes certain lives more "grieveable" than others.[27]

Hamlin and other critical legal scholars point out that reality is always much more complex than positivist legal categories and narratives would have us believe. "Economic development, political corruption, and armed conflict are closely linked processes," observes Hamlin. "Even on their own, economic factors are forces that can compel people to move." But legal regimes abhor complexity. And so too do circles of truth with hardened, settled boundaries. Those on the move because of environmental issues—issues also linked to economic development, political corruption, and armed conflict—represent the "impossible subject" within the modern sovereignty and human-rights project. They simply cannot be emplotted into contemporary nationalistic or legal narratives as either characters with rooted national identities or as refugees deserving the benevolence of receiving states. Environmental migrants are neither here nor there.

So then where do they appear in narratives of rights and justice? Where do they matter? As hinted at earlier, they matter to assuage anxieties over the increasingly porous borders that constitute nationalistic-based identities and the cherished concept of sovereignty. More than any other type of border crosser, environmental border crossers are easy targets for the exclusion needed to uphold the value and worth of some lives over others. Beltrán argues that "[f]or nativists who yearn for the freedom to police, punish, and exclude, targeting migrants makes them feel stronger, freer, more agentic, transforming acts of racialized violence—whether people are committing, witnessing, or merely describing such acts—into feats of heroism, democratic redemption, civic engagement, and virtuous sovereignty."[28]

Migrants generally are the fodder for preserving clear national identities and borders. Environmental border crossers specifically are seen as completely fictitious and opportunistic characters—and so utterly undeserving not only of legal protections but even of human dignity. Many in the public sphere, and certainly many neo-conservative and alt-right politicians, don't even accept the effects of climate change as real. To a significant portion of the population, it is nonsense to talk of sea-level rise along low-lying coastal areas, or about drought, desertification, drylands, loss of biodiversity, food insecurity, extreme weather, and climate-driven natural diseases. Even more foolish in their minds, then, is to link displacement and movement to these phenomena. Environmental border crossers simply do not register within the narratives of rights and sovereignty. They enter the imagination as an opportunistic pathogen in need of immediate policing through authorized violence—all to preserve borders. Their uncategorized status disrupts neat legal regimes and political justice talk.

PARTING THOUGHTS: INVITATION FOR THINKING (AND SPEAKING) OTHERWISE

At this point, many are perhaps expecting me to adumbrate some solutions to the plight of those uprooted due to environmental causes. Some scholars and activists point to the "hope" in liability and compensation mechanisms (such as the polluter pays principle), in possible international insurance claims, or in the possibility of another international instrument that includes migrants, specifically environmental ones. And still others hope to expand the definition of refugee as found in the Refugee Convention and its Protocol. Religious folk might look to Pope Francis's leadership on the environment. Indeed, in March 2021, the Vatican released "Pastoral Guidelines on Climate Displaced People." While I laud this, I wonder how many Catholics have heard of this document or even believe that environmentally displaced peoples exist. What are the limits of religious and theological language in social-justice claims?

Transformations in imagination will likely not come via authorized legal, political, or even religious imagination or language. Law and politics, as this essay has argued, justify the norms of existing centers of truth. Religion, even when oriented toward justice, also tends to normalize or privilege certain moralities, identities, knowledges, and practices that have and continue to limit the possibilities for being otherwise in the continual search for "liberation" as a one-time event. So where to look?

One suggestion might be conversations that seek to demystify concepts and rhetoric that simply keep the status quo—the dominant narratives—going. I have engaged Afro-pessimists and nihilism throughout my work and in this essay because epistemological nihilism in particular seeks to redress the epistemological and ontological violence caused by simplistic ethical scenes of instruction and the characters held up as normative by theological and political police powers, which are often two sides of the same coin.[29]

Space for nihilism and hopelessness can rupture what creates meaning and what holds subjects and objects in place to enact that meaning (such as hope and justice talk).[30] The death of stagnant imaginations and narratives is an essential step before moving on to imagining other worlds, selves, and scripts. Out of death emerges new life, which eventually must also be killed to allow the loop to continue—but in unforeseen ways. How to rid our minds and actions of the fascism within us all—of that urge to erect and protect fictitious borders around truly fleeting and shifting personal, social, and political identities?

Before proposing any solutions to large-scale global issues, let us start by daring to think and be otherwise as much as possible within the loop of history and of power's ongoing reconstitutions. Rather than seek "liberation grounded in political reconfiguration and emancipatory rhetoric,"[31] I seek to fragment totalities, even well-intentioned ones, that limit the endless possibilities of shifting and uprooted bodies and identities—identities that disrupt the fascism and egoism in us all, even if only for a few moments. Who knows what variation can emerge then? Who knows what compassion for broken and shifting bodies can arise within us all once fixed borders begin to shatter?

NOTES

1. Caroline Dick contends that "the concept of identity, as it is employed by identity-driven theories of group rights, obscures in-group differences and assigns a false homogeneity to groups and communities." See Caroline Dick, *The Perils of Identity: Group Rights and the Politics of Intragroup Difference* (Vancouver: UBC Press, 2011), 20.

2. I share Mark D. Jordan's sentiment: "I would like to believe that the words we use to tell our inmost truths are most of all our own words, but I know better." See Mark D. Jordan, "Roundtable on Ethnography and Religion: Writing 'the Truth,'" *Practical Matters* 6 (2013), http://practicalmattersjournal.org/2013/03/01/writing-the-truth/.

3. Calvin L. Warren, "Black Nihilism and the Politics of Hope," *CR: The New Centennial Review* 15, no. 1 (2015): 215–48, 219.

4. Ibid., 221.

5. Maggie Nelson borrows the distinction between liberation as a one-time event and the practice of freedom as ongoing from Michel Foucault. See Maggie Nelson, *On Freedom: Four Songs of Care and Constraint* (Minneapolis: Graywolf Press, 2021), especially 5–7.

6. Frank B. Wilderson III, "Afro-Pessimism and the End of Redemption," *Humanities Future*, https://humanitiesfutures.org/papers/afro-pessimism-end-redemption/.

7. An Yountae and Eleanor Craig, "Introduction: Challenging Modernity/Coloniality in Philosophy of Religion," in *Beyond Man: Race, Coloniality, and Philosophy of Religion*, ed. An Yountae and Eleanor Craig (Durham: Duke University Press, 2021), 9.

8. Ibid., 3–4. An Yountae and Craig note, "Coloniality is the universalization and normalization of matrices of power that historically enacted colonization itself and the presumption of superiority that these forces collectively grant to discourses articulated from colonizing and western perspectives."

9. See especially Douglas C. Bayton, *Defectives in the Land: Disability and Immigration in the Age of Eugenics* (Chicago: University of Chicago Press, 2016).

10. See Susan M. Schweik, *The Ugly Laws: Disability in Public* (New York: New York University Press, 2009).

11. Michel Foucault, "Nietzsche, Genealogy, History," in *The Foucault Reader*, ed. Paul Rabinow (New York: Vintage Books, 2010), 85.

12. Ibid., 86.

13. See Mahmood Mamdani, "Responsibility to Protect or Right to Punish?" *Journal of Intervention and Statebuilding* 4, no. 1 (2010): 53–67.

14. See Samuel Moyn, *Humane: How the United States Abandoned Peace and Reinvented War* (New York: Farrar, Straus and Giroux, 2021).

15. Cristina Beltrán, *Cruelty as Citizenship: How Migrant Suffering Sustains White Democracy* (Minneapolis: University of Minnesota Press, 2020), 18.

16. Burton L. Mack, *Christian Mentality: The Entanglements of Power, Violence, and Fear* (London: Equinox, 2011), 7.

17. Ibid.

18. Warren, "Black Nihilism and the Politics of Hope," 217.

19. Reinhold Niebuhr, *The Nature and Destiny of Man: A Christian Interpretation, Vol. 1: Human Nature* (New York: Scribner's Sons, 1964), 169.

20. Rebecca Hamlin, *Crossing: How We Label and React to People on the Move* (Stanford: Stanford University Press, 2021), 33.

21. Michel Foucault, "The Eye of Power," in *Power/Knowledge: Selected Interviews and Other Writings 1972–1977*, ed. Colin Gordon (New York: Vintage Books, 1980), 156.

22. Hamlin, *Crossing*, 18.

23. Ibid., 31.

24. Joseph-Achille Mbembé, *Necropolitics*, trans. Steven Corcoran (Durham: Duke University Press, 2019), 66.

25. United Nations, Convention and Protocol Relating to the Status of Refugees, https://www.unhcr.org/en-us/3b66c2aa10.

26. Hamlin, *Crossing*.

27. Judith Butler writes that "[a]n ungrievable life is one that cannot be mourned because it has never lived, that is, it has never counted as a life at all." See Judith Butler, *Frames of War: When is Life Grievable?* (New York: Verso Books, 2009), 38.

28. Beltrán, *Cruelty as Citizenship*, 99.

29. See César "CJ" Baldelomar, "A Reimagined Ethical Imagination: Considering Epistemological Nihilism and Afro-Pessimism as a Corrective to Ethics of Hope," *Perspectivas* 18 (2021): 23–42.

30. See De La Torre, *Embracing Hopelessness*.

31. Warren, "Black Nihilism and the Politics of Hope," 230.

5

Environmental Destruction, Forced (Im)migration, and Disaster Capitalism in Puerto Rico: Resisting a Colonialist "Puertopia"

Kristina I. Lizardy-Hajbi

ON JUNE 7, 1919, my grandfather Fernando Lizardi boarded the passenger ship *Grecian* in San Juan, Puerto Rico, and arrived on Ellis Island in New York Harbor just a few days later, on June 12.[1] He was accompanied by his mother Asunción (my great-grandmother), aunt, and older brother. My Grandpa Freddy, as I lovingly refer to him, was only eleven years old at the time. Woodrow Wilson had signed the Jones-Shafroth Act just two years earlier, granting Puerto Ricans on the island born on or after April 25, 1898, a limited form of US citizenship which remains in effect today.[2] Not so coincidentally, just two months after the signing of this Act, Puerto Rican males of age—now deemed citizens—were required to sign up for the draft for the First World War. Roughly 18,000 men from the island served in that war, many in racially segregated units if they were of African descent.[3]

Much of my great-grandmother's family, including her mother, were already living in Manhattan; so, it must have made sense to join her *familia* in a place where they could secure steady employment and enjoy the many freedoms granted by their new citizenship status. Unfortunately, those promised "freedoms" were never quite realized in their lifetimes, nor are they fully realized by Puerto Ricans today, regardless of whether we live on the island or are part of the massive diaspora present on the US mainland and abroad.

Puerto Rico—or Borikén, the island's Taíno name—has been a land impacted by movements of various peoples across time due to forces both colonial and environmental. More accurately, the colonial history of Borikén has exacerbated environmental challenges—such as hurricanes—in ways that have led to further loss, dispossession, and subsequent forced (im)migrations beyond "*la Isla de Encanto.*" However, if one identifies as Puerto Rican, one can never really "leave" the island itself. Our identities, our histories, our cultures contain such a deep connection to the notion of place in relationship to the land that extricating ourselves from Borikén becomes an impossibility. The stories—our stories—are breathed into being by the land, by acts of refusal and resistance to colonization and genocide, by sacred knowledges and practices passed down to us through our ancestors, and by the island's relationships with its surrounding worlds of water and sky.

ACTS OF THE GODS: JURAKÁN AND THE HURRICANES

When Taíno wind goddess Guabancex does not receive the respect she deserves from the people, she sends one of her strongest warriors, Jurakán (the storm god), to unleash hurricanes. "Jurakán" is the etymological origin for the English word "hurricane." As Puerto Rican artist Daniel Irizarri Oquendo remarked: "A Taíno word is part of the entire world's lexicon and that always brings a little smile to my face."[4] Hurricanes have been an enduring facet of life on Borikén; in the Taíno worldview, they are divine acts. What is purely non-divine and utterly mortal, however, are the ways that colonialism and degradation of the land create true catastrophes from these hurricanes. Historian Stuart B. Schwartz remarks: "Hurricanes, like other natural hazards, only become disasters because of the vulnerability of specific social and economic structures and because of political decisions and a variety of human actions before and after their impact."[5]

Before colonization, the biodiverse array of vegetables and fruits—mostly grown close to and underneath the ground—as part of traditional farming practices that were adapted to the land and weather patterns themselves ensured minimal hurricane damage to the food supply. In this manner, the people maintained a symbiotic, yet reverential relationship with Jurakán. Due to centuries of environmental colonization—and with most farms in Puerto Rico now existing as large-scale monocrop export systems for bananas, plantains, papaya, corn, and coffee—hurricane winds and rains can flatten entire crops in the blink of an eye.[6] This lack of sustainable ecological infrastructure is a primary reason why the most devastating hurricanes in the last 200 years have been so catastrophic. Without such infrastructure, migration from Borikén became inevitable.

Thanks to a changing climate, the frequency and ferocity of hurricanes is also on the rise, thereby impacting continuing migration to and from islands in the Caribbean as a whole. Climate scientists have determined definitively that there is a causal link between an increase in both the number and power of hurricanes and human-created atmospheric fluctuations.[7] Decolonial scholar Hilda Lloréns argues: "Unjustly, island societies and low-lying coastal areas in the Caribbean and the Pacific are on the front lines of climate change and will likely continue to experience its worsening effects and consequences, even though these societies contribute only a tiny fraction of all greenhouse gas emissions."[8] Ironically—or, rather, tragically—with the "modernization" of Puerto Rico by the United States and multinational corporations with electricity (which, for years, has been an old, poorly functioning electrical grid) and air travel/transport (which provides most of the food supply and other essentials), the island is dependent upon fossil fuels to such an extent that it is debilitated completely when hurricanes disrupt these aspects of modern life.

Such forces came to a pinnacle when Hurricane María, then a Category 4 storm, made landfall in Puerto Rico on September 20, 2017. This "act of the gods" caused billions of dollars in damages to both property (buildings) and economic productivity (primarily land/crops) and destroyed the power grid, leaving islanders without electricity for weeks and months. Though the estimated number of total deaths varied and was marred by a US administration that sought to minimize María's overall impact, the final accepted estimate from an independent study commissioned by the Puerto Rican government was 2,975 deaths.[9] Preceded by Hurricane Irma just two weeks earlier, María laid bare decades—topped upon centuries—of exploitation and neglect as a colony of empire. Four years later, the island and the people are continuing to struggle as recovery in the form of aid dollars and infrastructure support has moved at the rate of colonial "progress."

Part of this lack of support for infrastructure and aid—granted much more liberally to states than territories—included spending restrictions and procedures created during the Trump administration for Puerto Rican financial requests.[10] Such restrictions, however, are not new to the island, since in 2016 the Obama Administration enacted the Puerto Rico Oversight, Management, and Economic Stability Act (PROMESA), which created a board to oversee finances, develop a process for restructuring the island's debt, and assist with expediting infrastructure projects. With no local input or accountability incorporated into PROMESA (even though Puerto Ricans are taxed directly for all costs associated with PROMESA at around $200 million per year), this board has made decisions that only serve corporate interests at the expense of the people, thereby constituting a broken "promesa" (promise) for Puerto Ricans.[11]

In addition to enormous losses of life and environment, María prompted "the biggest migration from Puerto Rico since records have been taken," with over 400,000 people leaving between September 2017 and February 2018 (though half later returned to the island).[12] By all accounts, this migration was likened to a biblical exodus by media outlets, with CNN even creating a visual map of this "exodus" to the States.[13] Over the longer term between 2010 and 2020, the island encountered a cumulative population decline of 11.8 percent.[14] Demographers studying these trends believe that "steady migration, coupled with a declining birth rate that's lower than the death rate, is creating a 'demographic crisis' that will fundamentally alter Puerto Rico's society, economy and culture."[15]

Interestingly, media outlets reporting on Hurricane María began describing Puerto Ricans fleeing to the mainland as "climate refugees," both underplaying the role of colonial history and policies on the devastation that was caused and inaccurately including islanders in this ill-defined conception. Unfortunately, the term "climate refugee" is not one that is recognized by the United Nations' 1951 Refugee Convention, which is the standard that is still in use today for categorizing refugees.[16] In addition, Puerto Ricans are not refugees, since we are citizens and are not crossing international borders. Only about half of Americans even knew that Puerto Ricans were legal US citizens at the time Hurricane María made landfall.[17] Moreover, the notion of the refugee reinforces colonial imaginations about who can and cannot move freely between and among various geographic locations. Lloréns elaborates:

> Perhaps it is time to revisit the idea that people born on islands, such as Puerto Rico, are meant to remain there for the duration of their lives. Conceptualizing Indigenous and Black populations from the Global South as people who "naturally" belong to their ecosystem, like plant species, frames their mobility and migration as a pathological condition of uprootedness, contrasted with wealthy, cosmopolitan Westerners who are highly mobile, global citizens.[18]

Remaining as refugees whose migration is seen as "unnatural," Puerto Ricans are marginalized further and thereby considered more readily to be burdens on the state, taking up precious resources reserved for "actual" Americans (who were born in the United States, are white, middle-class, etc.). Such narratives maintain the colonial construction of islanders as non-American refugees whose own careless actions and misuse of government-endowed resources has led to their ill-preparedness for these "natural" disasters.

Ultimately, while María and other hurricanes of the past and future are certainly no less than "acts of the gods," the human-induced climate forces that create these more numerous and fiercer environmental phenomena—coupled with a decaying human-made infrastructure, so-called "relief" policies, and unabashed resource exploitation rendering the land incapable of withstanding hurricanes and their aftereffects—undermine true liberation and human flourishing and thus leave people with few choices regarding recovery and long-term subsistence on Borikén. In terms of the massive loss of life encountered during Hurricane María, Rachel Maddow summarized it quite appropriately: "This storm is no longer killing Americans—the federal government's response to the storm is now killing Americans."[19]

DISASTER CAPITALISM AND THE CREATION OF A "PUERTOPIA"

Within the colonial imagination, the colonizer himself is always portrayed as the "savior" who can rescue the people, the land, the economy, and the very soul of the place upon which he has set his sights. Such an imagination is aided significantly (and by design) through the process of disaster capitalism detailed by economist Milton Friedman. Coined the "shock doctrine" by Naomi Klein, this flavor of capitalism involves a process whereby "the original disaster—the coup, the terrorist attack, the market meltdown, the war, the tsunami, the hurricane—puts the entire population into a state of collective shock"[20] and is used "to push through radical pro-corporate measures, often called 'shock therapy.'"[21] In other words, these shocks create such disturbances to economic, social, political, and/or environmental systems that "residents are 'shocked and awed' into giving up taken-for-granted rights and private forces raid the public sphere."[22] Capitalism becomes the "savior" of the system when, in reality, it heaps continuing trauma, erasure, and exploitation upon an already shocked environment.

In the aftermath of Hurricane María, Klein described Puerto Rico as experiencing the effects of a "shock after shock doctrine," recognizing that the initial shock was not the hurricane but years of stringent economic policies grooming the island to be ripe for capitalistic exploitation the moment María arrived. Klein details:

> The Fiscal Control Board . . . already had all the policies; they didn't need to do any more planning. All they needed was the bloody-minded opportunism to push it through. It's harnessing trauma, the state of emergency, the fact that people are struggling to stay alive, and using that dislocation to ram through a pre-existing, totally articulated agenda.[23]

This struggle to stay alive during and after Hurricane María led to relocation—namely, mass migration from Borikén—leaving decimated structures, lands, and resources ripe for cheap purchase and development. With space to spare and a vision in sight of Puerto Rico as a "visitor economy" with fewer actual Puerto Ricans on the island, "in their place would be tens of thousands of 'high net-worth individuals' from Europe, Asia, and the US mainland, lured to permanently relocate by a cornucopia of tax breaks and the promise of living a five-star resort lifestyle inside fully privatized enclaves, year-round."[24] In this manner, migration moves in two directions, both mimicking movement patterns of Spanish colonization centuries ago and creating a wholly elevated and expedited gentrification process brought about by disaster capitalism.

Such movements have been aided by both older and more newly implemented tax breaks, one of which is Act 20/22, which allows wealthy individuals from the mainland to utilize the island as a tax haven if they reside there for at least six months out of the year. These breaks make Puerto Rico the only place under US jurisdiction where passive income and capital gains are untaxed (and are available only to newly arrived residents, not long-time inhabitants).[25] Additionally, corporations and wealthy entrepreneurs have been hosting multi-day seminars on the island for potential investors, not only for land development, but also for technological exploitation. One such seminar held in 2018 called Puerto Crypto sought to lure investors into making the island, through deregulation and blockchain (including the mining of Bitcoin), a haven for this technology.[26] Such "investments" from these blockchain technologies into Puerto Rico's economy are minimal and the overall environmental impact irredeemable. Global Bitcoin mining is estimated to produce approximately 22 to 23 million metric tons of carbon dioxide emissions a year, the same levels produced by entire countries over the same timeframe.[27] Countries in the Global South, including the Caribbean, are being targeted for this newer wave of colonialism, "perpetuating North-South trade and investment inequalities" and creating "a new power asymmetry enabled by the technology through data colonialism and surveillance capitalism."[28] Disaster capitalists such as these have named the island "Puertopia," a combination of "Puerto Rico" and "utopia," in carrying forward the Manifest Destiny doctrine of expansion and domination that served their forefathers so richly.

With a somewhat recent change in corrupt local leadership as the result of sustained protests in the summer of 2019—several of which I witnessed firsthand while on the island—many of these Puertopian dreams have not yet come to pass, thankfully.[29] As has been and will be the praxis of Puerto Ricans, there is no giving up without a struggle.

DECOLONIAL MOVEMENTS: RECLAIMING BORIKÉN

Miguel A. De La Torre notes: "Ethics becomes the process by which the marginalized enter a more human condition by overcoming oppressive or controlling societal mechanisms."[30] For many Puerto Ricans struggling for greater humanity, a return to the land is bringing about liberation from colonial systems underlying the Puertopian dystopia. Those on the island during Hurricane María survived without electricity and clean water sources because families, neighbors, and communities came together to support and care for one another in sharing food, supplies, and housing and clearing access to roads and community gathering places. In that moment, the failure of the colonizer's modern technologies created a different kind of "shock" for islanders and diasporans alike—a shock that raised the consciousness of many to the immediate life-and-death realities of centuries-long colonialism.

As a result, islanders have formed both new and stronger existing coalitions—direct resistance/recovery movements—to transform Puerto Rico (back) into a sustainable, locally-based environment. One longstanding project that was in existence before María is Casa Pueblo, a community organization located in the municipality of Adjuntas "committed to appreciating and protecting natural, cultural, and human resources."[31] During and after María, Casa Pueblo was one of the only places that had electricity and reliable shelter within the surrounding area due to its reliance on renewable energy sources. Another entity, the Alliance for Sustainable Resources Management (AMANESER 2025), is "an ecumenical network of grassroots organizations whose purpose is to promote sustainability in Puerto Rico."[32] Like Casa Pueblo, AMANESER 2025 works with local communities to develop their own plans for sustainability in response to climate change, while also relying on the skills and expertise of collaborating organizations depending on the unique needs of each community.[33]

The return to sustainable farming practices that can withstand Jurakán's storms is also well under way. One school in Orocovis, through its agriculture education program, is helping children and families recover from the trauma of the storm by reconnecting them with the land, creating deeper symbiotic, yet reverential relationships with *la tierra*. There are many other movements across the island like this where people are learning practices of agroecology, "a combination of traditional farming methods that promotes resilience and protects biodiversity, a rejection of pesticides and other toxins, and a commitment to rebuilding social relationships between farmers and local communities."[34] Organización Boricuá, a network of farmers committed to promoting agroecology "as a vehicle to achieve food sovereignty and environmental justice on the islands," relies on jíbaro-campesino knowledge passed down from the ancestors.[35]

The "shock" brought on by Hurricane María is continuing to awaken more and more islanders to the possibilities of a different kind of existence, one that breaks free from the chokeholds of colonial reliance and is based on the power of the community and the people, including those of us who live in the diaspora. Diasporans contributed significant support in the forms of time, money, resources, and shelter for relatives and friends after María; and we continue to do so, just as we have always done. For many residing in the States, art has become an important expression of solidarity, resistance, justice seeking, and consciousness raising. El Museo del Barrio in New York City was founded over fifty years ago by a group of Puerto Rican artists, activists, and educators to create a place for Latinx artists to showcase their work since other museums did not offer such space. One of my own ancestors, George L. Aguirre Miranda—an early developer of laser photography—was a founding sponsor and board member of El Museo del Barrio.[36] El Museo continues to this day and is a pivotal part of the Latinx and New York City art worlds, providing a platform that highlights the continued political, economic, cultural, and environmental struggles and resistances related to Puerto Rican life.[37] This is just one place among many that diasporan Puerto Ricans have carved out for creative expression, that defies the colonial hold and demonstrates solidarity, resistance, and resilience, and that makes clear our collective desires for self-authorship and reclamation of a decolonized Boricán.

CONCLUSION

Theologian Teresa Delgado, in her book *A Puerto Rican Decolonial Theology: Prophesy Freedom*, positions the movements of Puerto Ricans to and from the island—the "revolving door" of migration—as "an eschatological bridge of hope and promise that one day the journey between the two worlds will not be so long and arduous, so expensive and difficult; it will be as effortless and joyful as *fiesta*."[38] Acknowledging that many of these movements have been born from great suffering arising from environmental disasters and exacerbated by various colonial powers, do we dare hope that such migrations might become a source of joy and even reconciliation?

The promesa-filled revolving door that our people have passed through time and time again includes ancestors like my Grandpa Freddy and my great-grandmother Asunción who embarked on their first passage to Ellis Island over a hundred years ago. Such a door, therefore, will include those who come after us, our future promesas. Perhaps the greatest hope of reconciliation for us Puerto Ricans is that such movements—along with our collective struggles for justice and reclamation/restoration—might find favor with the gods of Borikén before it is too late.

NOTES

1. The spelling of my grandfather's last name is different from mine. On the ship's passenger list, my great-grandmother Asunción purposely changed the spelling of her children's last names. I've been told by a cousin that this might have been a way to distance them from their father after Asunción's divorce from him, in addition to attempting a fresh start in a new place. I recognize that this also may have been a way to ease the transition culturally for her children by trying to "Americanize/Anglicize" their last name (a common practice for migrants of that era). As the legacies of colonialism are never far from those of us with marginalized identities, our very names often reflect these deep traumas and complex histories.

2. Full citizenship, which includes having one's vote counted in US presidential elections, is only granted to Puerto Ricans who reside in one of the fifty states.

3. I have a copy of my great-grandfather Asisclo R. Lizardi Lebrón's draft card from the First World War, as well as my Grandpa Freddy's Korean War draft card.

4. Daniel Irizarri Oquendo, "Madre de Dios," in *Puerto Rico Strong: A Comics Anthology Supporting Puerto Rico Disaster Relief and Recovery*, ed. by Marco Lopez, Desiree Rodriguez, Hazel Newlevant, Derek Ruiz, and Neil Schwartz (St. Louis: The Lion Forge, LLC, 2018), 17.

5. Stuart B. Schwartz, "The Hurricane of San Ciríaco: Disaster, Politics, and Society in Puerto Rico, 1899–1901," *Hispanic American Historical Review* 72, no. 3 (August 1992): 303.

6. Naomi Klein, *The Battle for Paradise: Puerto Rico Takes on the Disaster Capitalists* (Chicago: Haymarket Books, 2018), 36–37.

7. See James B. Elsner, "Evidence in Support of the Climate Change—Atlantic Hurricane Hypothesis," *Geophysical Research Letters* 33, no. 16 (2006): 1–3.

8. Hilda Lloréns, "U.S. Media Depictions of Climate Migrants: The Recent Case of the Puerto Rican 'Exodus,'" in *Aftershocks of Disaster: Puerto Rico Before and After the Storm*, ed. Yarimar Bonilla and Marisol LeBrón (Chicago: Haymarket Books, 2019), 128.

9. Ed Morales, *Fantasy Island: Colonialism, Exploitation, and the Betrayal of Puerto Rico* (New York: Bold Type Books, 2019), 213.

10. Carolina Cardona, "Central Floridians Say $8.2 Billion in Relief after Hurricane Maria Is Long Overdue," News 6 CBS, June 23, 2021.

11. Yarimar Bonilla and Marisol LeBrón, "Introduction: Aftershocks of Disaster," in Bonilla and LeBrón *Aftershocks of Disaster*, 7.

12. Morales, *Fantasy Island*, 220.

13. See John D. Sutter and Sergio Hernandez, "'Exodus' from Puerto Rico: A Visual Guide," CNN, February 21, 2018, https://www.cnn.com/2018/02/21/us/puerto-rico-migration-data-invs/index.html.

14. "Percent Change in Resident Population for the 50 States, the District of Columbia, and Puerto Rico: 2010 to 2020," US Census Bureau, https://www.census.gov/library/visualizations/2021/dec/2020-percent-change-map.html.

15. Syra Ortiz-Blanes, "'A New Maria': Puerto Rico's Next Crisis Is a Demographic Crisis," *Tampa Bay Times*, May 25, 2021, https://www.tampabay.com/news/nation-world/2021/05/25/a-new-maria-puerto-ricos-next-crisis-is-a-demographic-crisis/.

16. Lloréns, "U.S. Media Depictions," 130.

17. Kyle Dropp and Brendan Nyhan, "Nearly Half of Americans Don't Know Puerto Ricans Are Fellow Citizens," *New York Times*, September 26, 2017, https://www.nytimes.com/2017/09/26/upshot/nearly-half-of-americans-dont-know-people-in-puerto-ricoans-are-fellow-citizens.html.

18. Lloréns, "U.S. Media Depictions," 129–30.

19. Rachel Maddow, "Doctor Quits Puerto Rico Medical Relief Team over 'Spa Day,'" *The Rachel Maddow Show*, October 12, 2017, https://www.msnbc.com/rachel-maddow/watch/doctor-quits-puerto-rico-medical-relief-team-over-spa-day-1072301123804.

20. Naomi Klein, *The Shock Doctrine: The Rise of Disaster Capitalism* (New York: Metropolitan Books, 2017), 17.

21. Naomi Klein, "How Power Profits from Disaster," *The Guardian*, July 6, 2017, https://www.theguardian.com/us-news/2017/jul/06/naomi-klein-how-power-profits-from-disaster.

22. Daina Cheyenne Harvey, "Social Policy as Secondary Violences in the Aftermath of a Disaster: An Extension to Naomi Klein's Disaster Capitalism," *Humanity & Society* 41, no. 3 (2017): 334.

23. Yarimar Bonilla and Naomi Klein, "The Trauma Doctrine: A Conversation between Yarimar Bonilla and Naomi Klein," in Bonilla and LeBrón, *Aftershocks of Disaster*, 23–24.

24. Klein, *The Battle for Paradise*, 14.

25. Bonilla and LeBrón, "Introduction," 8–9.

26. Klein, *The Battle for Paradise*, 16, 18.

27. Alexander Smith, "Factbox: How Big Is Bitcoin's Carbon Footprint?," *Reuters*, May 13, 2021, https://www.reuters.com/technology/how-big-is-bitcoins-carbon-footprint-2021-05-13/.

28. Peter Howson, "Climate Crises and Crypto-Colonialism: Conjuring Value on the Blockchain Frontiers of the Global South," *Frontiers in Blockchain*, May 13, 2020.

29. Adriana Hamacher, "Puerto Rico: A Haven for Crypto No More," *Yahoo!*, August 2, 2019, https://www.yahoo.com/video/puerto-rico-haven-crypto-no-155049648.html.

30. Miguel A. De La Torre, *Doing Christian Ethics from the Margins* (Maryknoll, NY: Orbis Books, 2004), 26.

31. Casa Pueblo, https://casapueblo.org/.

32. "AMANESER 2025, Puerto Rico," https://www.globalministries.org/partner/lac_partners_amaneser_2025/.

33. Queremos Sol, an organization committed to achieving "50 percent renewable energy generation by 2035 and 100 percent by 2050," is one such collaborator. See https://www.queremossolpr.com/.

34. Klein, *The Battle for Paradise*, 34.

35. Organización Boricuá de Agricultura Ecológica, https://www.mariafund.org/organizacin-boricua.

36. "George Aguirre, 62, Hispanic-Art Backer," *New York Times*, Obituaries, January 12, 1995. George was my second cousin on my paternal grandmother's side.

37. Learn more about El Museo del Barrio at https://www.elmuseo.org/.

38. Teresa Delgado, *A Puerto Rican Decolonial Theology: Prophesy Freedom* (Cham: Palgrave Macmillan, 2017), 171.

6

Off the Grid:
Climate Change, Immigration, and POWER in Texas

Rebecca M. David Hensley

DURING THE WEEK OF FEBRUARY 15, 2021, the state of Texas experienced its most drastic winter storm on record, ultimately costing 210 Texans their lives. As the death toll began to climb, an estimated 3.5 million Texans were left without power, while others existed on rolling blackouts. At one point, over twelve million Texans were under "boil water notices" as the state scrambled to ensure safe water distribution, while others were left with no water and extensive damage to their homes caused by burst pipes.[1] And while Texas prides itself on the saying "Everything's bigger in Texas," the storm itself was no "bigger" there than in multiple other impacted states, though none of these states suffered anywhere near the loss of power and ensuing disaster that engulfed the state of Texas. What was bigger in Texas that fateful week was the failure of the state's leadership in preparing its electric grid for the region's predicted climate shifts. While Governor Greg Abbott blamed the state's wind energy as the driving force for the outage, and ERCOT (the state's energy management council for its independent electric grid) blamed gas lines, the truth is, wind energy accounted for less than thirteen percent of the power outages and there were preventable reasons the gas lines froze. So, while it is correct that wind and gas energy sources were both part of the equation, the fundamental issue is that Texas governance set up its independent utility grid for minimum regulation and maximum profit. This choice reflects decades of deregulation and privatization of public services, while providing the lowest energy costs to large commercial users. Because of this, Texas never winterized its natural gas lines—*even after* a major winter storm in 2011 prompted a warning from federal regulators that the state's power plants were destined to fail in similar weather events. The Texas government's choice to save money by not winterizing the gas lines is the reason those lines froze; and its choice to keep over twenty-six million of its residents on an independent and isolated electric grid, disabling them from drawing power from either the Eastern or Western Interconnection, is the primary reason for this most recent energy disaster in Texas.[2] In prioritizing profit over people, Texas governance has, quite literally, legislated itself "off the grid."

This chapter explores how this climate disaster, combined with Texas state governance and infrastructure, created the perfect storm of intersecting injustices—from climate change to racial inequity to immigration policy—shedding painful light on the state's (and the nation's) structural foundations of white supremacy. Drawing upon this event as a clarion call for theological reflection and social action, this chapter explores connections between climate change and immigration in Texas and throughout Latin America. It then applies Ivone Gebara's ecofeminist theory of interdependency as a contextual and holistic epistemology for religious communities to engage in intersectional forms of activism to address these rapidly growing concerns.

In considering the impacts of climate change, it is important to remember that as a border state, Texas is home to the second largest immigrant population in the nation, with immigrants comprising seventeen percent of its residents, or approximately five million people. Of that number, over 3.2 million are from Latin American countries of origin.[3] When these communities—along with other communities of color—are hardest hit by crises like the February 2021 winter storm, ethical questions of intersecting injustices arise. Beneath this web of interconnected oppressions is the ever-present foundation of white supremacy, which was on clear display in aerial photos taken during the storm, where entire sections of impoverished minority communities were completely blacked out as city skylines in Austin and Houston remained lit like a beacon of whiteness for all to see. While these cities quickly responded to complaints about such discrepancies with the simple answer that downtown areas house critical services like hospitals, it is nevertheless important to take a critical look at how the decisions regarding which areas maintained or lost power are more complex in terms of how they impacted specific segments of the population. A report released in April by the Electricity Growth and Use in Developing Economies (e-GUIDE) Initiative analyzed the data from satellite photos of the blackouts that occurred between February 14–18 and found that "predominantly white areas had an 11% chance of suffering an outage compared to a 47% chance in high minority share areas."[4]

Comparing census data with the state's blackout information, this report found that across the board, areas with the highest minority populations suffered most from blackouts—even when accounting for wealth disparities—painting a clear and undeniable picture that the state's failure to address climate change and provide the most basic and essential services is having a significantly greater impact on its minority populations than its White population. Furthermore, while Texas law dictates that areas with critical facilities like hospitals, fire and police stations, and water and wastewater treatment must be prioritized during blackouts, this study found that predominantly white poor and middle-class areas have over four times as many critical facilities when compared with poor and middle-class high minority areas. Additionally, this report found that the blackouts impacted a "larger portion of the populations in the southern region of the state than elsewhere"[5]—the region that is home to the highest numbers of immigrant populations, with Harris County (where the city of Houston is located) ranking in the top five immigrant population counties in the United States.[6]

PREVENTION THROUGH DETERRENCE: THE EVER-EXPANDING MILITARIZED BORDER ZONE

Meanwhile, just across the state's southern border, migrant encampments filled with hundreds (previously, thousands) of asylum seekers waited out the frigid temperatures in a tent city—where they also waited out flooding and resulting swarms of mosquitoes, spiders, and snakes from Hurricane Hanna in July 2020—due to the Trump administration's "Migrant Protection Protocols" (MPP) policy. Many of these migrants are escaping environmental destruction in their homelands as the lack of regulations in a global capitalist market wreaks havoc in those regions. These climate, poverty, and gender violence refugees came to the US border legally seeking asylum. But under MPP, they were stranded between two worlds—existing on the margins of *la frontera*—for over a year.

The Trump administration is by no means solely responsible for the intersecting disaster of climate change and forced migration. Rather, Trump was well set-up by previous administrations to step into his authoritarian-style "leadership" role that further criminalized and dehumanized immigrants while completely ignoring the climate crisis, even going so far as to convince many of his followers that, despite the mounds of evidence from decades of scientific research, climate change is in fact "a hoax."[7] His predecessor, while being the first US president to actually use the term "climate change refugees" in a May 2015 speech to the US Coast Guard Academy, did so not with the intent to address the root causes of this kind of forced displacement, but rather as a way of informing the cadets that the Coast Guard would play a critical role in "guarding US territorial boarders and interests." The statement thus marked an important connection between a decades-long history of US policy choices focused on homeland security as the response to climate change and its inevitable impact on global migration.[8] It is worth noting here that to this day, no such "climate refugee" status is recognized by the US government. This is all part of a "Prevention through Deterrence" strategy that originated from the anticipation that migration from Mexico would increase after the signing of the North American Free Trade Agreement, which was enacted under the Clinton administration, constructed under the George H.W. Bush administration, but envisioned under the candidacy of Ronald Reagan in 1979. Since the passing of NAFTA, "the annual budget of the US Border Patrol has increased more than ten-fold, from \$363 million to nearly \$4.9 billion."[9]

Throughout these decades, prevention-through-deterrence strategies have met with the extremes of climate change, as the influx of NAFTA-era migrants have been purposely routed through the most severe of desert conditions. As anthropologist Jason De León illustrates in *The Land of Open Graves: Living and Dying on the Migrant Trail*, border zones have become "spaces of exception—physical and political locations where an individual's rights and protections can be stripped away upon entrance."[10] He goes on to describe the US borderlands as "a remote deathscape where American necropolitics are pecked onto the bones of those we deem excludable."[11]

The South Texas Human Rights Center (STHRC), a small, community-based organization in Brooks County, Texas, is acutely aware of this deathscape. Located at the county seat of Falfurrias, their methods include a water sanitation and distribution project, search and rescue, and forensic recovery and identification. Situated eighty miles north of the border, this county sees some of the highest numbers of migrant deaths in the United States. The reason? There is a checkpoint fifteen miles south of Falfurrias where border patrol officers search vehicles for illegal smuggling of drugs—or humans. Undocumented persons who cross the border with the assistance of coyotes are dropped off several miles before the checkpoint and left to fend for themselves in the sparse desert ranchlands, where some ranches cover the span of nearly 50,000 acres. Once migrants are dropped off, they must make their way to Highway 285, which runs east/west directly through the town of Falfurrias, in hopes that their arrangements for a new coyote work out and they will be driven to their next destination. As the STHRC co-director and forensic coordinator noted: "Crossing the border is the [relatively] easy part. It's the checkpoints that are deadly."[12] People often become disoriented and dehydrated as they try to make their way through this twenty-plus mile stretch of dense brush and desert heat, all the while hiding from Customs and Border Patrol officers who patrol the area heavily.

Brooks County is key to understanding the prevention-through-deterrence strategy because thus far in 2021, ninety-eight migrant deaths have been documented there—bringing the total estimate for this single county to 2,000 since 2008.[13] On the whole, more undocumented migrants have died after crossing the Texas border than anywhere else in the United States—totaling 3,523 *tallied* deaths over the last twenty-two years, while the total number is believed to be much higher because many are never found.[14]

THE TRUE COST OF "FREE" TRADE

Of course, death by environmental factors once migrants have crossed the border is only one part of the story. The reasons for forced migration vary, but since the passing of the Dominican Republic-Central America Free Trade Agreement (CAFTA-DR) in 2005, the ties between neoliberal capitalism, environmental destruction, and climate change are undeniable. This is largely due to provisions in the policy that privilege foreign corporations, allowing them to "bypass domestic courts and challenge domestic consumer and environmental protections."[15] More recently, multinational corporations seeking to bypass environmental regulations on emissions have even managed to find ways to profit off climate change at the expense of Central American countries. In Honduras, for example, this translated to thousands of acres being clear-cut for the planting of African palm, all "backed by bilateral and multilateral agencies such as the World Bank."[16] This rapid over-planting has not only had environmental costs, such as a massive fish kill caused by one palm oil supplier contaminating La Pasion River in Guatemala.[17] It has also robbed small-scale farmers throughout the region of their livelihoods. Additionally, CAFTA-DR has resulted in "mega-projects of commercial fishing, mining, drilling, and tourism," as well as the advent of special Economic Development Zones, or "model cities," which "have their own laws and judicial systems, and their own government, servicing the principles of free-market capitalism."[18] The first "model city," named Próspera, is currently being built and recruiting citizens on the Honduran island of Roatán.

In 2014, the United States saw a sharp rise in migrants from the Northern Triangle region of El Salvador, Guatemala, and Honduras. The Obama administration's response was to work with Mexico to implement "El Programa Frontera Sur," which touted objectives of safeguarding human rights for migrants, but ultimately ended up funding security, deportation, and immigration enforcement. With US funding and equipment, apprehensions in Mexico rose while detentions at the Texas border declined—but only temporarily. Ultimately, this prevention-through-deterrence tactic failed at cutting off migration to Texas; but it succeeded at making the journey through Mexico far more dangerous, as migrants were more vulnerable to gang activity, assaults, and of course, environmental elements.[19]

While the United States was in the business of outsourcing its border security to Mexico, a multi-year drought hit the "dry corridor" region of El Salvador, Guatemala, Honduras, and Nicaragua in 2015, costing approximately 400,000 farmers eighty percent of bean crops and sixty percent of corn crops in that single year. In the country of Honduras alone, where over half the population lives in severe poverty, this sustained loss only served to increase massive food insecurity and violence. An April 2021 Brookings report analyzed data collected on Honduran migrant apprehensions at the US southern border between 2012–2019. It showed that "decreases in precipitation are associated with increased migrant flows," where the "magnitude of this effect increases with higher levels of violence."[20] Climate scientist Chris Castro has described the Northern Triangle region as "ground zero" for the impact of global warming in the Western hemisphere, as it continues to see an "intensification of the mid-summer dry period."[21] And an April 2021 report from World Food Programme predicts even higher migration rates from this area in the near future, as "almost 8 million people don't have enough to eat."[22]

All the while, neoliberal capitalist market logic continues to clash with climate change in Mexico, as the current drought and its ensuing water shortage make clear. While this environmental threat could be seen solely as a weather pattern, weather patterns alone fail to account for the nearly twentyfold growth in population in the US-Mexico border region since the 1940s—a growth that is "powered by a booming, water-dependent manufacturing industry in Mexico that exports products to US markets. Irrigated agriculture, ranching and mining compete with growing cities and expanding industry for scarce water."[23] While these intersecting factors have been decades in the making—exacerbated since the 1990s by the implementation of NAFTA—when Mexico nearly failed to meet its water treaty agreement (enacted in 1944) to send 345,600-acre-feet of water to the United States in 2020, Texas Governor Greg Abbott's response was unwavering: "Mexico owes Texas a year's worth of Rio Grande water."[24] Mexico managed to meet its obligation to this outdated treaty just three days before the deadline—but meeting Texas's needs "jeopardized the supply of more than a million Mexicans living downstream of the Amistad Dam."[25]

Finally, for those who dared to hope that the Biden era might bring more compassion for forced migration through climate change, in January, a caravan of 8,000 migrants from Honduras—many of whom were migrating due to back-to-back Category 4 hurricanes in November 2020—were met by US-trained police in Guatemala who deported countless individuals before they even made it to the militarized Mexico border. For any who did make it all the way to the US border, there is still no climate-refugee status for asylum seekers, proving that even catastrophic hurricanes aren't strong enough to penetrate the prevention-through-deterrence strategy.[26]

And in September of 2021, an influx of 30,000 Haitian immigrants to the Texas border were met with no more compassion than the Hondurans, many of whom claimed that they were forced to relocate after the 2010 earthquake but had struggled to maintain jobs in Chile and other South American countries over the last year due to the COVID-19 pandemic. Over the course of a few weeks, Biden's border operations deported 8,000 Haitians "and more than 12,000 others were sent to federal immigration facilities across the southwest."[27] It's also important to remember that in addition to recent Haitian tragedies, neoliberal capitalism did Haiti no favors back when the Clinton administration negotiated a trade agreement "that gave US rice farmers subsidies if they sold their grain to Haiti. This essentially killed Haiti's rice farming industry, leading to a mass loss of jobs."[28]

WHERE DO WE GO FROM HERE?: CREATING A CULTURE OF INTERDEPENDENCE

What are we to do with the reality of these intersecting injustices in a state at the epicenter of state, national, and international immigration and environmental forces? Can religious communities help build a new social and political grid by reclaiming *environmental and humanitarian power* in Texas? To explore this from a theological perspective, it is helpful to revisit Brazilian theologian Ivone Gebara's 1999 groundbreaking book on ecofeminism in a Latin American context, *Longing for Running Water: Ecofeminism and Liberation*. Gebara argues that: "Religions have an undeniable role in helping us to develop the *sensibilities we need* in order to love the earth and the human community in light of the indissoluble communion among all beings."[29] If religious leaders, especially in a border state like Texas, take this statement to heart in light of global climate and migration trends, then such leaders must build coalitions of solidarity that energize constituents to fight for a truly comprehensive immigration reform policy, which at minimum includes a clear pathway to citizenship. But perhaps more importantly, comprehensive immigration reform needs to focus on interdependently just, equitable, and sustainable climate policies centered on the swift and mass reduction of carbon emissions; the swift and mass reduction of clear-cutting and over-planting of industrial agriculture paired with intentional reforestation efforts; and protection of oceans with swift and mass reduction of industrial over-fishing. All of these efforts would not only mean the salvation and restoration of countless forms of life throughout the planet. They would also drastically reduce the flow of migrants escaping climate change *and* neoliberal market logic.

While ecofeminism has been critiqued for its potential to whitewash environmentalism by not focusing on environmental racism, Gebara's voice comes from her personal experience in Latin America—from the voices of the poor who have long struggled to survive there, and especially the lived experiences of poor women.[30] Furthermore, she calls for a dialogue among the global range of differing religious and spiritual traditions and identities, while making numerous connections to the wisdom of Indigenous spiritualities in the context of preserving the environment. But perhaps most importantly, this work provides a detailed critical analysis of traditional Christian theologies and eurochristian epistemologies, with a specific focus on the harm caused by the hierarchical nature of trinitarian theology.

Core to Gebara's ecofeminist theology is the concept of interdependence, which she describes as: "the basic fact that any life situation, behavior, or even belief is always the fruit of all the interactions that make up our lives, our histories, and our wider earthly and cosmic realities."[31] She unpacks this concept of interdependence through five epistemological and theological frameworks: the human condition, the earthly condition, ethical reality, religious experience, and the cosmic condition. The remainder of this chapter will focus on the human, ethical, and religious frameworks.

In considering the human condition, Gebara provides a sharp critique of anthropocentric epistemologies, linking this kind of hierarchical thinking to the profound imbalances produced by human intervention "in the whole network of our relationships with the earth." She goes on to describe our "species evil" as the "excessive desire to take possession of life and make it our own . . . the appropriation of goods—and also of other persons" regarded as secondary by those who have appointed themselves as "proprietors of the earth."[32] This belief is undeniably at work in policies like NAFTA and CAFTA-DR, and the willful ignorance displayed by every recent presidential administration regarding the harms such policies would bring to people and the planet.

Gebara's hope for a new ethical reality is one where relatedness becomes "a whole educational process aimed at rebuilding our self-understanding."[33] In this sense, she is clear in her critique of hierarchical epistemologies, which "run parallel to the hierarchizing of society itself," a society that excludes "the majority of people [and] . . . monopolizes both power and knowledge." This system serves a "male elite" while presenting BIPOC communities as "those who know the least."[34] When we consider the driving forces of heteropatriarchy and White supremacy which are intrinsically bound up in capitalist market logic and the severe imbalances it has caused, her call for "introduc[ing] the notion of communion with, rather than conquest of, the earth and space" within our educational processes is a critical and timely foundation for addressing climate change.[35]

This educational-ethical step is key to moving into a new religious experience or theological pursuit. Here, she critiques the historical global impact of Christianity's deference to autonomy and self-determination, which has led to some "appalling behaviors because it was promoted in a dogmatic, absolute, univocal, and unlimited way." Because of this, Gebara asserts, "we have gone from promoting the autonomy of individual persons to the unrestrained exercise of our passion for possessing, for self-assertion, and for power."[36]

Ultimately, Gebara is interested in helping humans break out of dualistic views that inhibit our ability to understand ourselves as related not only to one another as humanity, but also to every aspect of the earth and the cosmos, and in fact, to the cosmos itself. The very concept of a man-made border epitomizes this kind of dualistic, hierarchical thinking that Gebara is pushing against. And certainly, the militarization of such a border as a "defense" against climate refugees is a sign of just how disconnected we have become from both the earth and the rest of humanity. How might Gebara's theological and epistemological approach shape the ways in which religious communities address the intersecting injustices of environmental destruction, immigration, racism, and sexism? Further, how might it call such communities into deep interrogation of their own complicity with and perpetuation of the very forces that have caused such imbalance to begin with?

Our first "defense" to mass forced displacement cannot simply be more walls, surveillance systems, border patrol agents, and ICE networks throughout the United States. Our first defense must be a defense of our planet that understands the delicate balance inherent in our interdependency with all forms of life. And it would seem the thing we most desperately need to defend our planet against is neoliberal capitalism.

The irony is not lost that while ecofeminism promotes interdependency, Texas's winter storm crisis was a direct result of the state's refusal to be part of the Eastern or Western "Interconnection" utility grids. In clinging to its deeply held (false) value of independence, Texas's government brought a disaster upon its people and the planet in February 2021. If this remains the driving ethic and epistemology for this border *and coastal* state, the forecast almost certainly predicts that it won't be long before other states begin seeing "climate refugees" escaping *from* the state of Texas. Perhaps the greatest gift religious communities can provide is a much-needed epistemological and theological shift to an ethic of interdependency. If the intersection of migration and climate change teaches us anything, it is that we are all, in fact, part of the "interconnection."

NOTES

1. Bill Chappell, "8.7 Million People Under Boil Water Notices In Texas," *National Public Radio*, February 22, 2021, https://www.npr.org/sections/live-updates-winter-storms-2021/2021/02/22/970241763/monday-update-8-7-million-people-under-boil-water-notices-in-texas.

2. "Fact Check: The Causes for Texas' Blackout Go Well beyond Wind Turbines," *Reuters*, February 19, 2021, https://www.reuters.com/article/uk-factcheck-texas-wind-turbines-explain/fact-check-the-causes-for-texas-blackout-go-well-beyond-wind-turbines-idUSKBN2AJ2EI.

3. "State Immigration Data Profiles: Texas," *Migration Policy Institute*, https://www.migrationpolicy.org/data/state-profiles/state/demographics/TX.

4. Mary Dettloff, "Frozen Out: Minorities Suffered Four Times More Power Outages in Texas Blackouts," University of Massachusetts, Amherst, April 14, 2021, https://www.umass.edu/news/article/frozen-out-minorities-suffered-four-times.

5. JP Carvallo, Feng Chi Hsu, Zeal Shah, and Jay Taneja, "Frozen Out in Texas: Blackouts and Inequity," The Rockefeller Foundation, April 14, 2021, https://www.rockefellerfoundation.org/case-study/frozen-out-in-texas-blackouts-and-inequity/.

6. Abby Budiman, Christine Tamir, Lauren Mora, and Luis Noe-Bustamante, "Immigrants in the United States: County Maps, 1960–2018," Pew Research Center's Hispanic Trends Project, August 20, 2020, https://www.pewresearch.org/hispanic/2020/08/20/facts-on-u-s-immigrants-county-maps/.

7. Todd Miller, *Storming the Wall: Climate Change, Migration, and Homeland Security* (San Francisco: City Lights Publishers, 2017), 60.

8. Ibid., 49.

9. "The Cost of Immigration Enforcement and Border Security," American Immigration Council, https://www.americanimmigrationcouncil.org/sites/default/files/research/the_cost_of_immigration_enforcement_and_border_security.pdf.

10. Jason De Leon, *The Land of Open Graves: Living and Dying on the Migrant Trail* (Oakland: University of California Press, 2015), 27.

11. Ibid., 84.

12. South Texas Human Rights Center presentation for Park Hill United Methodist Church Youth/Adult Mission Team, July 22, 2019.

13. Pablo De La Rosa, "Brooks County Sheriff Looks to Protect Migrant Lives Days after a Man Was Found Hanging from a Tree," Texas Public Radio, October 8, 2021, https://www.tpr.org/border-immigration/2021-10-08/migrant-hanging-brooks-county-investigation.

14. Jasmine Aguilera, "More Migrants Die Crossing the Border in South Texas Than Anywhere Else in the U.S. This Documentary Depicts the Human Toll," *Time*, August 20, 2021, https://time.com/6091742/migrant-deaths-texas-documentary/.

15. "Central America Free Trade Agreement (CAFTA)," *Public Citizen*, https://www.citizen.org/article/central-america-free-trade-agreement-cafta/.

16. Miller, *Storming the Wall*, 85.

17. Ben Lilliston, "Climate Change, CAFTA and Forced Migration," *Institute for Agriculture and Trade Policy*, May 16, 2019.

18. Miller, *Storming the Wall*, 87.

19. Johnny Harris, "How the US Outsourced Border Security," *Vox*, December 5, 2017, https://youtu.be/1xbt0ACMbiA.

20. Sarah Bermeo and David Leblang, "Climate, Violence, and Honduran Migration to the United States," Brookings, April 1, 2021, https://www.brookings.edu/blog/future-development/2021/04/01/climate-violence-and-honduran-migration-to-the-united-states/.

21. Miller, *Storming the Wall*, 75.

22. WFP Staff, "Honduras: Climate Change, Coronavirus and Caravans," *World Food Programme*, April 21, 2021, https://www.wfp.org/stories/honduras-climate-change-coronavirus-and-caravans.

23. Andrea K. Gerlak, Robert Gabriel Varady, and Stephen Paul Mumme, "'Mega-drought' Along Border Strains US-Mexico Water Relations," *The Conversation*, July 1, 2021, https://theconversation.com/megadrought-along-border-strains-us-mexico-water-relations-160338.

24. Ibid.

25. Ibid.

26. Todd Miller, "Why Did Border Security Firms Bet on Biden in 2020?," *The Nation*, March 25, 2021, https://www.thenation.com/article/society/border-security-biden/.

27. Uriel J. García, "'We Suffered a Lot to Get Here': A Haitian Migrant's Harrowing Journey to the Texas-Mexico Border," *The Texas Tribune*, October 1, 2021, https://www.texastribune.org/2021/10/01/haitian-migrants-texas-mexico-border/.

28. Ibid.

29. Ivone Gebara, *Longing for Running Water: Ecofeminism and Liberation*, trans. David Molineaux (Minneapolis: Fortress Press, 1999), 212. Emphasis added.

30. Ibid., 5–6.

31. Ibid., 52.

32. Ibid., 168.

33. Ibid., 90–91.

34. Ibid., 25–26.

35. Ibid., 52.

36. Ibid., 72.

7

It's Closer Than You Think:
Climate Gentrification as a Form of
Climate Migrancy in the United States

Emily Askew

"WE BUY HOUSES – AS IS & PAY CASH!" If a sign bearing these words appears on your block after a tornado hits, the chances are good that you are working-class or poor and are about to move very far away from your long-time neighborhood. This sign foreshadows dislocation, because when natural disasters hit under-resourced parts of town, predatory developers rush in to buy up damaged, under-valued houses usually located in historically redlined areas of town. Because homes in these areas have been so systemically undervalued, insurance often won't cover the cost of repairs. Knowing this, builders and developers are literally on the streets the day after flooding or tornadoes with cash offers, buying up blocks of damaged homes. They will raze these homes and replace what were once small single-family homes on modest lots with multiple large, tall, and thin houses—several of them to a lot with six feet (or less) between them. The new houses, in turn, become short-term rentals or are priced out of range for previous residents. Thus, these "flipped" neighbor-hoods quickly become expensive and white, when once they were afford-able and historically the home of African-American or immigrant residents. And owing to the crisis of affordable housing in the United States, residents forced to take the buyout cannot find a new home near their children's school or house of worship.[1]

This scenario of dislocation is one version of what a group of Harvard researchers investigating housing prices in Miami-Dade County, Florida have termed "climate gentrification."[2] Climate gentrification is simply the ongoing process of gentrification of neighborhoods exacerbated by the impacts of climate change. The National Resources Defense Council writes about gentrification and climate:

> The cycle is all too familiar: Affluent residents move into lower-income neighborhoods in cities and make their mark on the area's character and culture. Property values and the cost-of-living rise in tandem. While the process of gentrification may revitalize under-resourced neighborhoods, the skyrocketing costs of living displace longtime residents and businesses, leaving a new demo-graphic to enjoy the benefits.[3]

As climate change starts to play a more significant role in where we live, it has become a trigger for gentrification and displacement in its own right. Coastal cities that lie on the frontlines of global warming have seen an influx of investments to improve climate resilience. The efforts to rede-velop or build new structures that can withstand the impacts of intensify-ing storms, flooding, erosion, and sea-level rise may inadvertently pose new threats to low-income communities of color.[4]

I begin by briefly describing the politics of space and mobility that I believe should influence discussions about migration in general and dis-cussions about climate migration in particular. I follow that with a descrip-tion of the three pathways of climate gentrification illustrated by Keenan, et al. I then turn to two situations in my own home city of Nashville, Tennessee, where two tornadoes twenty years apart threatened to exacer-bate gentrification in two different areas of town. I conclude by lifting up some practices of resistance to climate gentrification from the aftermath of the 2020 tornado in North Nashville that may repel future attempts at climate gentrification.

The right to migrate or to remain is defined by privilege. The answer to the question of who should be able to move or stay in order to survive economic, climate, or social disaster is riddled with racism, classism, and xenophobia worldwide. Immigration rights activist and theorist, Aviva Chomsky, makes the case that national borders are social constructs that people with power, either military power or social power or both, use to designate boundaries for reasons of self-interest. As social-spatial constructions, boundaries of nations, states and, for our purposes, neighborhoods, vary in tandem with the self-interests of the powerful. Two places where this confluence of factors, boundaries, racism, and xenophobia are most evident are in redlining in mortgage lending and in the history of the line in the sand known as the United States/Mexico border, which now serves to designate whole classes of people as either "legal" or "illegal" persons.[5]

When we treat socio-geographic constructs as immutable, the power-laden determination of who belongs and who does not, of who is "in place" and who is "out of place," is whitewashed under layers of what seems to be "natural," i.e., essentialized categories. As the boundaries and ideologies sediment, a moral rhetoric grows up around them and their inhabitants. For instance, Western culture insists that the mobility of some people demonstrates their deviance.[6] Consider the unhoused in major urban areas. They may camp and live on the streets or in tent enclaves in abandoned lots. Cities forcibly move homeless encampments on the occasion of a large, politically important convention coming to town, on the supposition that these people are dangerous, dirty, and "out of place," an aesthetic blemish on an otherwise pristine illusion. Or consider the myriad ways in which structural racism and white supremacy enculturate white people into being suspicious of people of color in "white" spaces (which turns out to be any space with a white person in it). Historical examples of mobility as deviance include the ways that dominant cultures have treated both hoboes in the United States[7] and the Roma people throughout Europe. In these cases, people who move in order to survive are considered deviant. They are "out of place," thus deserving suspicion, scorn, and even violence.

Simultaneously, other groups have always perceived themselves to have the "right" of both mobility and of stasis. Chomsky makes the point that the right of mobility and the belief that European culture and religion *should* be spread universally motivated colonial expansion. "Europeans apparently belonged everywhere."[8] Colonialism was the physical expression of the idea that white, Anglo-European culture *should* be *everywhere*—and was thus justified in its movement and takeover of any space it chose. Accompanying the "right" of mobility is the belief that white, Anglo-European culture would *improve* the existing space wherever it went. Thus, the right of movement has been afforded to some and forbidden to most. Much like the illusion of "free trade" before it, as receiving nations resist climate migrants by hardening and militarizing their borders or creating offshore refugee camps, carbon emissions move unrestrained from the industrialized receiving countries to the less industrialized countries suffering the greatest climate consequences. Greenhouse gasses produced in the developed world have more freedoms than those fleeing the effects of these toxins.

Thus, the ways that boundaries are drawn and maintained serve to naturalize social power in geographic ways. More specifically, as we will see with climate gentrification, these boundaries, riddled with racism, classism, and xenophobia, seem only malleable when the desires of the most socially and economically powerful change.

Climate gentrification as a concept has been growing in use since its scholarly appearance in 2018. In an article entitled "Climate Gentrification: From Theory to Empiricism in Miami-Dade County, Florida," researchers investigated housing prices by elevation, from 1971–2017 across several neighborhoods in Greater Miami, Florida in the United States. From this study, the authors write that climate gentrification is based, "on a simple proposition: climate change impacts arguably make some property more or less valuable by virtue of its capacity to accommodate a certain density of human settlement and its associated infrastructure."[9] The implication is that such price volatility "is either a primary or a partial driver of the patterns of urban development that lead to displacement (and sometimes entrenchment) of existing populations consistent with conventional framings of gentrification."[10] They continue:

Climatic impacts should be understood within a broader array of influences driving gentrification, including historic racial segregation, income inequality, and the spatial distribution of jobs, transportation, and housing. However, with [climate gentrification], it can be argued that climatic influences will increasingly play an important role in the weighted factors driving investment and locational decisions of households, investors, and financiers.[11]

In addition to the standard markers of gentrification in which rich white people belong everywhere, or at least in the "best places," and working-class people, people of color, and immigrants belong nowhere—or out of sight—climate change becomes a threat multiplier. It increases and amplifies existing inequitable conditions. Like climate migration worldwide, these authors claim that climate change within the borders of the United States now highlights and exacerbates existing inequities in housing in our towns and cities.[12]

The authors identify three main processes or "pathways" of climate gentrification. The first is called the "superior investment pathway" and is the most common. In Miami, investors began investing in properties that were at higher elevations from the formerly preferred properties lining the coast. Properties at higher elevations became more desirable after it became clear that climate change would result in more frequent flooding of the properties at lower levels. The properties at higher elevations, which at one time were less desirable, were the home to immigrant communities and poorer communities, who were now being priced out of their homes and neighborhoods. The second pathway is called the "cost-burden pathway."[13] Here, neighborhoods gentrify when only the wealthiest can stay in place as climate change increases costs of insurance, property taxes, and the ability to afford to repair homes after a natural disaster.

The third pathway, called the "resilience investment pathway," is also a result of "Green Gentrification."[14] In this pathway, neighborhoods are rebuilt or retrofitted for resilience against increasingly devastating natural disasters. The resulting homes and community then become affordable to wealthy people who can "pay to stay." Their wealth insulates them (temporarily, at least) from the necessity to move.[15]

To that end, the authors expect to see climate gentrification nation-wide. They write:

> If [climate gentrification] proves to be an accurate description of economic processes and behaviors, high-elevation property, shaded or wind-cooled property, fresh water resourced property, geologically stable property, ecologically diverse property, pollution-free property, and property with resiliently designed buildings will all provide attributes of market valuation that complicate the existing capacities of society to house and shelter its most vulnerable populations.[16]

With the ideas of climate gentrification in mind, I want to turn to two case studies in which natural disasters set the stage for gentrification in my own home city of Nashville, Tennessee.

Increasingly, my city has seen a rise in devastating storms, tornadoes, and "once in a hundred year" floods. We are most definitely feeling the effects of climate change, and with it, climate gentrification. Though not an exact match, these case studies signal the ways that mobility and stasis are related to wealth and race and the processes that need to be in place to both keep people in their historic neighborhoods and build such communities back for resilience. I will look at the demographic changes that took place in the wake of two tornadoes that hit Nashville, Tennessee twenty years apart. The first occurred in East Nashville in May of 1998 and the second occurred in North Nashville just weeks before the country closed down due to the COVID-19 pandemic in March 2020.

Before I launch into the data, I want to say that this paper on climate gentrification is more than an academic exercise for me. It is also what I hope is a clear-eyed appraisal of the processes of climate gentrification and resistance to it in my home for the last twenty-five years. It is the story of how two tornadoes, twenty years apart, threatened under-resourced parts of town and the responses of the residents of those parts of town on two separate occasions. I hope that you will see that it is the story of the ways that the social construction of boundaries—of who should move and who should stay—with all of the racial and class narratives embedded in them, can be resisted and rewritten for just purposes.

Nashville, Tennessee is a city of 715,884 people situated in the American Southeast.[17] Like much of the southeastern portion of the United States, Nashville has a long history of racial brutality and injustice that has historically been countered by creative resistance and resilience from mobilized African Americans.[18] The tale of these two tornadoes is the tale of this history of injustice and resistance on two separate occasions. Sprawling across 562 square miles, Nashville is divided by the Cumberland River, which separates East Nashville from downtown and West Nashville. Prior to the gentrification following the 1998 tornado, many white Nashvillians proudly declared that they had never been "over the river" to East Nashville, which, at that time, was populated by mostly working-class white and African-American families.

For decades, East Nashville had been redlined by banks in mortgage lending, meaning that mortgage lenders deemed it a "hazardous" neighborhood (read: Black) and would not lend money for home ownership in that area.[19] Areas on a city map were sectioned off by red lines and red shading to designate where the least desirable areas were for lending. A 2019 study of the racial wealth gap created by redlining showed that in those areas of the city mortgage lenders had designated "best" (mostly white), homeowners had 131 percent more home equity than those who lived in areas that had been deemed "hazardous." This disparity in wealth accumulation results in an average of $648,000 for those who bought in the "best" parts of town versus $281,000 for those in the formerly "hazardous" parts of town. Thus, though the practice of redlining was officially banned by the 1968 Fair Housing Act, the huge wealth disparity between Black and white homeowners remains part of its legacy; as does, then, the ability to rebuild after a natural disaster.

The EF-4 tornado that cut a swath through this twenty-six square mile part of town, known as East Nashville, in May 1998 damaged or destroyed 300 homes and tore out football fields worth of old shade trees that kept cooling prices low in these neighborhoods.[20] Rebuilding from that tornado accelerated the gentrification of East Nashville away from its historical roots as an affordable place to live to a rich, white enclave. Demographics changed from 40 percent African American to 22.8 percent African American.

Insurance money and developers flooded the area and in rapid succession bought out damaged structures from distressed homeowners. The homes they razed or rebuilt, along with the businesses that sprung up, left East Nashville unaffordable for previous inhabitants, who were forced to move to outlying suburbs. The community that was once multiracial and affordable became overrun with upscale bars and restaurants, and housing prices soared as East Nashville became the new hip place to live. East Nashville, publicity proclaimed, was "revitalized," as if this multi-racial and multi-class part of town had been dead until rich white people took it over.[21] This kind of language used in gentrification schemes reflects the colonizers belief that whatever land they occupied became better for them having taken it. Now we fast forward twenty years to North Nashville in 2020.

On March 2–3, 2020, just weeks before the country closed down for COVID-19, an EF-3 tornado hit parts of central Tennessee and Nashville, including again East Nashville as well as an area seven miles from downtown on the west side of the Cumberland River called North Nashville. This description of North Nashville aptly describes its character:

> North Nashville has been the center of Black life in the city since the 1950s. During its heyday, many people shopped in the numerous businesses that peppered the area, worshiped in its churches, and danced in its live music venues. Additionally, Fisk University and Tennessee State University have long served as the academic bedrocks of Black Nashvillians.[22]

Comprising an area of just 7.8 square miles, North Nashville is 70 percent African American and 15.5 percent white, with Latinx, Asian, and Pacific Islanders making up the remaining 15 percent.[23] Like East Nashville, North Nashville was redlined for decades, resulting in the same undervaluation of homes and under-resourced neighborhoods.

Prior to the 2020 tornado, gentrification in North Nashville had been pushing in, but suddenly, as was true in East Nashville twenty years before, the destruction of so many Black-owned homes and businesses signaled open season for predatory builders interested in creating new residences for the average of eighty-two people moving to Nashville every day.[24] Indeed, by the end of the first full day of clean up, drones were flying over the damaged neighborhoods locating distressed property and property owners.[25] Just two days after the tornado in North Nashville, as I was helping a friend move out of her severely damaged rental home, we were met at her front door by someone offering her a cash for the damaged home. However, unlike twenty years before, this part of Nashville mobilized to stand against development and gentrification. Under the banner of #Don't Sell Out North, volunteers from organizations like The Equity Alliance and Stand-Up Nashville took to the streets as quickly as the developers to educate people on the options for keeping and repairing their homes. Reflecting on the destruction days after the tornado, Councilwoman Delishia Porterfield told a reporter: "In one fell swoop, the character and history that is so essential to the black experience in Nashville could be gone. We saw what happened before, and we are aware of the situation so we're trying to provide resources so that the community is not preyed on . . . ."[26]

Banding together, community members and activists held meetings where homeowners heard about ways they could stay in their homes and in their community. They heard tips from FEMA, The Small Business Association, real estate agents, attorneys, banking officials, and government representatives, along with area nonprofits. Together they formed an educated, mobilized group of residents ready to stand against the gentrification that climate change and increased tornadic activity had brought to their doorstep. Leaving these meetings, homeowners were given yard signs that read "Don't sell! Won't Sell! I am an informed homeowner!"

Unlike twenty years before, they were not turning over their neighborhoods to rich white people. This time would be different. And it has been. Reports one year after the tornado (March 2021) state that "the efforts have worked as many fewer properties were sold in this zip code than in the years prior to the tornado as gentrification threatened North Nashville. People see their homes as places to hand down through the generations."[27] North Nashville stayed put and fought back as it has fought back against racism in the South so many times before. Learning from the transformation of East Nashville twenty years before, North Nashville refused to be moved. It became a space of resistance defying the privilege of rich white people to move anywhere they choose.

To conclude then, the boundaries and borders of spaces like neighborhoods have racial, classist, and xenophobic assumptions woven throughout—in the case of much of the United States literally represented by redlines on maps. The politics of mobility and stasis, of who belongs where and why relies on the social constructs becoming naturalized as simply, "the way things are." Colonialism writ large has been founded on the belief that Anglo-Europeans belong everywhere and that people of color should make way for this reality, because white people will "improve" or "revitalize" the space. But the citizens of North Nashville mobilized, got educated, and thus thwarted this racist dynamic. They stayed. They rebuilt.

But as North Nashville continues to resist and rebuild eighteen months later, a new potentially dislocating dynamic may come forward as it has in many places around the United States, the one that Kennan et al. called the "resilience investment pathway."[28] "Building for resilience" or "green initiatives" is the language used to reengineer and retrofit communities so that they can withstand the increasingly dire effects of climate change. "Green initiatives" in cities have served to create a new class of people called "sustainability-class residents"[29]—people who can afford to live in areas that have been reshaped to be resilient to flooding, for instance. Many of the initiatives to build for resilience price out historic inhabitants. Often, these resilience measures—such as creating more green space in neighborhoods for rainwater runoff—decrease the population density and affordability of the neighborhood. Recent studies have shown that "green resilient infrastructure" results in reducing the minority populations of the neighborhoods they are used in,[30] which is caused by such projects' failure to: 1) investigate the structures of inequality that exist in the neighborhoods in question, and 2) consult the residents of the neighborhoods about what structures of injustice exist in these neighborhoods and what they see as necessary to keeping the character of the neighborhood. In other words, "green resilient infrastructure" initiatives are not community driven but "top down" impositions.[31]

This "resilience" reality tells us that it is not enough to mobilize against the racism that threatens communities after a natural disaster. Rather, we have to remain vigilant to ensure that our rebuilding responses do not reinscribe the racist, classist, xenophobic practices that have plagued the inscriptions of boundaries and the very notion of mobility and stasis for people worldwide, nationwide, and perhaps in neighborhoods like mine and yours—right next door.

NOTES

1. Habitat for Humanity, "2020 State of the Nation's Housing Report," https://www.habitat.org/costofhome/2020-state-nations-housing-report-lack-affordable-housing.

2. Jesse M. Kennan, Thomas Hill, and Anurag Gumber. "Climate Gentrification: From theory to empiricism in Miami-Dade County, Florida," *Environmental Research Letters* 13, no. 5 (2018): 1.

3. Shelia Hu, "What is Climate Gentrification?" *Natural Resources Defense Council*, August 27, 2020.

4. Ibid.

5. Aviva Chomsky, *Undocumented: How Immigration Became Illegal* (Boston: Beacon Press, 2014), 19.

6. See Tim Cresswell, *In Place/Out of Place: Geography, Ideology and Transgression* (Minneapolis: University of Minnesota Press, 2010).

7. See Idem., *The Tramp in America* (London, UK: Reaktion Books, 2001).

8. Chomsky, *Undocumented*, 26.

9. Kennan et al., "Climate Gentrification," 2.

10. Ibid.

11. Ibid., 4

12. Yale Climate Connections Team, "Why Climate Change is a Threat Multiplier," *Yale Climate Connections*, June 2019.

13. "Gentrification happens inversely by the fact that vulnerable populations are unable to afford to live *in situ*." In Kennan et al., "Climate Gentrification," 3.

14. "Yet, recent research suggests that green infrastructure planning for climate change is rooted in a green and resilient city orthodoxy that integrates nature-driven solutions into urban sustainability policy. This orthodoxy, as we have argued in previous research, either overlooks or minimizes negative impacts for socially vulnerable residents while selling a new urban brand of green and environmentally resilient 21st-century city to investors, real estate developers, and new sustainability-class residents." In Isabelle Anguelovsky, et al., "Opinion: Why Green "Climate Gentrification" Threatens Poor and Vulnerable Populations," *Proceedings of the National Academy of Sciences of the United States of America* 116, no. 52 (December 26, 2019): 26140.

15. Keenan et al., "Climate Gentrification," 2. The authors also note, as could be anticipated, that these pathways are "limited in their duration and intensity" as a variety of conditions change that make relocation more and more necessary. They conclude: "Eventually, even the most-wealthy will have to abandon" their residences.

16. Ibid.

17. United States Census Bureau, "Quick Facts Davidson County, Tennessee": www.census.gov/quickfacts/davidsoncountytennessee.

18. "Sit-ins: Nashville, Tenn.," *Civil Rights Digital Library*: crdl.usg.edu/events /sit_ins_nashville_tn/?Welcome

19. Dylan Aycock, "How Real Estate Redlining Shaped Nashville," *Community Impact Newspaper*, July 31, 2020.

20. William Jordan Miller, *A Model for Identifying Gentrification in East Nashville, Tennessee*, master's thesis (Lexington: University of Kentucky, 2015), 15.

21. Nate Rau, "1998 Tornado Traumatized and then Sparked Revitalization in East Nashville," *The Tennessean*, April 2018.

22. Staff, "The Struggle Against Gentrification in Nashville, Tennessee," *Liberation*, November 13, 2017.

23. "North Nashville Neighborhood in Nashville, Tennessee, 37208, 37209, 37228 Detail Profile," *City-Data.com*, August 2021: https://www.city-data.com/ neighborhood/North-Nashville-Nashville-TN.html

24. Melanie Layden, "Music City Continues to See a Boom in Out-of-State Residents," *News 4 NBC*, July 8, 2021.

25. Tee Wilson, "Don't Sell Out the North," March 2020 at The Equity Alliance website: https://theequityalliance.org/dontselloutnorf/.

26. Adam Tamburin, "Nashville Comes Together after Tornado, But Some Worry Accelerating Gentrification Will Push Them Out," *The Tennessean*, March 6, 2020.

27. Damon Mitchell, "Rebuilding Historically Black North Nashville, 1 Year After Deadly Tornado," *WBUR*, March 3, 2021.

28. Kennan, et al., 3.

29. Isabelle Anguelovsky, et al., "Opinion," 26140-41.

30. Galia Shokry, James Connolly, and Isabelle Anguelovski, "Understanding Climate Gentrification and Shifting Landscapes of Protection in Green Resilient Philadelphia," *Urban Climate* 31 (March 2020): 5.

31. Anna Beaman, "Climate Gentrification and Resilience Planning: What Is at Stake for At-Risk Populations," *Environmental Law Institute*, September 18, 2019.

On the Move:
Black People and the EnviroPolitics of Shifting Climates, Shifting People

Jennifer S. Leath

MIGRATION MANIFESTS IN MANY FORMS. This essay explores the relationship between different types of migration in the lives of Afrodiasporic people in the United States, offering a comparative analysis between 1) the forced immigration of people in the transatlantic slave trade and the contemporary climate-change driven migrations of people in and away from Africa; 2) the migration of Afrodiasporic people from slaveholding states to the North during the Great Migration and from the North *back* to those former slaveholding states today,[1] and 3) the relationship between historic redlining and contemporary gentrification. While these (im)migrations have often been read contemporaneously and retrospectively as political in motivation, there is evidence that they were and are also responding to environmental contexts. The forced (im)migrations Afrodiasporic people have historically endured due to commodification, racial bias, and sociopolitical profit are consistent with the present trends of disproportionate impacts of climate change and other detrimental environmental factors on people in Africa and Afrodiasporic people in the United States. Consequently, I suggest a multi-dimensional resistance strategy that builds on 1) the holistic spiritual insights of local Afro-indigenous religious movements and 2) deliberate migrations that maximize the political power and climate change survival preparedness of people of African descent as hallmarks of a new "we" and a new "community."

THE TRANSATLANTIC SLAVE TRADE AND CONTEMPORARY AFRICAN IMMIGRATION

The transatlantic slave trade commodified and forced the (im)migration of people of African descent not only for the sake of expanding the economic profits of slave traders, but also as a way of codifying white supremacy. Regardless of how the motivations for this trade are measured, the outcome was that people of African descent were forced to maximize the productivity of lands outside of Africa (and Europe) for the financial and political interests of Europeans looking to expand beyond their own borders.[2] In this process, people of African descent were conscripted into *both* participation in their own exploitation *and* participation in an increasingly exploitative relationship with the geographical spaces to which they were brought and confined—the land, water, and air of their enslavement. How does the historic relationship between enslaved people—themselves exploited—and the land they were conscripted to exploit compare with the current relationship between those (im)migrating from and/or within Africa and the lands from which they are (im)migrating?

The Institute for Security Studies reports: "Despite contributing only 7.1% of the world's greenhouse gas emissions, sub-Saharan Africa is one of the regions suffering the most from climate change impacts... In 2019, 195% more Africans were affected by extreme weather than in 2018."[3] According to the Institute, climate change will especially impact places like Addis Ababa and Dar Es Salaam, causing droughts and flooding, respectively. Consequent migration is inevitable; some of that migration will include immigration. Consistent with the ways people of African descent have been conscripted into the process of their own exploitation and the exploitation of the earth, *Africa* and its people now suffer the impacts of climate change largely on account of the violations of those outside of the continent of Africa. However, in marked contrast with the migrations of the slave trade—and notwithstanding contemporary stereotypes and assumptions about a generalized, universal interest of those living on the African continent to migrate to Europe and North America—most climate-impacted African population migration consists of movement between regions on the continent.[4]

Though there were already Africans in what is now known as the United States before August 20, 1619—and there is documentation of some African people arriving on the shores before Christopher Columbus in 1492—a specific type of record exists on this *particular* date. Ibram X. Kendi writes that when "twenty or so Ndongo people" arrived in Jamestown, Virginia in 1619, the presence of "thirty-two African slaves" had already been documented there. Unlike the Ndongo people who arrived on August 20, though, the *arrival* dates of those already enslaved in Jamestown had not been documented. Kendi writes:

> Virginia's recorder general John Rolfe, known as Pocahontas's husband, produced Black America's birth certificate in 1619. He notified Sir Edwin Sandys, treasurer of the Virginia Company of London, that "a Dutch man of Warr . . . brought not any thing but 20 and odd Negroes" and traded them for food.[5]

The import of Rolfe's record of the arrival of Africans is undeniable, even as the record feigns its insignificance. Kendi calls attention to Rolfe's "not any thing." Not any thing. Not anything. No thing. Nothing. The African people enslaved on *The White Lion* were nothing, nothing to speak of, next to nothing, nothing of much value, nothing much. They were *after* nothing. They were *after* nothing following the coordinating conjunction "but." They were nothing, *but* what was (already) little or nothing. Such clarity confirms that the die of racism had already been cast. Rolfe readily documented the Africans' arrival according to the economic and social context of his day. Rolfe's account reflected his understanding that the presence of Africans on *The White Lion* was an artifact of the economic expansion of European traders and was meant to be profitable to those traders. Rolfe's account also reflected his understanding that Africans on *The White Lion* signified white supremacy—and that he neither objected to Africans as cargo on the *The White Lion* nor to the logic of white supremacy that made cargo of Africans. The economic and social interest went hand in hand.

George Fredrickson writes: "In all manifestations of racism from the mildest to the most severe, what is being denied is the possibility that the racializers and the racialized can coexist in the same society, except perhaps on the basis of domination and subordination."[6] An even more insidious circumstance, he notes: "What makes Western racism so autonomous and conspicuous in world history has been that it developed in a context that presumed human equality of some kind."[7] *This* is the irony and hypocrisy of Jamestown—a community founded on a vision of human equality and self-determination born of a need for religious freedom. *This* is the irony and hypocrisy of building *community* on such virtues. *This* is the irony and hypocrisy of the ways that Europe and North America persist in efforts to under/mis-develop the people and land of Africa.[8] And yet, this irony and hypocrisy take up the power and prominence of the religious. Under the force of such foul religious fervor, contra-community is born. This contra-community is born again and again—and most especially when difference and power are enlisted for the work of domination and subordination. It is under such circumstances that a common drive for freedom unites otherwise disparate people; it is under such circumstances that migration is an obvious alternative to dangers seen and unseen; it is under such circumstances that contra-community, new community, truer community emerges as a simultaneous clap back and flight forward.

Notwithstanding the clarity of racism that frames the August 20, 1619 arrival of Africans, Kendi offers an important rejoinder to this occasion in the introduction to *Four Hundred Souls: A Community History of African America, 1619–2019*. He writes:

> Since 1619, the people of African descent arriving or born in these colonies and then the United States have comprised a community self-actualizing and sometimes self-identifying as African America or Black America. *African* speaks to a people of African descent. Black speaks to a people racialized as Black.[9]

And in an artistic flourish, Kendi sharpens this point:

Racist power constructed the Black race—and all the Black groups. *Them*. Racist power kept constructing Black America over four hundred years. *Them* constructed, again and again. But the antiracist power within the souls of Black folk reconstructed Black America all the while, in the same way we are reconstructing ourselves in this book. *We* reconstructed, again and again. *Them* into *we*, defending the Black American community to defend all the individuals in the community. *Them* became *we* to allow *I* to become *me*.[10]

Yes, a community, a "we" was made through the forced migration known as the transatlantic slave trade, such that by June 19, 1865, collective celebration for collective emancipation was possible.

Contemplating the contemporary conditions of African people leaving the continent for what is now called the United States and other sites of European conquest and empire—especially those moving due to the residual effects of the transatlantic slave trade, such as (neo)colonization—it is important to name some of the byproducts of the slave trade. Naming the byproducts of the slave trade can help clarify the motivations and significance of present day (im)migration. The transatlantic slave trade not only polluted the globe with an ethos of naturalized oppressive hierarchies that subjugate "others" based on melanin (first) and everything that can be categorized as nonwhite and/or non-heteropatriarchal (after), but *also* polluted the globe with climate changing particles and practices that accompany industrialization.[11] Crimes against humanity in the form of racism (i.e., a quintessential degradation of human life) and crimes against the planet (i.e., unfettered capitalist industrialization) fueled one another and were trafficked together with the transport and trade of people of African descent during the transatlantic slave trade. Moreover, Africans leaving the continent today (like so many of those forced to leave in chains) are often among the elite and/or *occasionally* the most persecuted in their places of origin. Those who (im)migrate to Europe and North America today are the exception, not the rule—even if their migration is exaggerated as if it were a terrible, incalculable invasion.

In this context, the sentiment of Lawrence Summers's infamous December 12, 1991, memo while serving as the World Bank's Chief Economist is unsurprising. He wrote: "'Dirty' Industries: Just between you and me, shouldn't the World Bank be encouraging MORE migration of the dirty industries to the LDCs [Least Developed Countries]?" One of the reasons he offered for this was:

> The costs of pollution are likely to be non-linear as the initial increments of pollution probably have very low cost. I've always thought that under-populated countries in Africa are vastly UNDER-polluted, their air quality is probably vastly inefficiently low compared to Los Angeles or Mexico City. Only the lamentable facts that so much pollution is generated by non-tradable industries (transport, electrical generation) and that the unit transport costs of solid waste are so high prevent world welfare enhancing trade in air pollution and waste.[12]

Summers concludes: "The problem with the arguments against all of these proposals for more pollution in LDCs (intrinsic rights to certain goods, moral reasons, social concerns, lack of adequate markets, etc.) could be turned around and used more or less effectively against every Bank proposal for liberalization."[13] Notwithstanding "intrinsic rights to certain goods, moral reasons, social concerns," and even "lack of adequate markets," Summers defends the migration of *pollution*, not *people*. Summers believes a strong case can be made for dumping trash in places with low wages, low population, and low life expectancy—African countries among these. According to the Summers memo, Africa and other "LDCs" can and should bear the brunt and pay the price for the excess, greed, planetary hazard, and environmental harm of industrialized so-called "developed countries." The subtext of Summers's claims is loud and clear: there is "not any thing but" over 1.38 billion Africans on the continent of Africa. The comparison is enraging: from trading imported African people for food so that a slave trader can live to exploit again (and enable others to follow suit) to trading exported waste (that African people have been conscripted to help create) to create room for the exporters to create more waste. The historic expectation is that the imported African people were not people at all—and as objects, neither sentient victims nor beneficiaries of an economy (of slavery) built on their objectification. The contemporary expectation is that African people on the continent are not people at all—and as objects, neither sentient victims nor beneficiaries of an economy (of waste dumping) built on their objectification.

Most absurd is the expectation that African people will (and should) remain on the continent of Africa in the wake of all the dumping and climate change that modern "development" has set into motion. However, due to the expense and requirements for those emigrating from Africa to have resources, certain knowledge, and connections, this expectation is likely to be realized. Racism is so ubiquitous that it drives both explanations for why people on the continent of Africa will (and should) stay amid environmental degradation for which African people are not primarily or exclusively at fault *and* why people on the continent of Africa make their way to Europe and North America at increasing rates.[14] It follows that the work of counteracting racism is no more likely to result in remaining in or leaving Africa. The Institute for Security Studies, in fact, maintains: "Climate change drives far more internal movement within a country than it does internationally. Of the migrants who do cross international borders, most stay within their region of origin."[15] And the best that can be done in the wake of climate change and other environmental challenges is not to overemphasize emigration to Europe and North America, but to prepare *in* Africa and its cities and regions. As researchers from the Institute for Environment and Human Security of the United Nations University conclude:

> The burden of assisting and protecting vulnerable populations cannot be borne by the most affected states and communities alone. All countries have a role to play in minimizing pressure on vulnerable populations and providing adaptation options, including for dignified, safe movement of people if this becomes unavoidable.[16]

The "we" created through practices of human and environmental terror cannot be reduced to a community of African Americans or Blacks but involves global communities on and beyond the continent of Africa. This broader "we" demands care, priority, and the cessation of harm—along with the dismantling of paternalism. This "we" is a migrating "we" that defies national borders while moving regionally and evoking solidarity globally. From the Niger Delta and Ghana, from Tanzania and Uganda, from Zimbabwe and Ethiopia, from Somalia and Nigeria[17]—in the wake of climate change and conflict, many African people are migrating, and by 2050 as many as 200 million could be in this number.[18]

BLACK FOLKS AND INTERSTATE US MIGRATIONS

A comparative reflection on forced migratory patterns during the transatlantic slave trade and contemporary African migratory patterns in the wake of climate change invite a reconsideration of migration in the United States. Between 1916 and 1970, about six million African Americans migrated from the formerly slaveholding South to the North in what is now known as the Great Migration. The post-emancipation conditions had improved the plight of the formerly enslaved for only a short time in the South. From 1890 to 1920, a new cloud hovered as Jim Crow took root in the nadir of African-American life and history. For people of African descent, lynchings increased steadily; political opportunities were blocked; sharecropping, chain gangs, and prisons took up where slavery left off to make sure that the Afrodiasporic population in the United States would remain subjugated, especially in the South. As Black people moved north, many left a forced relationship with land cultivation for possibilities of urban work in factories and intellectual outlets.

In his book, *The Devil You Know: A Black Power Manifesto*, Charles Blow observes that Afrodiasporic people in the United States have begun, in the early twenty-first century, to move back to those formerly slaveholding regions. He notes that this has been an intuitive move for many, but that there is also important political possibility in such migration. Blow commends efforts to add political consciousness to the movement that is already happening and that is, largely, driven by financial interest and opportunity already in place. There are already Black majority cities and states—or jurisdictions where at least a third of the population is already Black. Blow argues that such places just need Black people to migrate to them for reinforcement and to cultivate political strongholds. However, such intentional migration—especially with Black power interest—is not without its own risks and dangers. Blow writes: "Whenever

Black people make progress, white people feel threatened and respond forcefully."[19] This is not merely a historical observation.[20]

Beyond the possibilities that Blow perceives, I argue that there are environmental possibilities of reconnection with cultivation on healthier terms than are now in play as Afrodiasporic people of the United States move south. Yes, Blow aptly points out that migrants in the Great Migration were fleeing cotton fields and oppressive agricultural working conditions. He even quotes Fannie Lou Hamer reading Adam Clayton Powell, Jr. at the 1964 Democratic Party National Convention to remind him of the points that distinguished her and her Black delegation from Mississippi: "'Yeah, I know who you are. You are Adam Clayton Powell.' She continued, 'But how many bales of cotton have you picked? How many beatings have you taken?'"[21] No, Blow does not envision an agricultural return for Blacks who return south, but "a somewhat organic galvanizing of collective conscious that produced collective action" and "unlocked opportunity and unleashed creativity."[22]

I agree with Blow. *And*, notwithstanding the devastating impacts of climate change on port cities in the US Northeast, Louisiana, and Texas, there are climate-change-resilient possibilities for select southern locations to which Black people and communities can relocate according to Blow's advice (and are already relocating). Blow knows this.[23] To Blow's recommendations I add: such relocation must be concerned with both the micropolitics of urban geography that have historically resulted in greater environmental vulnerabilities in predominantly Black communities and the macropolitics of regional climate change trends. Moreover, I would also recommend a more conscientious reconnection with agriculture through deepened cultural connections with agriculturally oriented communities Indigenous to Turtle Island. I recommend reconnection with Indigenous communities and people who are mutually concerned about planetarily, pluriversally responsible land cultivations for a holistically healthful, liberative future for (normative) life.

GENTRIFICATION AND OTHER TRAGIC LEGACIES OF REDLINING

Interestingly, the infrastructure proposal that the Biden Administration put forward in 2022 responds directly to legacies of redlining and other systemic political, economic, and social policies that maintained segregation.[24]

However, it remains to be seen how effective this proposal will be in responding to the new and ongoing violence of gentrification. Interestingly, *both* infrastructural neglect *and* attention, *as well as* environmental neglect *and* attention have been complicit in the deleterious impact of redlining and gentrification on the lives of Afrodiasporic people. However, the connection between infrastructure and the environment *together* as they impact Afrodiasporic people has yet to be adequately studied. And still, the fate of environmental interests with respect to the infrastructure bill are as uncertain as those aspects of Biden's agenda that respond to histories of redlining.

Between the new community possibilities for Afrodiasporic people that exist globally as a result of common experiences of migration and the new possibilities of community that exist as Black and Indigenous communities reconnect through migratory patterns on Turtle Island are the dual hauntings of gentrification and redlining. Both threaten to contravene the formation of a politically effective and collective "we" among people of African descent in the United States, an interracial "we" *in* the United States, and a planetary "we" that corrects for plaguing racist exploitations. When, in one city, eighty-seven percent of the areas designated as "hazardous" according to historical Home Owners' Loan Corporation (HOLC) redlining maps are now gentrifying, on the one hand, but also bearing the burden of disproportionately high impacts of climate change, on the other, one wonders how long it will take for neo-redlining gentrifiers to get hot and move on, improve the acute conditions, improve the global conditions, and/or otherwise redistribute the burden onto people of African descent and other people of color.[25]

MOVE: COMBATTING COMMODIFICATION, RACISM, AND SOCIOPOLITICAL GREED

I close with a controversial, but complex invocation of a "we," a "community" *defined* by being "on the move"—fundamentally and unequivocally linked to Africa as Afrodiaspora through the refining fire of "the United States." On May 13, 1985, the Philadelphia police bombed a row house at 6221 Osage Avenue in West Philadelphia. Mayor Wilson Goode, Philadelphia's first Black mayor, and Gregore J. Sambor, the police commissioner, had classified the inhabitants as terrorists. The bomb intended for this single location destroyed about sixty-five houses and killed eleven people. The six adults and five children who died in the bombing were John Africa, Rhonda Africa, Theresa Africa, Frank Africa, Conrad Africa, Tree Africa, Delisha Africa, Netta Africa, Little Phil Africa, Tomaso Africa, and Raymond Africa. Those in the house were part of a group that John Africa led called MOVE. The 1996 pamphlet "25 Years on The Move" explains the organization and its name:

> The word MOVE is not an acronym. It means exactly what it says: MOVE, work, generate, be active. Everything that's alive moves. If it didn't it would be stagnant, dead. Movement is the principle of life, and because MOVE's belief is life, our founder, JOHN AFRICA, gave us the name "MOVE." When we greet each other we say "ON THE MOVE!"[26]

MOVE was countercultural. MOVE maintained: "We don't believe in this reform world system—the government, the military, industry and big business." MOVE modeled itself as family—united followers of John Africa who took the name "Africa" and followed the religious teachings he presented. Beyond the dangers of their countercultural lifestyle, which disrupted the comfort of others in the "we" of Philadelphia's Black community, MOVE presented a spiritual, political, and environmental alternative. "MOVE's work is revolution," the 1996 document explains: "JOHN AFRICA's revolution, a revolution to stop man's system from imposing on life, to stop industry from poisoning the air, water, and soil and to put an end to the enslavement of all life."[27] Could it be that the only safe place to be "on the move" is *in* the place that is forging revolutionary community, moving (only) at the behest of revolutionary purpose that serves the liberation of subjugated people and nature?

In *The Devil You Know*, Blow invokes the Provisional Government of the Republic of New Afrika (RNA) formed a year after the 1967 Detroit riots. Blow explains: "The group called not only for reparations, but also for the creation of an independent country in 'the subjugated land' of Louisiana, Mississippi, Alabama, Georgia, and South Carolina, states with large Black populations and which had been the sites of extreme oppression."[28] The RNA was to be a new and separate republic. Blow

writes: "My proposition differs. I am not advocating for a Black national-
ism, but a Black regionalism—not to be apart from America but stronger
within it, through consolidation and concentration. The goal is not sedi-
tion but liberty."[29] But what if Blow, and what if we, heard the more defen-
sible parts of the radical, revolutionary, and religious countercultural call
of MOVE? What if migration was an opportunity to participate in
ecospiritual, just ways of being, beyond an expansion of "democratic" participation in the geopolitics of nation states?

Recognizing the certainty and necessity of migration—physical and
spiritual, across space and time, between new and transforming versions
of intra-African and extra-African Afrodiaspora—it stands to reason that
Blow may be right: it is time for a collective political Black community to
regroup and move. However, his hope in an American liberty through
regionalism may be misguided. What if the fullness of the RNA vision
was not moving to "an independent country of 'the subjugated land,'" but
the MOVE of revolutionary work to liberate all life, including the full
family of people, creatures, and land? Though the fate of MOVE demonstrates just how dangerous such intention and clarity can be, the unequiv-
ocal call for revolution is truth. What less than such revolution, what less
than being "on the move" could (re)situate and (re)constitute a "we" that
is for people and planet?

But is MOVE the right *rhetorical* move? As a Black person who loves
Black people and who grew up in Philadelphia, I did believe and hope
that MOVE was the right move when I began this essay. I could see and
have shared holistic spiritual insights that characterized MOVE's identity
and mission. However, not long after completing this essay, through the
work of Aishah Shahidah Simmons,[30] I learned about June Stokes, Maria
Hardy, Josh Robbins, Michelle-Whit Sims, Salina Robbins, and Sara
Robbins: survivors who witnessed and experienced abuse in MOVE as
children, citing "coercive sexual relationships, child marriages, death
threats, financial crimes, and several forms of psychological control."[31]
Having encountered these testimonies,[32] it is hard to believe that MOVE
was the right move then—or is the right move now. However, I will not
deny that MOVE quenched a thirst and, as bell hooks explained the des-
peration of certain thirsts: "Because you are thirsty you are not too proud

to extract the dirt and be nourished by the water."[33] So, even as we move toward MOVE to drink what is potable from its fountain, we must move from MOVE to where the earth is not scorched, where there is "water of thirst" that needs less purification, where there is an ecospiritual safety that includes the protection children, women, and all who are vulnerable to sexual abuse.

Katherine McKittrick quotes Ruth Gilmore in *Dear Science and Other Stories*: "there is no life that is not geographic."[34] In irony, in effigy, Osage Avenue is geographically engraved, immovable in the minds of those who dared to be "on the move." As this essay shows, there are different ways that Afrodiasporic people in and beyond the United States—including those presently being geographically, atmospherically forced into diaspora—can deliberately draw on the insights of resistance-based, earth-friendly communities and migrate with political, spiritual, and environmental savvy. As we *move*, "we" can—"we" must—self-determine the geographies of our lives. Perhaps we can be "on the move" toward revolutionary, environmentally conscious, sound possibilities—even if this also means moving toward the constructive and holistically sound aspects of the social, political, philosophical, and religious peripheries of Black community and culture? Even if "we" move at the risk of stultification: better to have faltered on the move as community than never to have moved as community at all.

NOTES

1. See Charles M. Blow, *The Devil You Know: A Black Power Manifesto* (New York: Harper, 2021).

2. Ta-Nehisi Coates, "Slavery Made America," *The Atlantic*, June 24, 2014, https://www.theatlantic.com/business/archive/2014/06/slavery-made-america/373288/; "Economics and the Accumulation of Wealth," http://archive.understandingslavery.com/index.php-option=com_content&view=article&id=362 &Itemid=212.html.

3. Aimée-Noël Mbiyozo, "African Cities Must Prepare for Climate Migration," *Institute for Security Studies*, January 15, 2021, https://issafrica.org/iss-today/african-cities-must-prepare-for-climate-migration.

4. David Eltis and David Richardson, "Overview of the Slave Trade Out of Africa: 1500–1900," in *Atlas of the Transatlantic Slave Trade* (New Haven: Yale University Press, 2015), 1–20; Guy J. Abel, Michael Brottrager, Jesus Crespo Cuaresma, and Raya Muttarak, "Climate, Conflict and Forced Migration," *Global Environmental Change* 54 (January 1, 2019): 239–49.

5. See Ibram X. Kendi and Keisha N. Blain, eds., *Four Hundred Souls: A Community History of African America, 1619–2019* (New York: One World, 2021), xvi.

6. George M. Fredrickson, *Racism: A Short History* (Princeton: Princeton University Press, 2002), 9.

7. Ibid., 11.

8. See Walter Rodney, *How Europe Underdeveloped Africa* (Washington, DC: Howard University Press, 1981).

9. Kendi and Blain, *Four Hundred Souls*, xiv.

10. Ibid., xvii.

11. David Eltis and Stanley L. Engerman, "The Importance of Slavery and the Slave Trade to Industrializing Britain," *The Journal of Economic History* 60, no. 1 (2000): 123–44.

12. Basil Enwegbara, "Toxic Colonialism: Lawrence Summers and Let Africans Eat Pollution," *The Tech* 121, no. 16 (April 6, 2001): 7.

13. Ibid.

14. Marie-Laurence Flahaux and Hein De Haas, "African Migration: Trends, Patterns, Drivers," *Comparative Migration Studies* 4, no. 1 (January 22, 2016): 1.

15. Mbiyozo, "African Cities Must Prepare for Climate Migration."

16. Koko Warner, Tamer Afifi, Kevin Henry, Tonya Rawe, Christopher Smith, and Alex De Sherbinin, *Where the Rain Falls: Climate Change, Food and Livelihood Security, and Migration* (Bonn: CARE France and United Nations University – EHS, 2012), 22.

17. See "The Climate Change and Migration in Africa Series," Africa Portal, https://www.africaportal.org/features/climate-change-migration-africa-series/.

18. Abel et al., "Climate, Conflict and Forced Migration," 239–49; and Renata Brito, "Report: Climate Change Could See 200 Million Move by 2050," *The Associated Press*, September 13, 2021, https://apnews.com/article/africa-climate-environment-and-nature-immigration-europe-69cada32a7c13f80914a2a7b48fb5b9c.

19. Blow, *The Devil You Know*, 96.

20. Todd J. Gillman, "Texas House Finalizes Gnarled U.S. House Map That Gives GOP Bounty from Decade of Hispanic Growth," *Dallas News*, October 17, 2021, https://www.dallasnews.com/news/politics/2021/10/16/texas-house-finalizing-gnarled-us-house-map-that-gives-gop-the-bounty-from-decade-of-hispanic-growth/; "Race & Movements Across the Map," *Yogi Berra Museum and Learning Center*, https://yogiberramuseum.org/when-baseball-led-america/lesson1-race-and-

movements/; Yahoo Finance, "A Look at How a Reverse Great Migration to the South Could Impact States' Power and Business," uploaded January 26, 2021, YouTube video, https://www.youtube.com/watch?v=NTMyC24fxwU; and US Environmental Protection Agency, "Future of Climate Change," Overviews and Factsheets: https://19january2017snapshot.epa.gov/climate-change-science/future-climate-change_.html.

21. Blow, *The Devil You Know*, 182.

22. Ibid., 209.

23. Ibid., 45.

24. "FACT SHEET: Biden-Harris Administration Announces New Actions to Build Black Wealth and Narrow the Racial Wealth Gap," The White House Website, June 1, 2021, https://www.whitehouse.gov/briefing-room/statements-releases/2021/06/01/fact-sheet-biden-harris-administration-announces-new-actions-to-build-black-wealth-and-narrow-the-racial-wealth-gap/.

25. Urban Displacement Project, "What are Gentrification and Displacement," https://www.urbandisplacement.org/about/what-are-gentrification-and-displacement/; Bruce Mitchell and Juan Franco, "HOLC 'Redlining' Maps: The Persistent Structure of Segregation and Economic Inequality" (Washington, DC: NCRC, 2018).

26. "25 Years on The Move," *Pamphlet* (MOVE, 1996): https://azinelibrary.org/approved/25-years-move-1.pdf.

27. Ibid.

28. Blow, *The Devil You Know*, 127.

29. Ibid., 128.

30. Aishah Shahidah Simmons, "In Survivor Solidarity: I BELIEVE June, Maria, Josh, Michelle-Whit, Salina and Sara," *Medium* (blog), July 30, 2021, https://medium.com/@AfroLez/in-survivor-solidarity-i-believe-june-maria-josh-michelle-whit-salina-and-sara-e89ffe97c544.

31. "Former MOVE Members Are Speaking out about Abusive Behavior within the Organization," *Billy Penn* (blog), https://billypenn.com/2021/08/04/move-philadelphia-abusive-behavior-child-marriage-leaving-members/.

32. *Murder at Ryan's Run*, Apple Podcasts, https://podcasts.apple.com/us/podcast/murder-at-ryans-run/id1561552064.

33. bell hooks, "Paulo Friere," *Teaching to Transgress: Education as the Practice of Freedom* (New York: Routledge, 1994), 50.

34. Katherine McKittrick, *Dear Science and Other Stories* (Durham: Duke University Press Books, 2020), x.

9

Multinational Oil Companies and Environmental Racism in the Global South: Evidence from the Niger Delta, Nigeria

Luke Amadi

THIS CHAPTER DISCUSSES evidence of environmental racism in the Niger Delta and considers how, where, and why environmental racism occurs more generally. The chapter builds on Marxian political ecology in analyzing the deleterious, lethal, and asymmetrical practices of capitalist oil resource appropriation in the Niger Delta by foregrounding the activities of multinational oil companies (MNOCs). It also engages with ecological justice, resource accounting, transparency, and equity as central to overcoming environmental racism. The chapter critically examines the various dimensions of environmental racism that have contributed to ecological breakdown in the Niger Delta. It argues that environmental racism is the direct and underlying source of environmental degradation, destruction of the ecosystem, and underdevelopment of the Niger Delta and suggests some solutions on how to move towards a more ecologically just and eco-friendly policy discourse about natural resource appropriation in poor societies.

Environmental racism denotes the fact that people of color and low-income groups are not only disproportionately exposed to pollution but are also disadvantaged by biases in natural resource policy, uneven enforcement of environmental regulations, and the exclusionary nature of mainstream environmentalism. According to Robert Bullard, the term "refers to any policy, practice, or directive that differentially affects or disadvantages (whether intended or unintended) individuals, groups, or communities based on race or color. Environmental racism combines with public policies and industry practices to provide *benefits* for whites while shifting industry *costs* to people of color."[1] Its impacts in low-income countries, however, have not been adequately explored in recent scholarship.[2] Mainstream environmental policymakers have long ignored ecological justice and the unequal effects of pollution and environmental hazards on people of color and low-income countries of the Global South.

Environmental racism is an evolving dynamic of immense ecological significance. It has harmful effects on both the ecosystem and host communities. The complex challenges of environmental racism have informed recent interest in its causes and implications.[3] Across the natural-resource rich, low-income countries of the Global South, capitalist resource appropriation by multinational oil companies taints the environment. In the United States, environmental racism impacts racial minorities such as Hispanics, African Americans, and Native Americans, but as Bullard notes, corporations from the United States and other Western industrialized nations also inflict environmental harm on countries of the Global South.[4]

One of the earliest immediate post-Cold War efforts to address the problem of environmental racism was the January 1990 conference on Race and the Incidence of Environmental Hazards held at the University of Michigan. Despite the attention the conference gave to environmental racism, it has persisted as a grave problem. Environmental racism remains part of the wider debate on "ecological injustice," which comprises various forms of deleterious capitalist resource appropriation and pollution that have a disproportionate impact on minorities, formerly colonized countries, and countries of the Global South.[5]

Across Africa, environmental racism is evident. Post-apartheid South Africa experiences environmental racism associated with the built environment and mineral resource extraction.[6] Similarly, there are diverse forms of environmental racism among the least developed resource-rich African countries. They have an average growth of around five percent.[7] Among these least developed countries, including oil exporters (Angola, Chad, Equatorial Guinea, and Sudan) and mineral producers (the Democratic Republic of the Congo, Guinea, Mali, Mauritania, Mozambique, and Zambia),[8] have experienced an exponential rise in environmental racism. For instance, in Mozambique, the Mozambique Gas Project accounted for environmental degradation as local communities were dispossessed for offshore drilling in Cabo Delgado.[9] These Indigenous communities are vulnerable and internally displaced as a result of European drilling companies capturing their land for resource appropriation. They are subjected to a racialized form of land degradation.

In Nigeria, Africa's leading crude oil producer, there is complex environmental racism—a colonial legacy linked to postcolonial hegemony and the marginalization of communities in the oil-rich Niger Delta. One example of environmental racism is the dumping of 18,000 drums of hazardous waste near residents of Koko—a small port community in the Niger Delta—in 1988 by two Italian firms, which later resulted in chronic diseases.[10]

Appropriation of natural resources for economic rather than ecological ends has been an evolving process of increasing significance, particularly in low-income countries. Appropriation is a Marxian term that denotes "the transfer of ownership, use rights and control over resources that were once publicly or privately owned—or not even the subject of ownership—from the poor (or everyone including the poor) into the hands of the powerful. It is an emotive term because it involves injustice."[11] Appropriation becomes a vehicle of environmental racism when it is undertaken by Western, majority-white nations and corporations while shifting its costs—first and foremost environmental degradation—onto communities of color in the Global South. Powerful multinational corporations marginalize these communities in multiple ways, one being the destruction of the environment upon which they depend for their livelihoods.

Against this backdrop, this chapter builds on a Marxian political ecology approach and provides evidence of environmental racism in the Niger Delta. It argues that, despite deleterious and lethal implications of environmental racism by foreign multinationals, ecological justice has been in the margins.

COLONIAL ORIGINS OF ENVIRONMENTAL RACISM

Environmental racism is a serious problem in contemporary Africa. To understand the specific form of environmental racism in Africa, we first need to review its colonial origins.

Environmental racism builds on long histories of colonial resource appropriation. The colonial origins of environmental racism have involved resource theft, exploitation, coercion, marginalization of Indigenous peoples, the destruction of the natural environment, and the institutionalization of structures that favored the colonial state. These "enduring absolutist structures" of the colonial state[12] in Nigeria appropriated both human and material resources through the transatlantic slave trade, the Colonial Public Land Acquisition Ordinance, the Minerals Ordinance, forest policies, land tenure systems, introduction of cash crop production, and similar actions by the colonial administration.

Racism is a relatively modern concept that traces its origins to the era of European imperialism, the rise of capitalism, and the Atlantic slave trade.[13] It can be broadly defined to encompass individual and group prejudices and acts of discrimination that result in material and cultural advantages conferred on a majority or a dominant social group.[14] The concept of white racism centers on societies with a majority-white population. Racist actions have subjected Indigenous peoples to discrimination, marginalization, genocide, and the deportation of Indigenous minorities.[15] Modern racism, as Louis Althusser argues, emerged in the early modern period as the "discourse of race struggle" and encompassed various historical and political contexts.[16] A key aspect of colonial racial subjugation was slavery and slave trade. Daron Acemoglu and James A. Robinson argue that the appearance of Europeans all over the coast of western and central Africa eager to buy slaves had a huge impact on African societies: "The huge amount of money to be made capturing and selling slaves led to an intensification of warfare across the continent fueled by huge imports of guns and ammunition which the Europeans exchanged for slaves."[17]

After the Second World War, processes of decolonization often led to neocolonialism, "a form of global power in which transnational corporations and global and multilateral institutions combine to perpetuate colonial forms of exploitation of developing countries."[18] With neocolonialism, multinational corporations perpetuate domination by exploiting natural resources and labor power for profit. In Nigeria, "the departing [British] colonial authority ensured the vast petroleum reserves in the Niger Delta area were under the control of two foreign monopoly concerns before independence. The foreign firms are the British Petroleum and the Royal Dutch Shell Company."[19]

As discussed previously, environmental racism refers to the disproportionate and deleterious appropriation of natural resources and the indiscriminate destruction of the natural environment through a racialized logic that subordinates and adversely impacts populations of color. Environmental destruction caused by multinational corporations in formerly colonized countries—in this case, the majority Nigerians—can, in line with Bullard's definition, be considered environmental racism because it represents white-dominated institutions overwhelmingly saddling Black populations with the negative environmental effects of their corporate practices. The racialized logic continues to undermine resource justice and equity and prioritizes the vested capitalist interests of the MNOCs. In short, multinational corporations, and particularly fossil-fuel corporations, perpetuate environmental degradation and the destruction of the natural ecosystem in a manner that disadvantages postcolonial communities of color.

All these forms of appropriation have, in different ways, dislodged local inhabitants or drastically curtailed their land and resource use rights and practices,[20] and they are especially apparent in the Niger Delta.

ENVIRONMENTAL RACISM IN THE NIGER DELTA

The Niger Delta is an oil-rich, majority-minority region in South Nigeria that extends more than 70,000 square kilometers (27,000 square miles) and makes up 7.5 percent of Nigeria's land mass. Crude oil was found in commercial quantity in 1956 at Oloibiri, a community in the region, by a

Dutch multinational, Shell Oil. Despite its vast oil reserves, the region remains poor. Gross national product (GNP) per capita is below Nigeria's national average of 280 US dollars.[21]

Prior to the discovery of crude oil, Nigeria's economy relied on agricultural exports. After nearly fifty years of prospecting for oil in the country, Shell-BP discovered oil at Oloibiri in the Niger Delta in 1956. The first oil field commenced production in 1958.[22] Towards the end of the 1950s, other multinational oil companies were granted operational licenses: Mobil in 1955, Tenneco in 1960, Gulf Oil and Chevron in 1961, and Elf and Agip in 1962. Ahead of Nigeria's political independence in 1960, a total of 847,000 tons of crude oil was exported. While oil resource extraction has generated enormous profits for the multinational oil companies, it decimates the natural environment, humans, and nonhuman species. Water pollution, deforestation, oil spills, soil contamination, gas flaring, and acid rain are just a few of the devastating environmental impacts caused by oil drilling.

Across the Niger Delta, oil exports have averaged two million barrels per day since the mid-1970s.[23] Oil drilling has brought with it oil spills, land degradation, and water contamination.[24] Oil spills represent a key form of pollution caused by drilling. For instance, in 2018, Amnesty International reported that, since 2014, Eni, an Italian oil and gas corporation, has caused 820 spills in the Niger Delta, with 26,286 barrels lost. Since 2011, Shell has reported 1,010 spills, with 110,535 barrels lost.[25] That amounts to about seven Olympic swimming pools. These are huge numbers, but the reality may be even worse. The companies' figures are vastly different than those of the Nigerian government, which recorded 1,369 Shell spills and 1,659 Eni spills in the same timeframes.[26]

Going back further, the last five decades of oil appropriation by multinational oil companies have seen numerous oil spills. Although there is uncertainty regarding the precise figures, the Nigerian National Petroleum Corporation (NNPC) puts the volume spilled each year at 2,500 cubic meters (660,430 gallons per year), with an average of three hundred individual spills per year, or almost one spill per day.

This record excludes "minor" spills.[27] The World Bank reports that the true quantity of oil spilled into the environment in the Niger Delta could be as much as ten times this number, or twenty-five thousand cubic meters each year (6.6 million gallons per year). Between 1958 and 2010, the World Bank and other organizations such as Nigeria's Department of Petroleum Resources (DPR) estimate that somewhere between nine and thirteen million barrels of oil have been spilt in the Niger Delta by individuals and by industry.[28]

The destructive effects of oil spills are manifold. They include water pollution as well as the devastation of animal habitats and the communities that depend on hunting and fishing for sustenance and income. The 2011 *Environmental Assessment of Ogoniland* report sought to "underline that there are, in a significant number of locations, serious threats to human health from contaminated drinking water [and] concerns over the viability and productivity of ecosystems."[29] Pollution not only affects fishing in the coastal communities. It also destroys other aquatic animals, such as crab, crayfish, and periwinkle, which are sources of food and income. The *Environmental Assessment of Ogoniland* reports that while "fishing was once a prime activity in Ogoniland, it was evident from community feedback and field observations that it has essentially ceased in areas polluted by oil."[30] It also states that "fish tend to leave polluted areas in search of cleaner water, and fishermen must therefore also move to less contaminated areas in search of fish."[31] Water pollution exerts pressure on the ecosystem. In Oyorokoto, in the alluvial Rivers State, which is the largest fishing community on the west coast of Africa, there is increasing decline in the quantity and quality of catch by fishermen and women. This is largely attributed to pollution by multinational oil companies.[32]

The lands, water, and creeks of oil-bearing communities are consistently degraded with oil spills and soil contamination. Sugi, Bodo, Mgbede, Nisisioken, and Ogale, among other communities in the Niger Delta, have been affected by oil pollution. Shell's impact on the Bodo community in Ogoni provides evidence of complex lethal feedbacks such as soil contamination arising from oil spills, water pollution, and deforestation. The United Nations Environment Programme concludes that "pollution of soil by petroleum hydrocarbons in Ogoniland is extensive in land areas, sediments and swampland."[33] Meanwhile, the UN Development Programme highlights that the "primary threats to biodiversity in the region are pollution, habitat degradation, land-use change, over-harvesting of natural resources, and invasive alien species."[34] Finally, the United Nations Environment Programme states that the environmental restoration of Ogoniland is possible but may take twenty-five to thirty years.[35]

All of these environmental problems caused by multinational oil corporations may be seen as instances of environmental racism. As Sina Ayanlade and Ulrike Proske demonstrate in their work, in those places where large tracts of land are polluted by oil multinationals, both households and the entire community are disempowered for years, as the pollution renders the land unproductive.[36] As corporations transfer profits to wealthy, white-majority countries, Indigenous communities of color are robbed of their means of subsistence and are exposed to toxic substances. Indeed, the United Nations Environment Programme reports that "since average life expectancy in Nigeria is less than 50 years, it is a fair assumption that most members of the current Niger Delta community have lived with chronic oil pollution throughout their lives."[37] For instance, on January 30, 2013, a Dutch court ruled that Shell is liable for the pollution in the region. In January 2015, Shell agreed to pay eighty million US dollars to the Ogoniland community of Bodo for two oil spills in 2008 after a court case in London.[38] In 2018, Amnesty International released a report that indicted Shell and Eni, two leading multinational oil companies, for being perpetrators of environmental racism. The report stated that both ignored oil spills in the region, as the region is one of the most polluted places on earth.[39]

Aside from these relatively minor penalties, however, corporations have generally been allowed to exploit the Niger Delta's resources and pollute with impunity. Various environmental policy responses by the Nigerian government, such as the Environmental Protection Agency Act of 1988 (FEPA Act), which was replaced by the National Environmental Standards Regulation Agency (NESREA) Act 2007, have been ineffective due to imperialism, neocolonialism, corruption, and rent seeking. To date, the polluted communities have not been cleaned, despite recommendations for a cleanup by the United Nations Environment Programme. Restoration and cleanup programs that the federal government launched in August 2017 have been ineffective.

Another central issue of concern regarding environmental racism linked to the oil multinationals is that local communities bear much of the cost. Oil spills, dredging of larger rivers, and reclamation of land for oil and gas extraction have been on the increase in the region and cost about 758 million dollars every year.[40] One study found that seventy-five percent of the cost is borne by the host communities, who experience biodiversity loss,[41] sea level rise, and coastal flooding, which undermine rural livelihoods. For instance, several fishing and farming communities increasingly experience decline in food production caused by racialized capitalist oil appropriation.[42]

Another instance of environmental racism is deforestation arising from oil appropriation by MNOCs. Deforestation has endangered many plant and animal species. UNDP highlights that Nigeria is one of the most deforested regions of the world.[43] Trees and shrubs, which provide shade and habitat for marine species while reducing fluctuation in water temperature, are destroyed.[44] Mangrove deforestation undermines the production of fish stock, as most fish inhabit the mangroves, where they reproduce. An estimated sixty percent of the fish in the Gulf of Guinea breed in these mangroves.[45] The exploitation of oil and seizure of natural resources destroys environmental resources and biodiversity in a way that has a disproportionate impact on Indigenous Nigerian communities of color. The lower tidal floodplain has more than twenty large estuaries and 7,700 square kilometers of mangrove forests, which is more than seventy percent of Nigeria's estimated 10,000 square kilometers of mangrove forests, Africa's largest mangrove area and the world's third largest.[46] The mangroves are made up of six species in three families: Rhizophoraceae (*Rhizophora racemosa, R. harrisonii*, and *R. mangle*), Avicenniaceae (*Avicennia africana*), and Combretaceae (*Laguncularia racemosa* and *Conocarpus erectus*).[47] High tidal effects in the mangrove zone in the Niger Delta reach amplitudes of one to three meters. The zone extends to the coast and reaches between fifteen to forty-five kilometers inland. The deep belt of the forests protects the freshwater wetlands in the Inner Delta. However, these forests have been cut down by oil corporations.[48] The destruction of mangrove zones should also be grasped as a form of environmental racism, because it will have long-term negative effects on the ability of communities of color to sustain themselves.

Another instance of environmental racism associated with MNOCs and oil appropriation is gas flaring. In an empirical study, Okecha determined that a large quantity of gas is flared in the region in addition to oil pollution.[49] While gas flaring has been declared illegal since 1984 under section 3 of Nigeria's Associated Gas Reinjection Act, flaring has been on the increase.[50] Recent estimates suggest that of the 3.5 billion cubic feet (100 million cubic meters) of associated gas produced annually, 2.5 billion cubic feet (70 million cubic meters), or about seventy percent, is wasted by flaring.[51]

Nigeria has huge natural gas reserves (5.29 trillion cubic meters, or about three percent of the world total) that are underutilized.[52] In some cases, gas flaring causes a rise in temperature within the environments of local communities, thereby producing heat that destroys crops and plants as well as microorganisms that facilitate biological processes for a healthy ecosystem.[53] The Department of Petroleum Resources reports 117 flaring sites in the Niger Delta region. The most pervasive are the five giant gas burners at the Nigerian Agip Oil Company (NAOC) Ebocha Oil center, which is the company's largest oil refinery. It is located in the Egbema community in Rivers State.[54] Gas flaring contributes to changes in local climate conditions as toxic substances are released, which cause acid rain. A study examined the spatial variability effects of gas flaring on the growth and development of crops in the region, including cassava and pepper. There is evidence that it has negative effects on crop development, especially those close to the point of flares.[55]

Statistical analysis also reveals that cassava yields are higher at locations further away from the flare point.[56] In addition, the amount of starch and ascorbic acid in cassava decreases when the plant is grown closer to gas flares. High temperatures around gas flares appear to be the most likely cause of underdeveloped crops.[57] Evidence of the impact on crops is common across the region, particularly in Egbema in Rivers State as well as Opuama and Sekewu communities in Warri, Delta State. Empirical evidence shows that gas flaring has affected the ozone layer of the region, which accounts for localized climate change unhealthy to cultivation of crops.[58]

CONCLUSION

This chapter has offered some insights into the problems of environmental racism, possibilities of transformation, and reflections on how environmental racism increasingly undermines environmental justice, leading to concerns and clamor for change in how multinational oil companies appropriate resources in developing countries. The lack of consequence for oil corporations combined with their destruction of the environment upon which Nigerian communities depend for their livelihoods make the case of the Niger Delta a textbook example of environmental racism.

More ecologically efficient use of resources would alleviate pressure on the mangrove forests, waters, creeks, aquatic creatures, and the natural environment generally. This would help protect the natural environment and animals that inhabit the mangroves. Environmental racism presents a fundamental challenge to environmental justice and indeed to all those concerned with both the analysis and transformation of the natural environment. This has led Daniel Tanuro to argue that "green capitalism" cannot work.[59] Moving towards a more ecologically just and eco-friendly policy discourse demands that we critically reexamine environmental racism and resource appropriation of multinational oil companies within social, ecological, and economic contexts. It demands that we design global policy in a way that values resource transparency and the natural environment.

Issues of pollution, land degradation, soil fertility decline, deforestation, and desertification are deeply entrenched problems. As James Keeley and Ian Scoones observed, such problems are confronted with policy crises.[60] In several ways, environmental racism is discernible in the Niger Delta and has taken multiple dimensions. Driven largely by the multinational oil companies, rent seeking, neoliberalization of nature, and capitalist resource appropriation, environmental degradation and its disproportionate impact on Black Nigerians are major problems. Thus, in the Niger Delta, the racist inclinations of capitalist natural resource appropriation by multinational oil companies have accounted for the destruction of the ecosystem.

However, if new enforceable global policies were implemented, environmental racism could be stopped. Such initiatives might include a bottom-up policy response that draws on local knowledge and that forefronts environmental justice, resource transparency, and equity. This response might involve civil society organizations, movements against environmental racism, and relevant stakeholders. Is deleterious capitalist resource appropriation of multinational oil companies inevitable, or are there alternatives?

NOTES

1. Robert D. Bullard, *Dumping in Dixie: Race, Class, and Environmental Quality*, 2nd ed. (Boulder, CO: Westview Press, 1994), 98.

2. Laura Pulido, "Introduction: Environmental Racism," *Urban Geography* 17, no. 5 (May 1996): 377–79.

3. Luke W. Cole and Sheila R. Foster, *From the Ground Up: Environmental Racism and the Rise of the Environmental Justice Movement* (New York: New York University Press, 2000), 257.

4. Carl A. Zimring, *Clean and White: A History of Environmental Racism in the United States* (New York: New York University Press, 2015); Bullard, *Dumping*, 14.

5. Dorceta Taylor, "The Environmental Justice Movement," EPA Journal (March/April 1992): 23–24; and Robert D. Bullard, "The Threat of Environmental Racism," *Natural Resources and Environment* 7, no. 3 (1993): 23–26.

6. Greg Ruiters, "Environmental Racism and Justice in South Africa's Transition," *Politikon* 28, no.1 (2001): 95–103.

7. André-Michel Essoungou, "Africa's Least Developed: Lands of Opportunity: At the UN Conference on LDCs, Focus Moves Away from Aid," *Africa Renewal* (August 2011): https://www.un.org/africarenewal/magazine/august-2011/africas-least-developed-lands-opportunity.

8. Ibid.

9. Camila Rolando Mazzuca, "Mozambique Gas Project, Villagers Dispossessed for Off Shore Drilling, Cabo Delgado, Mozambique," Environmental Justice Atlas, https://ejatlas.org/conflict/cabo-delgado-communites-impacted-by-gas-exploration-projects; Isilda Nhantumbo, "REDD+ in Mozambique: A New Opportunity or Land Grabbers?" International Institute for Environment and Development (IIED) September 15, 2011, https://www.iied.org/redd-mozambique-new-opportunity-for-land-grabbers; and James Fairhead, Melissa Leach, and Ian Scoones, "Green Grabbing: A New Appropriation of Nature?" *Journal of Peasant Studies* 39, no. 2 (2012): 238.

10. Segun Gbadegesin, "Multinational Corporations, Developed Nations, and Environmental Racism: Toxic Waste, Exploration, and Eco-Catastrophe," in *Faces of Environmental Racism: Confronting Issues of Global Justice*, ed. Laura Westra and Bill E. Lawson, 2nd ed. (Lanham, MD: Rowman & Littlefield, 2001), 187–202; Stephanie Buck, "In the 1980s, Italy Paid a Nigerian Town $100 a Month to Store Toxic Waste—and It's Happening Again: Toxic Colonialism at Its Worst," *Timeline*, May 26, 2017; Luke Amadi and Henry Alapiki, "Environmental Security Threats and Policy Response in the Niger Delta, Nigeria 1990–2016," in *Environmental Policies for Emergency Management and Public Safety*," ed. Eneanya Augustine (Hershey, PA: IGI Global Publishers, 2018), 189–208.

11. Fairhead et. al, "Green Grabbing."

12. Daron Acemoglu and James A. Robinson, "Why Is Africa Poor?" *Economic History of Developing Regions* 25, no. 1 (August 2010): 26.

13. See George M. Fredrickson, *The Arrogance of Race: Historical Perspectives on Slavery, Racism, and Social Inequality* (Middletown, CT: Wesleyan University Press, 1988), 311; Leonard Lieberman, "'Race' 1997 and 2001: A Race Odyssey," in *General Anthropology Division Modules in Teaching Anthropology* (Mount Pleasant: Central Michigan University, 1997), 2; Dennis Rutledge, "Racism," in *The Social Science Encyclopedia*, 3rd ed., ed. Adam Kuper and Jessica Kuper (London: Routledge, 2004), 2:715–17.

14. Joe R. Feagin, *Racist America: Roots, Current Realities, and Future Reparations* (New York: Routledge, 2000), 440.

15. Terry Martin, "The Origins of Soviet Ethnic Cleansing," *The Journal of Modern History* 70, no. 4 (1998): 813–61; and Dina Gilio-Walker, *As Long as Grass Grows: The Indigenous Fight for Environmental Justice, from Colonization to Standing Rock* (Boston: Beacon Press, 2019).

16. Louis Althusser, *Essays in Self-criticism*, trans. Grahame Lock (London: NLB, 1976), 224.

17. Acemoglu and Robinson. "Why Is Africa Poor?" 28.

18. Encyclopedia Britannica, s.v. "Neocolonialism," https://www.britannica.com/topic/neocolonialism.

19. Noah Echa Attah, "The Historical Conjuncture of Neocolonialism and Under-development in Nigeria," *Journal of African Studies and Development* 5, no. 5 (2013): 70–79, 72.

20. Ibid., 239.

21. J. Singh, D. Moffat, and O. Linden, "The Niger Delta: A Stakeholder Approach to Environmental Development," in *World Bank Group Africa Region Findings and Good Practice*, no. 53 (Washington, DC: World Bank, 1995), 1.

22. Andrew Walker, "The Day Oil Was Discovered in Nigeria," *British Broadcasting Corporation*, March 17, 2009.

23. S. Okecha, "Environmental Problems of the Niger Delta and Their Consequences," in *Environmental Problems of the Niger Delta*, ed. Akinjide Osuntokun (Lagos: Friedrich Ebert Foundation, 2000), 52–58.

24. See United Nations Development Programme (UNDP), *Niger Delta Human Development Report* (Lagos, Nigeria: Perfect Prints, 2006); and United Nations Environment Programme (UNEP), *Environmental Assessment of Ogoniland* (Nairobi, Kenya, 2011).

25. Amnesty International, "Nigeria: Amnesty Activists Uncover Serious Negligence by Oil Giants Shell and Eni," March 16, 2018, https://www.amnesty.org/en/latest /news/2018/03/nigeria-amnesty-activists-uncover-serious-negligence-by-oil-giants-shell-and-eni/.

26. Ibid.

27. United Nations Development Programme (UNDP), *Niger Delta Biodiversity Project Federal Ministry of Environment* (Nigeria, 2012), 76.

28. Singh, Moffat, and Linden, "The Niger Delta," 5.

29. UNEP, *Environmental Assessment of Ogoniland*, 6.

30. Ibid., 17.

31. Ibid., 10.

32. Ruth Maclean, "The Fisherwomen, Chevron, and the Leaking Pipe," *New York Times*, July 25, 2021, https://www.nytimes.com/2021/07/25/world/africa/nigeria-fisherwomen-chevron.html; Eze Simpson Osuagwu and Eseoghene Olaifa, "Effects of Oil Spills on Fish Production in the Niger Delta," *Plos One* 13, no. 10 (2018): e0205114.

33. UNEP, *Environmental Assessment of Ogoniland*, 9.

34. UNDP, *Niger Delta Biodiversity Project Federal Ministry of Environment*, 31.

35. UNEP, *Environmental Assessment of Ogoniland*, 12.

36. Sina Ayanlade and Ulrike Proske, "Assessing Wetland Degradation and Loss of Ecosystem Services in the Niger Delta, Nigeria," *Marine and Freshwater Research* 67, no. 8 (August 31, 2015): 10.

37. UNEP, *Environmental Assessment of Ogoniland*, 204.

38. Margaret Coker and Benoît Faucon, "Shell to Pay $80 Million Compensation for Oil Spills in Nigeria," *Wall Street Journal*, January 7, 2015, https://www.wsj.com/articles/shell-to-pay-80-million-compensation-for-2008-oil-spills-in-nigeria-1420617029.

39. Amnesty International "Nigeria: Amnesty Activists Uncover Serious Negligence by Oil Giants Shell and Eni," March 16, 2018, https://www.amnesty.org/en/latest /news/2018/03/nigeria-amnesty-activists-uncover-serious-negligence-by-oil-giants-shell-and-eni/.

40. Ayanlade and Proske, "Assessing Wetland Degradation."

41. Ibid.

42. "Climate Change, Peasantry and Rural Food Production Decline in the Niger Delta Region: A Case of the 2012 Flood Disaster," *Journal of Agricultural and Crop Research* 1, no. 6 (2013): 94–103.

43. UNDP, *Niger Delta Human Development Report*, 217.

44. Manuel C. Molles Jr., *Ecology: Concepts and Applications* (New York: McGraw-Hill, 2005), 592.

45. UNDP, *Niger Delta Biodiversity Project Federal Ministry of Environment*, 26.

46. UNDP, *Niger Delta Human Development Report*, 212.

47. Ibid.

48. UNDP, *Niger Delta Biodiversity Project Federal Ministry of Environment*, 27.

49. Okecha, "Environmental Problems of the Niger Delta," 52–58.

50. Robin Hinsch, "WAHALA," *International Photography Magazine*, 2019: http://internationalphotomag.com/robin-hinsch-wahala/.

51. Ibid.

52. UNDP Project Document, "Niger Delta Biodiversity Project," 13, https://info.undp.org/docs/pdc/Documents/NGA/Niger%20Delta%20Biodiversity_Prodoc.pdf.

53. Ibid., 35.

54. Julius Iyorakpo and P. Wagio Odibikuma, "Impact of Gas Flaring on the Built Environment, the Case of Ogba/Egbema/Ndoni Local Govt Area, Rivers State, Nigeria," *European Scientific Journal* 11, no. 26 (September 2015): 83–95.

55. Elisha Jasper Dung, Leonard S. Bombom, and Tano D. Agusomu, "The Effects of Gas Flaring on Crops in the Niger Delta, Nigeria," *GeoJournal* 73, no. 4 (September 2008): 83–95.

56. Ibid., 290.

57. Ibid., 295.

58. R. K. Pachauri and A. Reisinger, eds. *Climate Change 2007: Synthesis Report, Contribution of Working Groups I, II and III to the Fourth Assessment Report of the Intergovernmental Panel on Climate Change* (Geneva: The Intergovernmental Panel on Climate Change, 2007), 104.

59. See Daniel Tanuro, *Green Capitalism: Why It Can't Work* (London, UK: Merlin Press, 2013).

60. James Keeley and Ian Scoones, "Understanding Environmental Policy Processes: A Review" (University of Sussex: Institute of Development Studies Working Paper 89, 1999), 1–50.

 **10**

Vaha'a Ngatae:
A Pacific Island Response to the Global Issue
of Climate Change and Rising Sea Levels

Ikani Fakasiieiki

THIS CHAPTER IS A PACIFIC-ISLAND, SPECIFICALLY TONGAN, RESPONSE
to the global issue of climate change, which is causing the sea level and
sea temperature to rise. It consists of two parts. First, I will address some
of the problems happening in the Pacific because of climate change.
Second, I will explore the Tongan concept of *Vaha'a ngatae* as an islander
or Indigenous way to counter climate change. I use it as a springboard to
assert that including Indigenous knowledge in the conversation is crucial
to fighting climate change.

CLIMATE CHANGE AND THE PACIFIC ISLANDS

Climate change is one of the most threatening issues that the earth is facing.
The islands of Tonga and of the Pacific are on the frontline and are the
most vulnerable to its effects. This disaster is not happening in the future.
It is already happening, and it is getting worse. As a result of climate change,

the Pacific Islands are experiencing more damaging cyclones, drought, rising sea levels, warming sea temperatures, floods, and other disasters.

In 1990, Cyclone Ofa hit Samoa and flooded many low-lying coastal regions. In 1997, Cyclone Gavin hit Fiji, breaching the sea wall at the north coast of Vanua Levu and flooding the provincial capital of Lambasa. In 2009, a major 8.1 magnitude earthquake created a tsunami that struck Samoa and the northernmost islands of Tonga, leaving more than 189 people dead and hundreds injured or without houses. As a result of this tsunami, many people in my birth island Niuatoputapu in Tonga were forced to relocate from the coastal side to the higher part of the island. In 2014, Cyclone Heta devastated the island of Niue and caused damage to the islands of Tonga and American Samoa.[1] In 2015, Tropical Cyclone Pam, with winds of up to 280 kilometers per hour, struck Vanuatu and killed sixteen people. In 2016, Tropical Cyclone Winston, one of the strongest cyclones ever to hit Fiji, with winds up to 285 kilometers an hour,[2] devastated both Fiji and most of Tonga, with Fiji the hardest hit; it left forty-four people dead and many homeless. These extreme weather events and their impact on the islands show that uncharacteristic weather patterns are becoming the norm not only in the Pacific but also in other parts of the world.

The rising of the sea level is one of the most threatening climate issues facing low-lying coastal areas and small islands, especially the Pacific Islands. Some islands in the Solomon Islands, Kiribati, and Tuvalu are already being engulfed by the sea.[3] In the Marshall Islands, climate change and the risk of the rising sea level are magnifying ongoing pollution and toxicity produced by nuclear weapons tests conducted there by the United States. The rising of the sea level affects atolls, beaches, and low-lying areas, forcing migration to higher ground, to other islands, or overseas.

Furthermore, the rising sea level has led to other issues. Underground water is becoming salty, affecting islands that depend on it for their drinking water. Saltwater intrusion causes soil salinization, resulting in decreasing crop yields. When farmers cannot provide for their families and for local communities, island nations turn to bigger foreign countries to supply their food.

When the sea temperature warms, it affects coral and sea life, disturbing the entire ocean ecosystem. Fish migrate to deeper areas, making it more difficult for local fishermen to find fish nearby, which means that only commercial fishermen from rich countries with bigger boats and equipment can fish in deeper waters. This has led to overfishing, which risks doing severe damage to the main food resources of these small islands. When local fishermen with limited resources cannot provide for their families, they become dependent on outsiders for food. Galumalemana Steven Percival shares how a Samoan fisherman talked about how he was strongly discouraged to fish where his father used to fish due to the "changeable and less predictable nature of the sea."[4] Another Samoan fisherman explains that "in the two years he had been fishing in two areas he had noticed a drop from around 4–5 fish species caught to 3–4."[5] He also "observed smaller fish sizes and an increasing volume of rubbish caught in the net."[6]

With dependence comes control and domination—continuations of colonization in a different form. This makes formerly independent islands dependent poor countries, losing their food security while receiving unhealthy food products and the waste of bigger and richer countries. Currently, external multinational companies are vying for and competing over opportunities for deep-seabed mining in the Pacific Ocean, which will contribute to the further destruction of deep-sea environments.

Scientific researchers assert that climate change is caused by humans expelling greenhouse emissions from fossil fuel consumption. Not surprisingly, the biggest contributors to the climate disaster are the wealthiest countries. By relaxing measures to limit and decrease fossil fuel use and emissions, they demonstrate their prioritization of short-term profit over the survival of island nations and the life of this planet. It points to deeper root causes of climate change: human greed, lust for wealth, and obsession with power have led to the depletion of resources and the destruction of planet earth. However, most of the national plans unveiled to stop this disaster have enacted no concrete policies to stop human greed and avarice. Global calls have challenged countries to work together to fight this disaster. It is our critical moment. We must limit greenhouse emissions. We must plan for cleaner energy. We must work together to restore marine and coastal environments before it is too late. It is our *vaha'a ngatae* to our Mother Nature.

In saying that, my intention is to promote Indigenous/native knowledge—not only of Tongan and the Pacific Islanders but also of all Indigenous populations around the world—as being crucial for the future of planet earth, especially in light of the global issue of climate change. Therefore, I propose a Tongan epistemology/concept of *Vaha'a Ngatae* or *Tauhi Vaha'a Ngatae* as one vision emerging from Indigenous or native knowledges that can provide another perspective on this critical situation.

THE CONCEPT OF VAHA'A NGATAE

Vaha'a ngatae is a Tongan concept of space. *Vaha'a ngatae* literally means "space" between the *ngatae* trees. The first word, *vaha'a*, means "between" or "in-between." The second word, *ngatae*, is the name of the coral tree. The word "ngatae" literally means "end," as in "end here," but it can also mean "beginning," as in "begin here." It is a mark of the end and the beginning of the land between two neighbors. The people of Tonga grow the *ngatae* tree between their homes as a boundary that connects and separates them. There are several reasons why they plant *ngatae* trees: *ngatae* is a tree that easily grows; *ngatae* grows to be a big tree that provides shade for both homes; *ngatae* does not produce falling leaves that can burden the neighbors; *ngatae* attracts birds when it flowers.

When the *ngatae* tree is planted, it grows and belongs to both neighbors and at the same time to neither. Since it belongs to both and neither, it requires equal responsibility from both neighbors to keep and nurture this line of *ngatae* trees. So, *Vaha'a ngatae* literally refers to the space between the *ngatae* trees and it refers to the line of *ngatae* trees that marks the boundary between the two neighbors. *Vaha'a ngatae* also refers to the space between or the in-between space between the two neighbors. This is the origin of the saying: *tauhi vaha'a ngatae*. The word *tauhi* means "to keep, look after, maintain or manage." Therefore, *tauhi vaha'a ngatae* means "to keep, look after, or manage the space between the *ngatae* trees or the space between the neighbors." It refers directly to the shared responsibilities two neighbors each have to maintain the *ngatae* tree line as well as their relationship with each other. So, when we say *Vaha'a ngatae* or *tauhi vaha'a ngatae*, we are referring to both neighbors' responsibilities to nurture the *ngatae* tree line that belongs to them both. It shifts the emphasis and the focus from the two subjects to the space in between the two subjects, the space that equally belongs to both and neither. This action moves us to the metaphorical aspect of the concept of *Vaha'a ngatae*.

Vaha'a ngatae thus metaphorically refers to people's socio-cultural, political, and moral responsibilities. Socio-culturally, it refers to our relationship and our responsibilities not only to each other but also to nature, including our responsibilities to our families, relatives, clan, communities, land, and nature. In that in-between space, the responsibilities two subjects have for each other is defined. Those relationships and responsibilities define who these subjects are and their status in society and culture. This means that our identity is defined not only by how we relate to one other but also how we manage the relationship and how we fulfill the responsibilities that come with that relationship. This social-cultural concept is embedded in Tongan language, discourse, narrative, stories, art, song, music, and dance—the wisdom we pass down from generation to generation. The political aspect of the *Vaha'a ngatae* refers to the responsibilities between two national governments. *Vaha'a ngatae* appeals that international and national well-being should be based on how countries manage their relationships and fulfill their responsibilities to each other.

Vaha'a ngatae as "a space in-between" is a relational space or the space in-between two subjects. It is not an empty space. It is not the Western conception of space as defined by Michel Foucault: "Space was treated as the dead, fixed, the undialectical, the immobile."[7] There is a line of *ngatae* trees, and that in-between space is already filled with relation and responsibilities. In fulfilling those responsibilities, Tongan neighbors make our connections through these related subjects, which make our relationships stronger. It is dialectical space. When two neighbors appropriately fulfill their responsibilities to each other it empowers both.

That in-between space recalls the concept of "Third Space" introduced by Homi Bhabha.[8] For Bhabha, "all cultural statements and systems are constructed" in the "Third Space."[9] Bhabha seemed to refer to the Third Space as a space of negotiation.[10] However, *Vaha'a ngatae* moves beyond negotiation into equal responsibilities. For *Vaha'a ngatae*, there is no time for negotiation, only relationship and equal responsibilities.

Vaha'a Ngatae refers also to our moral responsibilities for each other and for our Mother Earth. It reminds us that climate change is also a moral issue that calls for moral responsibility. When relationships are properly managed and responsibilities are considered and taken seriously, then we will be able to alleviate and even stop this climate change disaster. When the global table is set for negotiation, bigger and wealthier countries always win. Only one voice is heard, while other voices are suppressed and silenced. It leads to control, domination, and exploitation, which is forbidden by the concept of *Vaha'a ngatae*. The *Vaha'a ngatae* perspective reminds bigger and richer countries that since they create larger amounts of pollution and greenhouse emissions through fossil fuel consumption, they should take more responsibility to resolve this issue.

VAHA'A NGATAE AND CLIMATE CHANGE

For Indigenous people, including Pacific Islanders, the life of human beings and the earth and ocean are intertwined and mutually connected. They cannot be separated. From a *Vaha'a ngatae* perspective, we view the earth as our good neighbor. We have mutual and equal responsibility for each other. We are equally important, and no one is more valuable than the other. We must learn to live in harmony. The land, air, and ocean are sacred and need to be treated with care, respect, and love. Every place is a sacred space, and every time or moment is a sacred time. We do not have to be in a particular place, space, and time to feel the sacredness of our Mother Earth. She is not property to own and commodify. She needs to be treated with respect, love, and care.

Tongan and other Pacific Islanders relate to the ocean, land, and nature as our mother. Our Tongan word for "land" is *fonua*. *Fonua* is also our word for "mother's womb." We also call the "grave" *fonua*. In some families, when the placenta is cut from the mother's womb, they wrap it with a tapa cloth and bury it into the ground; then they usually plant a tree in that place. When a person is buried, we always hear the word, *kuo kelekele'aki*, "she/he was part of land," which means that person becomes part of the *fonua* or land in which she/he was buried. This reminds us that our lives are intertwined with Mother Earth, which comes with responsibility and duty, our *Vaha'a ngatae*.

The ocean also represents our *Vaha'a ngatae*: the in-between space between one island and another and between one island nation and other nations. In our understanding, the ocean comes with a sense of greatness and awe, yet at the same time we live with the reality of insecurity and vulnerability, as people living on small islands surrounded by the great ocean in the context of the rising sea level and the unpredictability of earthquakes, volcanoes, and tsunamis. In the midst of this vulnerability, we still have responsibilities for each other. And by fulfilling these responsibilities, we change this vulnerability into opportunity.

Living in the midst of a vast liquid space, which is always moving and active, we recognize that our islands are always fluid and sinking. This leads us as Pacific Islanders to understand space as active and alive rather than as fixed, dead, and immobile. Through the ocean we are connected. It unites us and brings us together. It defines our identity, responsibilities, and relationships. Our responsibility is to sustain and clean it instead of dumping nuclear and other waste into it. We understand that the fluidity and the liquidity of oceans can, at the same time, be conduits for transportation that can be flexible, while serving as a signpost that the connection between islands is always vulnerable. Because of this instability and flexibility, our small islands always fear bigger countries, especially when they do not uphold their responsibilities. However, in the midst of this vast ocean, our ancestors made these small islands their home, while living with risks and responsibilities throughout their lives. They recognized these spaces, both the islands and the vast ocean, as their responsibility to steward and sustain. These island spaces separated them while at the same time connecting them.

The *Vaha'a ngatae* concept challenges us to revisit how we manage our relationship with our fellow human beings and with nature. We need to rethink the concept of development. We must use technology in a way that protects, rather than harms the earth. We must fulfill our responsibilities to others and our Mother Earth and learn how our ancestors lived in harmony and related to Mother Earth as our good neighbor, not as property to be owned. We have a responsibility and a duty to nurture and replenish her just as she is responsible to provide for us. Thus, the climate crisis is a moral issue between two subjects. The *Vaha'a ngatae* concept reveals a wise insight to the bigger and richer countries that it is their moral duty to fix the damage that they cause to nature. Keeping the *Vaha'a ngatae* or the *ngatae* tree line provides safety for both neighbors. The *ngatae* tree line between neighbors represents protection for both neighbors. Having this relationship and responsibility for each other allows us to see that our survival really depends on each other.

Human greed and desire for power undermine that good neighbor relationship with our mother. It shows how humanity ignored our *Vaha'a ngatae*. That ignorance led to the destruction of Mother Nature. Our Mother Nature, including the land and the ocean, is mourning and is hurt. It is almost unbearable. This exhaustion inhibits our Mother Nature from being able to fulfill her responsibility accordingly and appropriately. We can only understand the exhaustion of nature if we see her bleeding, if we stay connected and have a good relationship with her. We should not be alienated from the earth or view the earth as an endless supply of resources to be exploited and taken advantage of to satisfy our human needs.

Knowing our responsibilities and faithfully keeping them will help us undo the damage of greed and the desire to acquire more than we should. It is through the *Vaha'a ngatae* concept that we are able to keep the *nofo'a kainga*, "kin living together," uniting us in mutual love and care. *Vaha'a ngatae* helps us understand that deforestation, destroying farmland, and replacing natural places with supermarkets and parking lots is not development. It hurts us when oil and waste are dumped into the ocean, chemicals intoxicate the land, nuclear testing continues, and deep seabed mining increases. Our continual enjoyment of and obsession with technology and development blind us from knowing they are destroying our home, the earth.

INDIGENOUS KNOWLEDGE

I am not calling for us to ignore scientific research and knowledge or to say that one kernel of wisdom is more important than another. I only want to include Indigenous knowledge in the conversation. For Pacific Islanders, the fight against climate change is a fight for our life. That fight cannot be won with scientific knowledge alone. There is a need to draw on more wisdom in addition to scientific knowledge. Therefore, Indigenous knowledge and practices should be included in responses to the environmental crisis that we are facing now. It is important for the bigger and wealthier countries to open up a space at the decision-making tables and provide time to listen to the wisdom of these keepers of the earth, whose knowledges have been suppressed, subjugated, and ignored for too long. Michel Foucault coined the term "subjugated knowledges," referring to them as "a whole set of knowledges that are either hidden behind more dominant knowledges but can be revealed by critique or have been explicitly disqualified as inadequate to their task or insufficiently elaborated: naive knowledges, located low down on the hierarchy, beneath the required level of cognition or scientificity."[11]

Although Foucault seemed to point to the knowledges of those inside the system, like doctors, nurses, and patients in opposition to the knowledge of formal medicine or the knowledge of prisoners in relation to the formal knowledge of criminology, I go further to include in these subjugated knowledges the knowledge of Indigenous communities. This body of knowledge includes the knowledges of local farmers, fishermen, and native healers. The same respect should also apply to Indigenous knowledges about the nature of the world in fighting climate change. As Percival says, "it is the Indigenous people who are in direct and constant contact with their changing environment who, after centuries of exposure to a wide range of vulnerabilities, acquired and continue to acquire knowledge aimed at minimizing risks to livelihoods brought about by the changes experienced."[12] Indigenous people are the "the primary custodian of the land"[13] and the ocean. He assesses, "within the Indigenous populations of each country there are many people who share common knowledge about environment and the interlinkages within it."[14]

However, 'Epeli Hau'ofa, a Tongan scholar, speaks of the beginning of how Indigenous knowledges and cultures were forces to be ignored and suppressed in Oceania:

In Oceania, derogatory and belittling views of Indigenous cultures are traceable to the early years of interactions with European. The wholesale condemnation by Christian missionaries of Oceanic cultures as savage, lascivious, and barbaric has had a lasting and negative effect on people's view of their histories and traditions. In a number of Pacific societies people still divide their history in two parts: the era of darkness associated with savagery and barbarism, and the era of light and civilization ushered in by Christianity.[15]

This led to the abandonment of native knowledges and customs. However, Hau'ofa claims that if we look at the myths, legends, oral traditions, and cosmologies of peoples of Oceania, it becomes evident that they did not engage only with land surfaces but also with the surrounding ocean as far as they could traverse and exploit it, the underworld with its fire-control and earth-shaking denizens, and the heavens above with their hierarchies of power gods and named stars and constellations that people could count on to guide their way across the sea.[16]

The people of Tonga have relied on traditional understandings of the weather cycle, which has proven effective in their survival. One element of traditional knowledge relates to the breadfruit season at the beginning of every year. When the breadfruit tree produces heavy fruit, it indicates that there will be a cyclone coming that year. This knowledge helps them prepare ahead.

Indigenous knowledges, as a result of being suppressed and ignored, are not well collected, preserved, or documented. We have to retrieve, preserve, and utilize these knowledges before they are washed away and lost. These Indigenous knowledges have been passed down from generation to generation. They have already proven effective not through scientific experiments but through real life experiences throughout generations. If we learn more about traditional knowledges from different Indigenous communities, we may discover that there are close connections/relations between Indigenous knowledges and some scientific knowledges and recognize that their co-existence will provide more resources to fight this climate disaster.

Our ancestors who dwelled in these islands in the South Pacific were voyagers and navigators, who acquired great knowledge of the ocean, wind, stars, and surroundings. Their knowledge of the stars helped them navigate around the ocean from one island to another. When they settled in these islands, they became farmers and fishermen, building community in creative ways. Their familiarity with the moon cycles helped them know when to grow and what kind of plants to grow. Those knowledges helped them know when, where, and how to fish and the specific kinds of fish to fish. They would fish for their daily needs. These knowledges helped them not only to survive in these islands for centuries, but also to preserve their environment. Looking after each other and their surroundings was their *Vaha'a ngatae*. These knowledges helped them to survive from generation to generation.

However, when the Europeans through exploration, colonization, and Christianization arrived at the shore of these islands, some of the Indigenous knowledges were forced to be abandoned and rejected. They were forced to move their *tauhi vaha'a ngatae* "keeping the relationship" from nature and their native Gods to an unknown and unseen God, who only existed when they wanted Him to exist. They exchanged their *tauhi vaha'a ngatae* from Mother Earth down here where we see and dwell, to a heavenly world up there, a kingdom yet to come, treating it as more important than the earth down here. Bigger and richer countries developed an economic and education system that made our little islands dependent on them, forcing us to ignore the rich heritage of our own Indigenous resources and moving our *tauhi va* to these bigger countries, not knowing that they would use our own resources to keep us continuously dependent on them. Christian missionaries and churches, together with bigger and richer countries, should deeply regret what they did and open spaces for conversations with Indigenous knowledge that have been rejected and forbidden.

CONCLUSION

Our Mother Nature as our good neighbor is already hurt and is in many ways dying. If we ignore her cries, we are consciously destroying her and ourselves. In that sense, we are living a suicidal mission. This is not a political debate in which we have time to wait for who will provide a good argument to determine who is right and wrong or wait for the wealthiest countries to make national and international political decisions. It is the reality of the daily lives of people who are facing the actual death and destruction of their native islands. This environmental crisis that we are facing is a result of our human failure to understand and stay true to our *Vaha'a ngatae*. It is our failure to listen to the keepers of the earth and the important knowledge and wisdom they have to share. Therefore, in order for us to heal and to make right that mistake, we must return to and revisit our *Vaha'a ngatae*, uphold it and continue to be good neighbors of our beloved Mother Earth if we are to survive.

NOTES

1. John Cox, Glen Finau, Romitesh Kant, Jason Titifanue, and Jope Tarai, "Disaster, Divine Judgment, and Original Sin: Christian Interpretations of Tropical Cyclone Winston and Interpretations of Tropical Cyclone Winston and Climate Change in Fiji," *The Contemporary Pacific* 30, no. 2 (2018): 380–411.

2. Glen Finau, Jope Tarai, Renata Varea, Jason Titifanue, and Romitesh Kant, "Social Media and Disaster Communication: A Case Study of Cyclone Winston," *Pacific Journalism* Review 24, no. 1 (2018): 123–37.

3. George Carter, "Establishing a Pacific Voice in the Climate Change Negotiations," in *The New Pacific Diplomacy*, ed. Greg Fry and Sandra Tarte (Acton, ACT: Australian National University Press, 2016), 205–20.

4. Galumalemana Steven Percival, "An Assessment of Indigenous Environmental Knowledge (IEK) in the Pacific Region to Improve Resilience to Environmental Change" (New South Wales, ASTL: The Climate Change Research Center, 2008), 10.

5. Ibid., 9.

6. Ibid., 10.

7. Michel Foucault, "Questions on Geography," in *Power/Knowledge: Selected Interviews and Other Writings 1972–1977*, ed. and trans. Colin Gordon (New York: Pantheon Books, 1980), 70.

8. Homi K. Bhabha, "Cultural Diversity and Cultural Differences," in *The Post-Colonial Studies Reader*, ed. Bill Ashcroft, Gareth Griffiths, and Helen Tiffin (London and New York: Routledge, 2006), 156–57.

9. Ibid., 156.

10. Ibid., 157.

11. Michel Foucault, "Two Lectures," in *Power/Knowledge*, 82.

12. Percival, "An Assessment of Indigenous Environmental Knowledge," 6.

13. Ibid., 6.

14. Ibid.

15. 'Epeli Hau'ofa, "Our Sea of Islands," in *Inside Out: Literature, Cultural Politics, and Identity in the New Pacific*, ed. Vilsoni Hereniko and Rob Wilson (New York: Rowman & Littlefield, 1999), 27–38.

16. Ibid., 31.

11

Talking God in a Divided House:
Renewing Spirituality in God's Pacific Household

Faafetai Aiava

*It is no measure of health, to be well adjusted
to a profoundly sick society.*

—JIDDU KRISHNAMURTI

HOW HAS SYSTEMIC RACISM suppressed Pacific Indigenous knowledge?
How has it shaped the way we do God-talk? What has it meant for
Pacific spirituality, which cannot be fully understood apart from ecology?
This chapter tries to answer these questions while also evaluating the role
of theological education in identifying some of these racially motivated
hierarchies. Organized around the symbol of the house, it begins with a
discussion of housekeeping and introduces my location as a Samoan-born
theologian in Fiji. The second section explores some of the systemic factors that have controlled and continue to divide the houses of ecology,
economy, and ecumenism. The third overlapping segment addresses the
problem of access to formal and higher education for non-Western scholars.

143

144 SHIFTING CLIMATES, SHIFTING PEOPLE

The final part proposes a renewed spirituality for God's household in the Pacific and beyond.

HOUSEKEEPING

This work is written through the eyes of an immigrant residing in the island of Viti Levu in Fiji, a place with picture-perfect beaches and a haven for some of the world's most destructive cyclones. Since I am not a tourist, it is appropriate that I first acknowledge the hospitality of the *vanua*[1] for their gracious acceptance of me to teach and learn at the Pacific Theological College (PTC) over the past decade. I also admit that I am a foreigner; a beneficiary of colonial activities that have displaced the Suvavou people Indigenous to the lands that have become my second home. For this reason and the ignorance entrenched in our colonial and Christian heritage, it is only proper that I seek pardon and lift these Indigenous communities, as I share from their platforms.

Secondly, I wish to situate within these interspaces of shifting climates and shifting people, longing and belonging, son and migrant, this *talanoa* of a renewed spirituality.[2] The attempt is not to "speak for" the people of Fiji, Samoa, or the Pacific Islands, but rather to open up spaces to "speak with" and celebrate our interconnected stories and wisdoms.

Thirdly, in relation to scope, much of this chapter takes its cues from some of the classroom struggles raised by students throughout the Pacific Island region. To that end, the chapter does not deal extensively with global discrimination policies, immigration law, or climate science. What I have argued and continue to advocate is that the prevailing ideologies or oppressive systems found in the secular, scientific, and political world are not dissimilar to the hegemonies found in theological education; for instance, those that suppress the rich tapestry of intergenerational stories and cosmologies procured in Pacific languages.[3]

Lastly, this chapter aims to highlight some of the racially motivated hierarchies dominant in education today without categorizing peoples into victims and perpetrators, or colonizers and the colonized.[4] By addressing systemic racism through the lens of "systems and subscribers," my intention is to illustrate that the will to power almost always leads to exclusive practices, irrespective of the race or the color of those in control. Being cognizant of the fact that the delivery and administration of theological training is now fully localized in the Pacific—except for those countries in the process of establishing a theological school—it is an important discussion to have if we plan not to repeat the oppressive systems we have inherited from our mission forebears.[5] Paramount to that discussion is being able to remain critical of the colonial systems "out there" as well as the presence of tyranny "in here."[6]

GOD'S PACIFIC HOUSEHOLD AND THE PROBLEM OF CONTROL

The thematic organization of this chapter around God's Pacific household is deliberate. The longer phrase, "Household of God in the Pacific," is part of a renewed trajectory endorsed by the Pacific Church Leaders Meeting in 2017 to be its new ecumenical focus. The former theme, "Unity in the Body of Christ," which drove the ecumenical efforts of the World Council of Churches within the region in the 1960s, came under scrutiny for its rather dated emphasis on visible unity and its arguable inclinations toward uniformity. Though the change might appear hostile, the overall consensus among the leaders was that the ecumenical drive had to come from within. It signaled a "turning point in the history of our islands; from how *we* understand ecumenism, ecology and politics to development."[7] It was not only a timely change, as ecumenical participation within the region had reached a stage of stagnancy.[8] It was also a radical response by member churches to the ecological challenges facing its countries.[9]

Although the change was welcome, it called for a paradigm shift beyond the dichotomies normalized by the church. One example is in the various translations of the Greek *oikos* or "house," where the definitions of the word have been associated more with independence than relation. In translating ecumenism or *oikumene*, for example, some suggest it means "the whole inhabited earth," comprising human and nonhuman life. Others, for sound reason, argue that the biblical usage was a political reference to "the known world of the Roman Empire,"[10] emphasizing human habitation over the earth and its inhabitants.

A corresponding argument was raised in a recent publication from PTC regarding the Greek translations of ecology and economy. The authors claimed that the study of the house (*oikos-logos*) and discourse about the rules of the house (*oikos-nomos*) were not supposed to be separate disciplines or houses for that matter. Instead, "they were meant to relate in ways that would and should make the home work for the common good."[11] It thus evokes the question as to why ecology, economy, and ecumenism have remained separate for so long.

Offering one explanation, professor of theology and ethics Upolu Vaai argued that these "oikos triplets" were stolen and nurtured for generations by different empires for the purpose of serving their individual agendas. In his words:

> Ecology was stolen by the scientific research empire, turned into a mere object that can be extracted, categorized, and objectively studied. Economy was stolen by the capitalist empire, stripped of its original intention of "managing a home," and turned into a money-making institution. As a result, we see today a climate narrative that dominantly revolves around economic development. Climate talks and agreements are determined by whether the dominant economic models would be affected or not. And the creators of these models would do whatever it takes to protect their economy while many countries are suffering. Oikoumene was stolen by Christianity, turned into a human-centric system that serves the interests of the Christian empire.[12]

Worthy of note is the manner in which the controlling powers had a direct impact on the demarcation of what was meant to be a unified household. The great Alexandrian formula of "divide and conquer" was not far from the truth.

The separation, as seen in the complacency of Pacific Churches with respect to climate change, has kept Christian pastors and practitioners somewhat confined to "the flock" and less involved in advocating for justice.[13] Politicians within the region have been notorious for reacting crudely and even fatally to Christians protesting colonial rule and development policies as if they have no business in the "management" of the house. This continues while the life of the nonhuman remains at the mercy of their human roommates. To make matters worse, the imperial systems are allowed to exert their powers unchecked because the household members are accustomed to an *afato* mindset. An *afato* in the Pacific is a worm that bores holes into wood without ever cutting into the path of the next worm. It was a euphemism used to describe the ecumenical movement within the Pacific region,[14] but it is just as true for society at large.

Christians daring to speak up about economic inequalities are quickly dismissed as Marxist, socialist, radical leftist, or something insinuating an unholy collusion. Similarly, Christians rallying for climate justice are called to bear the shame of "virtue signaling," as if the problems they raise are strictly individual and not collective. Such a position is held by Australian Christian lobbyist Martin Isles, who reminded Christians not to "get too big for our boots."[15] Using his influence as a lawyer and media personality, Isles reinterprets Genesis 1 as being a sobering lesson in "divine control" or "God's business." His concluding message is that Christians should not interfere with global policy discussions about the climate because "it won't change much."[16] But the issue with Isles is not his cross-cutting commentary between politics and theology. In fact, that would be an encouraging venture. The issue is the obvious fact that he does not come from a country facing the realities of sea-level rise, thus reducing his rhetoric to a power-hungry ploy to gain control of the climate change narrative.

Jerusha Neal's analysis of how the climate problem has been preached within the Fijian Methodist context identifies two unmistakable hallmarks of this systemic problem. The first is an underlying mistrust between Fijian Christians and Western climate science in general.[17] The second is the nerve-racking tendency for preachers to internalize the problem, blaming themselves for the climate catastrophes and not the most destructive actors in the house.[18] This is not surprising in the Pacific. It is a familiar slant aligned with other elitist narratives that were documented and "monumentalized" by the victors who wrote our Pacific histories.[19] Though scholars have begun rewriting and re-righting our stories,[20] going against the status quo remains an uphill battle.

THE GATEKEEPERS: THE PROBLEM OF ACCESS

While overlapping with control, the problem of access requires some unpacking because it plays a pivotal role in encouraging *afatoism* and mistrust within the household. During the pre-colonial times of Samoa, racial mixing was not uncommon. Inter-island travel was most frequent between Samoa, Fiji, and Tonga, and intercultural marriage happened often. When Europeans (usually male) arrived, the same hospitality was extended even to the extent that *afakasi* (half-caste) children were openly accepted by their maternal families.[21] But all of this changed during the German annexation of Samoa from 1900 to 1903. Under the infamous Wilhelm Solf, the teaching of the German language was mandated in Samoan schools. Next came the appalling segregation of the Samoan-mixed[22] races from their European-mixed superiors.[23] The European-mixed consisted of those with European surnames or those who were adopted by Europeans in order to get into an urban school or find employment. The Samoan-mixed, classified as "natives," had almost no access to formal education or eligibility for employment.

By restricting access, the German government turned state services into a privilege. But instead of contesting the systems responsible for the inequality, people began competing against one another in vying for eligibility over justice. It was at this point when the realities of racial hegemony set in and the distaste for foreign rule had become part of Samoa's history. The climate of mistrust was at an all-time high and a self-defeating process of differentiation had begun. According to Roland Boer, this process might have started externally, but it will continue "in its inexorable path from outside to inside" until the entire thing becomes an "inside job."[24] Unfortunately, this competition between full and half-caste Samoans still exists in contemporary schools today. The ongoing challenge for future generations would be to unsubscribe from such exclusive ideologies.

Despite its colonial origins, the advantages of a common language such as English are countless. But this does not mean that the problem of access should be ignored. The students that I teach are from predominantly oral cultures. Though many have been trained in Western institutions or those established by the West, the majority are more proficient in spoken English than literacy. Another catch is the fact that English is usually a second, third, or fourth language. If Martin Heidegger was accurate when he said that "language is the house of Being" and it is "the creators of the words" that guard the home,[25] then for many of my students, English is more like a rundown motel than a home; a mere stopover on the way to the desired destination (read: academic qualification). As Jione Havea put it, "language makes some belong, and some people not belong. Language connects as well as discriminates and displaces."[26]

Since authentic "Being" connotes participating and belonging to a particular language, a language barrier is not simply an obstruction of knowledge. It is a displacement of the living truths that aid the understanding of the student. Speaking about his cross-cultural experience in Vanuatu, Randall Prior argued that "primary orality and primary literacy are not simply two different modes of communication; they constitute two different worlds."[27] For students of non-English speaking backgrounds, access to higher education is near impossible without scholarships. Yet even access to scholarships is partial to wealthier families that can afford private tutors and schools. Again, the problem of access endures. Students that manage to gain access continue to struggle with grasping concepts and expressing their experiences fully, while educators never come to appreciate wholly what a student has to offer.

In her groundbreaking treatise on colonial methodologies, Linda Tuhiwai Smith argued that exclusive access is a foundational premise on which Western "research" was created:

> It appalls us that the West can desire, extract and claim ownership of our ways of knowing, our imagery, the things we create and produce, and then simultaneously reject the people who created and developed those ideas . . . deny[ing] them further opportunities to be creators of their own culture and nations.[28]

For Smith, the methodical production of what constitutes "research" caters only to its creators and those deemed worthy enough to wield it. The double-oppression is when Indigenous or colonized peoples are forced to read about themselves "through the eyes of the West."[29]

What perplexes students more than having to provide evidence for a claim is being told that the reliable or verified sources were written by foreigners. Research also functions on the assumption that "academic knowledge" is the center of life and the only kind of knowledge worth guarding. In an effort to destabilize these centers, I have openly supported the initiative of our college to encourage students to locate parallel insights sourced locally from their elders, Indigenous customs, languages, and traditional art forms.

RENEWING SPIRITUALITY IN GOD'S PACIFIC HOUSEHOLD

In this section I want to focus on two major questions. First, why is a holistic spirituality necessary? Second, why is ecology important to spirituality? For the sake of convenience, I have provided a visual diagram below.

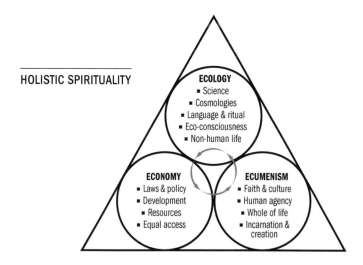

WHY IS A HOLISTIC SPIRITUALITY NECESSARY?

As alluded to earlier, systemic inequalities are not only systems that were imposed, but also those that we allowed in, adopted, and left to their own devices. As portrayed in the diagram, the current practical understanding of the household divides the activities within the house as though ecumenism should focus only on heavenly matters while the other two (ecology and economy) deal with the worldly. This conventional view of the church operating solely within the confines of the old *oikumene* has not been successful in addressing the climate crises. What it requires is a holistic spirituality; a relational event that summons all sectors of life together and holds each of its members responsible to and accountable for one another. The *afato*-minded Christian, policymaker, academic, or scientist might find this unsettling because it disrupts those systems and practices to which we have knowingly or unknowingly subscribed.

Vaai compares this spirituality to an eco-relational consciousness; a way of thinking that is not limited to "the one" but rather treats "the one" as inextricably connected to "the many."[30] This Trinitarian principle is important because it cautions us not to conflate the distinctions within the household. In other words, the household sectors are not being asked to replace the work of the other or drown out their own unique voices. Rather, each is being called to view their collaborative goals, interconnected responsibilities, and life-giving fellowship as worship of the Triune God. The current paradigm of management has been a lot more conducive to greed than need. Unless everyone in the household is willing to open channels of dialogue through a more holistic spirituality, the household sectors will continue to work independently instead of interdependently.

WHY IS ECOLOGY IMPORTANT TO SPIRITUALITY?

Going back to ecology, Christians should also be mindful not to reduce spirituality into *mea faalelagi* or "heavenly matters" by over-spiritualizing. The problem with this is that it misconstrues the teachings of the incarnation, as seen in the efforts of nineteenth-century Pacific missionaries who came to "save souls," promoting a heavenly Christ at the expense of Jesus's earthly ministry. Aeryun Lee describes this as a "half-Christology" with reference to the Roman Catholic missions in Korea.[31] The negative outcomes were that it reduced the Christian message to being other-worldly, it denied the bodily resurrection of Christ (John 20:27), and finally, it led to the demonization of the cultures and beliefs of those being converted.

In terms of learning, the bigger opportunity missed is failing to see how God has manifested Godself through other cultures. For instance, in various languages of the Pacific, the words *vanua* (Fiji), *fanua* (Samoa), *fonua* (Tongan), *fenua* (Maohi), and *whenua* (Aotearoa, NZ), translate as womb, the placenta, and land simultaneously. To date, this motherly image is maintained in its meaning and in the common ritual of burying the placenta after birth. The ritual is symbolic of a life being lived from "womb to womb," something Vaai preached as the "umbilical consciousness" connecting life to Mother Earth. A corresponding insight from Samoa is the translation of *palapala* or blood, which is synonymous with mud or dirt.

The meaning is consistent with the Judeo-Christian view that we are dust (Genesis 3:19), but also with the Samoan cosmological view that humans and the earth share the same ancestry. Unaisi Nabobo-Baba, the first Indigenous Fijian woman to be appointed professor at the University of Guam before returning to serve at the Fiji National University, made this unequivocally clear when she said that "the Self becomes the Self fully because the *Vanua* is. The Self is because the *Vanua* is."[32]

The overwhelming disregard for ecology has been detrimental to both Pacific spirituality and the wellbeing of the earth. On the world stage, Joseph Sittler argued over fifty years ago that "nature is the theatre of God's grace."[33] In his own way, Sittler was calling for a more holistic spirituality that goes beyond a theology of stewardship—which he believed was still rooted in the idea of environmental "managers"—and towards actually treating nature as God's creation.

AFTERTHOUGHTS: MOVING FORWARD

The call for a renewed spirituality invites theologians, educators, and practitioners of other disciplines to start embodying the change they seek in the world. The call is equally for the church to rethink the boundaries of its religious mission and the elitist systems rife within its ranks. As Manulani Meyer insists, "religion is the bureaucracy, spirituality is the great great grandmother."[34] Such a faith warrants an elevated sense of relationality that transcends the rifts holding us back into a liberating embrace of life and knowledge in all of its diversities.

The same sentiments were echoed in a statement released by the Pacific Theological College in response to the adverse impacts of the pandemic within the region. It was a reminder to faith communities that wellbeing entails more than physical health. It is a task too big for medical science, physicians, healthcare, and frontline workers. During a crisis, the role of the church is "to be the conscience of society. To speak out against imperial dominating systems at the root of many crises."[35] In this light, Christians must be called to task and not retreat into their own asylums or work to tear down other sectors.

In the current paradigms of theological education, the prominence of Western thought over the particularities of minority cultures has succeeded only in intensifying the gap between the center and the margins; the haves and have nots; humans and nonhumans. Though the landscape of Pacific education is changing with reference to language and research methods, the bigger questions relate to timeliness. How long should Pacific students deny their Indigenous selves and ecological worldviews just to get a qualification? How long should Pacific Christians carry on blaming themselves for climate catastrophes?

I contend that the longer it takes for us to identify the unjust hierarchies within the church and society at large, the longer it will take to start mending the fractures they have caused. The invitation, therefore, is not to trade one system for another. It is an invitation into a restorative process that involves the whole of life, including the earth. It is not about ticking boxes to meet environmental quotas. Nor is it a political position as often assumed. Rather, it is an eco-relational consciousness that is "bloody aware"[36] that justice for the earth affects the whole of life and should not be treated haphazardly by the political left or right. It is worth repeating here that the ecological consciousness of the Pacific is not a movement by any measure, but a way of life.[37] The story of the earth is our story. Failure to recognize the colonial-objectivist logic that continues to exclude Indigenous spirituality from the climate narrative is also a failure to see the miscarriage of justice within God's creation. It reminds me of an adage often attributed to Einstein: "we cannot solve a problem with the same level of consciousness that created it."

NOTES

1. Among a host of other symbolic meanings, *vanua* refers to both the people and the land of Fiji. See Ilatia S. Tuwere, *Vanua: Towards a Fijian Theology of Place* (Suva, Fiji: Institute of Pacific Studies, University of the South Pacific, 2002).

2. *Talanoa* is made up of *tala*, meaning speak or stories, and *noa*, meaning open and boundless. *Talanoa* therefore means to speak freely or tell stories openly. For multiple perspectives of *talanoa* in the Pacific see Matt Tomlinson, "Talanoa as Dialogue and PTC's Role in Creating Conversation," *Pacific Journal of Theology*, Series II, no. 59 (2020): 35–46.

3. Faafetai Aiava, "Taking Selfies: Honouring Faces (Alo) in Theology and Hermeneutics," in *The Relational Self: Decolonising Personhood in the Pacific*, ed. Upolu Luma Vaai and Unaisi Nabobo-Baba (Suva, Fiji: University of the South Pacific and PTC, 2017), 257–70.

4. It is not my intent to ignore the atrocities of blackbirding in the nineteenth century, where South Pacific peoples, especially those from Melanesia, were kidnapped and deceived by Australian-based colonists for the purpose of cheap labor. Nor do I wish to avoid the racial or ethnic tensions evident in Fiji between the Itaukei and the Fijian-Indian population; in Tonga and Samoa with the influx of Chinese migration; in the ongoing colonization of West Papua by Indonesia; or in France's rule over Maohi Nui and the Kanak people of New Caledonia. The deliberate focus on systemic racism in this chapter is based on the conviction that it is ideological motives and the will to power that ultimately give birth to the prejudicial acts.

5. Jione Havea, "Engaging Scriptures from Oceania," in *Bible, Borders, Belonging(s): Engaging readings from Oceania*, ed. Jione Havea, David J. Neville, and Elaine Wainwright (Atlanta: Society of Biblical Literature, 2014), 3–19.

6. Upolu L. Vaai, "Relational Hermeneutics: A Return to Relationality of the Pacific Itulagi as a Lens for Understanding and Interpreting Life," in *Relational Hermeneutics: Decolonising the Mindset and the Pacific Itulagi*, ed. Upolu L. Vaai and Aisake Casimira (Suva, Fiji: University of the South Pacific and PTC, 2017), 32.

7. Pacific Conference of Churches, "The Story of our Pacific Household in the New Normal," A statement issued by the moderator, Rev. Dr. Tevita Havea (Suva, Fiji: Pacific Conference of Churches, 2020). Emphasis mine.

8. See Manfred Ernst and Lydia Johnson, *Navigating Troubled Waters: The Ecumenical Movement in the Pacific Islands Since the 1980s* (Suva, Fiji: PTC, 2017).

9. Upolu L. Vaai, "We Are Therefore We Live: Pacific Eco-Relational Spirituality and Changing the Climate Change Story," Policy Brief no. 56, Toda Peace Institute, 2019, https://toda.org/assets/files/resources/policy-briefs/t-pb-56_upolu-luma-vaai _we-are-therefore-we-live.pdf.

10. See Pablo Richard, *Apocalypse: A People's Commentary on the Book of Revelation*, trans. Phillip Berryman (Maryknoll, NY: Orbis, 1995); Barbara R. Rossing, "(Re)claiming Oikoumene?: Empire, Ecumenism, and the Discipleship of Equals," in *Walk in the Ways of Wisdom: Essays in Honor of Elisabeth Schuessler Fiorenza*, ed. Shelly Matthews, Cynthia Briggs Kittredge, and Melanie Johnson-Debaufre (Harrisburg, PA: Trinity Press International, 2003).

11. Cliff Bird, Arnie Saiki, and Meretui Ratunabuabua, *Reweaving the Ecological Mat Framework: Toward and Ecological Framework for Development* (Suva, Fiji: PTC, 2020), 2.

12. Vaai, "We Are Therefore We Live," 7.

13. James Bhagwan, the General Secretary of the Pacific Conference of Churches, lamented this lack of responsiveness from the region's leaders with regard to justice issues. "Our eloquent statements are often hollow, as we are too slow, too passive, and do too little too late." See James Bhagwan, "Back to the Future: Reappropriating Island Time and a Return to Kairos," in *From the Deep: Pasifiki Voices for a New Story*, ed. James Bhagwan, et al. (Suva, Fiji: PTC, 2020), 43.

14. Winston Halapua, "Pacific," in *A History of the Ecumenical Movement 1968– 2000*, vol. 3, ed. John Briggs, Mercy Oduyoye, and Georges Tsetsis (Geneva: WCC Publications, 2004); Upolu Vaai and Jathanna Gladson, "'Let the House Speak': Memorialising the Islander Missionaries Chapel for Re-Storying Ecumenism as the Pacific Household of God," *Pacific Journal of Theology*, Series II, no. 59 (2020): 4–20.

15. Martin Isles, "The Truth of It: Confidence or Fear? | Climate Change Part II," uploaded on November 3, 2019, YouTube video, https://www.youtube.com/watch?v =N55MT_WpLI4.

16. Ibid.

17. Jerusha M. Neal, "The Edge of Water: Preaching Sovereignty in Rising Tides," *Interpretation: A Journal of Bible and Theology* 75, no. 2 (2021): 115–16.

18. Ibid., 118.

19. See Vaai and Gladson, "'Let the House Speak.'"

20. Aisake Casimira, "The Dance of the Frigates: Reframing the Ecumenical History of the Pacific Theological College from the Perspective of the Pacific Household," *Pacific Journal of Theology*, Series II, no. 59 (2020): 15–39.

21. Malama Meleisea, *The Making of Modern Samoa: Traditional Authority and Colonial Administration in the History of Western Samoa* (Suva, Fiji: University of the South Pacific, 1987), 163.

22. This group comprised mixes of Samoan and other Pacific races.

23. Ibid.

24. Roland Boer, "Thus I Cleansed Them from Everything Foreign: The Search for Subjectivity in Ezra-Nehemiah," in *Postcolonialism and the Hebrew Bible: The Next Step*, ed. Roland Boer (Atlanta: Society of Biblical Literature, 2013), 227.

25. Martin Heidegger, "Letter on Humanism," *Martin Heidegger: Basic Writings*, trans. F. A Capuzzi and J. Glenn Gray, ed. D. F. Krell (London: Routledge, 1977), 193.

26. Jione Havea, "Foreword: Polytick'g Translation," in Mosese Ma'ilo, *Bible-ing My Samoan*. (Apia, Samoa: Piula Publications, 2016), xi.

27. Randall G. Prior, *Contextualizing Theology in the South Pacific: The Shape of Theology in Oral Cultures* (Eugene, OR: Pickwick Publications, 2019), 147.

28. Linda Tuhiwai Smith, *Decolonizing Methodologies: Research and Indigenous Peoples* (London, UK: Zed Books and Otago University Press, 1999), 1.

29. Ibid.

30. Vaai, "We Are Therefore We Live," 12.

31. Aeryun Lee, "In Search of a Christ of the Heart," in *Faith in a Hyphen: Cross-Cultural Theologies Down Under*, ed. Clive Pearson (Adelaide: Openbook Publishers, 2004), 88.

32. Unaisi Nabobo-Baba, "In the Vanua: Personhood and Death within a Fijian Relational Ontology," in *The Relational Self: Decolonising Personhood in the Pacific*, ed. Upolu Luma Vaai and Unaisi Nabobo-Baba (Suva, Fiji: University of the South Pacific and PTC, 2017), 174.

33. Joseph Sittler, "Essays on Nature and Grace," in *Evocations of Grace: Writings on Ecology, Theology, and Ethics*, ed. Steven Bouma-Prediger and Peter Bakken (Grand Rapids, MI: William B. Eerdmans Publishing, 2000 [1972]), 157.

34. Manulani A. Meyer, "Native Hawaiians and Pacific Islanders: Systemic Racial Challenges," uploaded on August 1, 2021, YouTube video, https://www.youtube.com/watch?v=0-jYrgKB7lQ.

35. Pacific Theological College, "A COVID-19 Wellbeing Statement: Rethinking Health from a Theological and Pasifika Cultural Perspective" (Suva, Fiji: PTC, 2021), 9.

36. This is a pun to the common belief in the Pacific that humans and land share the same bloodline.

37. Faafetai Aiava, "Eleele Interrupts the Eden Wedding: From Mother Earth to Mistress," in *Decolonizing Eco-theology: Indigenous and Subaltern Challenges*, ed. S. Lily Mendoza and George Zachariah (Eugene, OR: Wipf and Stock Publishers, 2021), 104.

12

Subalterns as "Eco-Missionaries" and "Eco-Prophets" in the Context of Climate Change

Vinod Wesley

"CAN THE SUBALTERN SPEAK?" Gayatri Chakravorty Spivak's riveting question is especially pertinent in the age of climate change, which affects the subalterns most. The reply to this question that, "yes, the subalterns are speaking. Are we able to hear?" calls us to acknowledge and learn from their responses, resistance, and resilience in the context of climate change. The capitalist-industrial mode of production that has led to the climate crisis has exacerbated the life struggles of subalterns, who are already victims of racism and casteism. Today, we cannot discuss climate theology and eco-mission without considering environmental racism. We discover that subalterns are not only victims of climate change, but also people with agency who are prophetically questioning the socio-economic and religious causes of climate change and providing us with alternatives.

Subaltern is a very expansive term, as it encompasses subjugated communities throughout the globe.[1] This essay employs the term to specifically address the struggles and resurgence of Dalit communities in India. The first part of the essay mainly focuses on how the Dalit communities are among the subaltern communities facing the worst consequences of climate change. This section problematizes the concepts of "environmentalism" and "climate crisis" from a Dalit perspective, challenging the dominant Brahmanical Hindu understanding of environmentalism while articulating the environmental crisis from the experience of subjugation, marginalization, and resurgence.

The second part of the essay highlights how contemporary Dalit struggles and resistance contribute to a grassroots or subaltern perspective to climate theology and climate mission. The work of the Tamil Nadu Women's Collective (TWC), a subaltern movement, is explored using the methodological framework of ecowomanism propounded by Melanie L. Harris. I conclude by showing how the TWC may be seen as eco-prophets and eco-missionaries in the contemporary climate crisis.

DALITS AND THEIR SUBALTERNITY

The word Dalit comes from the Sanskrit word "dal," which means broken, scattered, downtrodden, and destroyed.[2] This community is excluded from the four-level *varna* (caste) system of Hinduism and treated as untouchables. The origin of the caste system is associated with the Aryans, who canonized its structures within their sacred scriptures. The *Rigvēda*, one of the oldest Hindu scriptures, dating to around 1500 BCE, contains the *Purusha-skūta* hymn, which speaks about the origin of the four castes, or *chaturvarās*, from the body of God. Dalits are absent from this body. They are thus excluded from society and considered "impure," with no way of attaining redemption.[3]

India is home to over 200 million Dalits, which comprises about 16.6 percent of the country's population. In many villages, Dalits are still not allowed to reside among upper caste groups and are forced to live outside of the villages.[4] Because of their impure status, the Dalit community is relegated to dangerous and unhealthy occupations, such as working with leather, disposing of dead animals, manual scavenging, sanitation work, cleaning the streets, etc. Many other Dalits work as agricultural laborers, depending on natural resources for their livelihood. This makes their lives more vulnerable to the climate crisis and environmental degradation. Because of the internalization of discrimination and exclusion from social, economic, and political rights as well as economic opportunities, the climate crisis further demoralizes them.

IMPACT OF CLIMATE CHANGE ON THE LIVELIHOOD OF DALITS

The National Dalit Watch of the National Campaign on Dalit Human Rights and Society released a pathbreaking report on the impact of climate change upon the lives and livelihoods of Dalits. This report highlighted the various ways in which Dalits are affected by the climate crisis and, in particular, how floods disproportionately impact Dalits because they live in low-lying areas. Denied access to services, relief does not reach them in time. They are not allowed to take refuge in upper-caste areas during floods and are denied safe haven (by the upper caste) even within common shelters set up by the government. When Dalit women take shelter from floods, they are attacked and harassed by upper-caste men. In the aftermath of these floods, they lack access to clean drinking water and they are denied water from the common borewell due to caste-based discrimination. During the 2007 Bihar floods, Dalits had to drink the floodwater.[5]

EXCLUSION OF DALITS IN CLIMATE DISASTER REHABILITATION

One of the most important challenges Dalits face is that in their suffering to adapt to climate change, they also are faced with exclusion from relief and rehabilitation programs. When Cyclone Fani swept through Bihar in May 2019, it destroyed several Dalit villages. Around 4,000 people lost their crops, marginal farmlands, and their houses. Without food, money, water, or shelter, many Dalit families waited for relief from the government. But these relief materials reached them too late because they live far from the main village. By the time the materials reached them, the communities had already faced the worst of the storm.[6]

In 2018, Cyclone Gaja devastated several Dalit villages in the coastal areas of the Nagapattinnum and Kadalur districts in the southern part of India. Birla Thangadurai, a victim of this cyclone, explains that "relief material came through the main roads and people in interior areas, like ours, could not access it. You have to cross so many upper-caste villages before you reach our village . . . Relief may be caste-blind, but the local situation is not."[7] This is a very common story that occurs during every climate disaster in India. The Dalit communities are the last to receive relief—if, that is, they are not totally left out of the government's response. There are incidents where Dalits have gone for twenty-four to thirty hours without food, waiting for the rains to stop while watching helplessly as their houses and crops are washed away by the floods.[8]

DALIT WOMEN: THOSE MOST AFFECTED BY CLIMATE CHANGE

Climate change impacts Dalit women most since they must also struggle against caste and patriarchy. Their lives are sacrificed in favor of their husbands, family members, and children. Several places in India face acute water shortages due to climate change during summer. In many upper-caste villages, Dalit women are not allowed to fetch water for their households. Hence Dalit women and girls sometimes walk long distances to fetch water, exposing them to incidents of physical and sexual violence.[9] Ritwajit Das, a global climate change and human rights activist, states: "Even prior to any extreme weather events like drought, floods, typhoons or cyclones, Dalit women are more vulnerable and exposed to disasters. Their social exclusion means they often live outside of main villages, with less access to the amenities and information of administrative centers."[10]

MIGRATION AS AN ADAPTIVE STRATEGY

Climate change negatively impacts rural livelihoods more. Because Dalits lack elaborate coping mechanisms when facing flood hazards, many are forced to migrate. Many Dalits migrate to urban areas as their favored "adaptation strategy" in the aftermath of climate change, shifting from the agricultural to the non-agricultural sector. They often take hazardous jobs on the urban fringes. It is mostly the men of the Dalit villages who migrate to support their families; the Dalit women are left behind, becoming vulnerable to greater sexual harassment and poverty.

ENVIRONMENTALISM AND CLIMATE CRISIS FROM A DALIT PERSPECTIVE

According to Mukul Sharma, the history of the environmental crisis has been approached from different perspectives in India. The dominant perspective begins with the arrival of European powers, which colonized India's natural resources and sought to control the natural world and people through a centralized, bureaucratic, scientific, and modern system of management. Political ecologists of India have focused upon issues of ownership, access, and availability of resources, while environmental academicians and activists discuss the increasing alienation and displacement of the poor from resources and the negative aspects of development and modernization. Feminists and anthropologists raise critical questions concerning "naturalness" and the nexus of power from a gender and caste perspective.[11]

The Dalit perspective, on the other hand, argues that the ecological destruction in India began with the Aryan colonization of India, which brought the caste system that existed many centuries before British colonization. A Dalit perspective strongly acknowledges and addresses the interrelationship between the environment and caste. Mukul Sharma affirms that prior to the European colonial enterprise in India, the history of environmental subjugation had been shaped by Brahmanical Hinduism. He explains this interrelationship between environment and caste as follows:

> Caste and nature are intimately and inextricably interwoven in India; and yet their interconnectedness has rarely been a subject of examination. However, Dalit experiences and narratives constantly underline their everyday ecological burdens in a marked hierarchal order. Images of land animate caste anxieties around labor, blood and bondage. In dry regions, Dalits must often sacrifice their lives to recharge ponds and water resources. From village to city and temple to school, caste metaphors of pollution, impurity and dirt dominate places and spaces through imaginaries of dangers posed by the presence of Dalits. Forests can be heaven or hell for Dalits. A river is someplace to dispose of your body. Nature, entwined with fear and violence, horror and hardship, bloodbath and war, makes environmental experiences of Dalits distinctive and different.[12]

Mukul Sharma vividly calls this influence of caste on the environment "Eco-casteism." While clearly pointing out the influence of caste on Indian environmentalism, Sharma formulates the following observations, which guide a Dalit perspective on the climate crisis:

1. Caste created a concept of natural and social order in which people, place, occupation, and knowledge are characterized either by pollution

or ritual cleanliness; where bodies, behaviors, situations, and actions are isolated, "out of place," and "untouched," because of deep hierarchical boundaries. The places, knowledge system, temples, and ritual and cultural practices of the upper caste Brahmin communities are considered pure and divine, while the villages, occupations, religious practices, and cultural knowledge of the Dalits are considered impure, unclean, and polluted.

2. Caste has shaped environmental attitudes and values of both Brahmins and non-Brahmins.

3. Caste has made it possible for Brahmins to appropriate and exploit natural resources by segregating and subordinating certain sections of the population.

4. Low castes, especially "untouchables," have developed their own understandings of environment and its resources, which were cohabitations of love and sorrow, pain and joy, and alienation and attachment.[13]

While the Dalit perspective highlights how caste has influenced the environmental life and history of India, Sharma points out that it also challenges two important ideas that emerge from the dominant Brahmanical perspective: eco-organicism and eco-naturalism. Sharma explains that eco-organicism is an "Indian" approach to nature that considers the environment to be divine, cosmic, and intrinsic. It is a concept of nature that identifies protecting the environment with protecting Indian culture and its religious and socio-economic structure, which are built upon the Brahmanical caste system. Eco-naturalism asserts that to protect environmental life, we need to follow the natural order, which is identified with the caste system. An ecological society is run by nature's rules and cycles. Sharma says that "eco-naturalism uses nature to affirm the supremacy of 'natural order' in major spheres of life—food, animal, livelihood—which is many a time synonymous with conservative Hindu Brahmanical belief."[14] Sharma points to the sacred status of the bull and the cow in Brahmanical Hinduism, which makes them holy animals that must be preserved. The *Manu Smriti*, the basic law book of Hinduism, considers the animal killer to be a murderer. Dalits eat cow meat and many work as butchers. Thus, according to eco-naturalism, such butchers and eaters of meat are liable to nature's punishment.

While the Dalit perspective criticizes the idea of eco-organicism and eco-naturalism, it affirms a rich and diverse environmental history and sensibility, which is not explicitly "environmental," but rather "social" with a strong adherence to justice.[15] Sharma states that "Dalits are active ecological agents in their own right, and their understandings of nature and ethics, planning and management of resources, labor and environment are intertwined with narratives of social justice."[16] Dalit life with nature is also characterized by the complexities of the forced roles and sacrifices they have had to make to maintain a sustainable environmental community. Sharma describes the complex roles, sacrifices, and contributions of the Dalits as their "eco-role, eco-sacrifice, and eco-dynamism."[17]

DALITS AS SUBALTERN ECO-PROPHETS AND ECO-MISSIONARIES

While we are all indebted to the scientific, academic, and activist world for providing data, solutions, alternatives, and courage to challenge capitalist economies, it is important to also learn from subaltern movements, whose struggles and resurgences in the climate crisis are defined by mitigation and appropriate adaptation strategies. From a Christian theological perspective, I recognize the subaltern movements as eco-prophets and eco-missionaries. Hebrew Bible scholar Walter Brueggemann claims that it is the role of prophetic ministry "to nurture, nourish, and evoke a consciousness and perception alternative to the consciousness and perception of the dominant culture around us."[18] The prophets' alternative consciousness, or prophetic imagination, helps us dismantle the dominant consciousness while energizing us in journeying towards a new just world. Subaltern movements that reveal the reality of climate change are the organic prophets who assist in the formation of an alternative consciousness. Howard R. Macy shows how many prophets in the Bible were ordinary folks who lived with extraordinary faithfulness. So, too, are the lives of those in subaltern movements today, who demonstrate extraordinary faithfulness to save the earth. Three Dalit women from India were in the news for protesting at the COP15 UN Climate Conference in Copenhagen. They were protesting because they felt that their voices were not heard in the climate conferences. One of the three participants, Narasamma, said: "Climate communities must have a place in such a forum. It is important to bring in the voices of the small and the excluded. If you really want to understand climate change, then come and talk to people like us."[19] The Dalit women represent the prophetic voices of many subaltern communities who challenge us to learn from grassroots movements.

Indian Dalit theologians like Shanthi Sudha Monica and Y.T. Vinayaraj explain how mission history in India illustrates that many Dalits worked as local missionaries to uplift their communities.[20] An article in *Al-Jazeera* titled "From Untouchable to Organic: Dalit Women Sow Change in India"[21] gives compelling witness to how Dalit women who belong to the Tamil Nadu Women's Collective (TWC), a grassroots people's movement and organization, are combating climate change and poverty through organic and community-based farming. Grassroots subaltern movements like the TWC are calling for an ecological turn focused on living in the ways of God—living peacefully with our fellow beings and our neighbor earth. They are the eco-missionaries who carry the goodness to save the earth and the earth communities through their mitigation and adaptation strategies.

The following section interprets the work of the Tamil Nadu Women's Collective (TWC) through the Ecowomanist methodology in order to demonstrate that subaltern movements like the TWC are eco-prophets and eco-missionaries in a world defined by climate change.

TAMIL NADU WOMEN'S COLLECTIVE: UNDERSTANDING THROUGH AN ECOWOMANIST FRAMEWORK

The Tamil Nadu Women's Collective (TWC) was started in 1994 as a small grassroots initiative in the state of Tamil Nadu, South India. The collective has grown to more than 150,000 poor, Dalit, single, landless, and marginalized women. This collective practice promotes agroecology—an organic and low-budget agricultural method that involves growing many crops together such as grains, lentils, beans, and oilseeds in order to sustain biodiversity.[22] This initiative helps poor women attain self-reliance and autonomy while combatting climate change by using adaptive and organic agricultural methods. Crop failures caused by climate change and the dominance of agriculture by large corporations has spurred many men to migrate to cities for jobs. The women are left behind as caretakers of their family and farmlands. The TWC teaches these women agroecology, helps them organize collective farming, empowers them to challenge violence and caste-based discrimination, and encourages them to participate in politics. Moreover, the TWC challenges the dominant capitalist, industrial agriculture and provides an alternative organic model for Indian agriculture in the era of climate crisis. Appreciating their work, the US Food Sovereignty Alliance recognized the grassroots initiative by granting it the Food Sovereignty Prize in 2013.[23]

Ecowomanism is a methodology developed by Melanie L. Harris in her book *EcoWomanism: African American Women and Earth-Honoring Faiths*. This ecowomanist lens helps to highlight how the work of the TWC affirms that subaltern movements are eco-prophets and eco-missionaries in the context of climate change. The ecowomanist methodology is both a prophetic and a practical methodology, and it opens space for bringing together Afro-American social movements and Dalit social movements. My intention here is to point out how subaltern projects like Afro-American ecowomanist methodology and the TWC in India are both alike and unique; how they, in their own ways, contribute to subaltern prophetic work everywhere.

Harris explains the concept of ecowomanism as follow:

> Ecowomanist approaches can be described as the reflective and contemplative study of the ecowisdom that is theorized, constructed, and practiced by women of African descent. The discourse validates their lives, spiritual values, and activism as important epistemologies (i.e., sets of knowledge) in ecowomanism.[24]

This ecowomanist method follows a nonlinear approach with seven interchangeable steps. It is both deconstructivist and constructivist.[25] According to Harris, it is a social justice agenda for earth justice that is intersectional and interdisciplinary and that utilizes a political, liberationist, theological, and religio-spiritual methodology.[26] Furthermore, it combines resources and methods from various disciplines, such as environmental studies, ethics, sociology, religion, anthropology, agricultural studies, history, geology, health, medicine, and more. The analytical framework employs a race-class-gender analysis[27] that pays attention to the complex subjectivity and genius of African-American women and focuses on Black women as "moral agents."[28] The seven steps of the ecowomanist methodology are as follows: 1) Honoring Experience and Mining Ecomemory, 2) Critical Reflection on Experience and Ecomemory, 3) Womanist Intersectional Analysis, 4) Critically Examining African and African American History and Tradition, 5) Engaging Transformation, 6) Sharing Dialogue and 7) Take Action for Earth Justice: Teaching Ecowomanism. These seven steps of the ecowomanist methodology are useful here in explaining the complex subjectivity and wisdom of Dalit women in India and the work of TWC.

Honoring Experience and Mining Ecomemory: In this first step, Harris defines ecomemory as "the collective and individual memory of the earth and its relationship to and with the earth. It can be a collective set of values that guide the earth commitments of an entire community or a singular story that reflects themes or values about the environment and one's connection to the earth."[29] For Harris, ecomemeory is agency-producing, and sharing ecomemory is an empowering act that is also an act of earth justice.[30]

Y.T. Vinayaraj, a Dalit theologian, strongly advocates the necessity of recollecting forgotten Dalit memories for emancipation.[31] The first step of the TWC is to revive Dalit women's immense agro-memory of sustainable agriculture and make it fruitful for their collective agroecological practice. The TWC helps women remember and articulate agricultural practices, seeds used, and the understanding of ecology and the natural world passed down through the generations. Shiney Varghese, in her study on the TWC, points out that Dalit women in the TWC recited their agro-memory about making decisions regarding crop selection in their villages and families. The TWC uses these agro-memories to rekindle the agency of Dalit women to fight ecological challenges posed by climate change.[32] Moreover, the group trains women in order to advance their agricultural knowledge so that they might be able to adapt to the newer agricultural challenges posed by the climate crisis. The TWC organizes meetings where women are allowed to share their farming experience. To enhance their agro-memory and agro-knowledge, TWC conducts training programs on ecological farming, seed banking, collective farming, water conservation, and methods for dealing with the impacts of climate change. They also work to raise awareness around the impacts of chemical farming, genetically modified organisms (GMOs), and resource grabs by big corporations.[33]

Critical Reflection on Experience and Ecomemory: Harris points out that the ecological memory and the eco-experiences of enslaved Afro-Americans were very paradoxical. On the one hand, the enslaved community developed a divine relationship with the earth, and on the other, they experienced brutality and oppression in their work with the land by their oppressive enslaver. Hence, Harris says that they had a paradoxical relationship with the earth as they understood its beauty while experiencing the burden of forced labor. She calls this paradoxical relationship the beauty-to-burden paradox.[34]

Dalit women in India have experienced a similarly paradoxical relationship with the earth. Working with the land evoked memories of sexual violence that they suffered at the hands of upper-caste men and the unclean situation they are forced to live in, while upper-caste farm owners live in better conditions. Coupled with this devastating experience is the patriarchy that they face within their own families and the heavy burden that they have to shoulder working in the farms after the men in the house have migrated to cities for other jobs. Jean Friedman-Rudovsky, in her study on TWC, narrates the story of Kasiammal, one of the collective's members: "Kasiammal says, she knew to keep her mouth shut. Despite the narrow canal of sewage that runs from the upper-caste neighborhood to her home in Erachi's Dalit section and her uneven access to potable water."[35] In spite of such difficult experiences, Kasiammal and many Dalit women still cherish their work in agricultural fields every day. Many Dalit women would recite their abuse stories along with their agricultural stories. Subaltern experiences such as these bring out the prophetic dimension of being critical about their ecological experiences and ecomemory. Romanticizing subalterns' ecological relationship with the earth covers over the complexity of their paradoxical beauty-to-burden relationship with it.

Womanist Intersectional Analysis: According to Harris, "womanist intersectional analysis uses a multidimensional lens designed to uncover how racial, economic, gender, sexual, and environmental injustice may constrict the building of moral communities living with and in the earth."[36] TWC is very particular in helping the women in their collective understand the intersectional aspect of their subjugation. In an interview, one of the founders and president of the TWC, Sheelu Francis, explains that casteism combined with colonialism devastated the traditional agricultural knowledge of Dalit communities. She states that "the main values (sustainable agricultural knowledge) are already there; they are part of Indian culture. But the long exposure to western colonial and imperial powers operated many changes and in many cases, people became alienated from their cultural roots."[37] On many occasions, Dalit women working in agricultural fields were not treated as farmers and are not registered as farmers in government records.[38] In most cases, their land holdings are registered only in the name of the men in the family. The TWC helps the women grapple with this nexus of caste, gender, and colonialism that has impacted their lives. They empower the women to dismantle the forces or structures that affect their lives and bring these marginalized women to the decision-making table.

Critically Examine African and African-American History and Tradition: Harris says that the ecological vision of Afro-American communities should be interrogated through the lens of the history of the colonization of African people. She warns that Western observers might romanticize a return to African culture and knowledge, which may again lead to the danger of ecological colonialism. For Harris, one should always question the parallels between the history of colonization of African peoples and ecological colonialism.[39] In India, too, upper-caste political leaders or parties have often romanticized the ecological practices of the Dalit communities and their contributions to sustainable living. However, they generally ignore the casteist and capitalist forces that have undermined the Dalit ecological vision. Sheelu Francis shows how the Green Revolution,[40] as a Western-oriented agricultural approach, and the market-based, capitalist agricultural policy of India destroyed traditional farming, which ushered in the shift from cultivating millet to producing rice.[41] She explains that caste oppression is also responsible for this shift. Many of the women of Tamil Nadu who have traditionally grown millet are Dalits, whereas rice is associated with lighter-skinned and richer castes. She identifies the intersection of government policies and caste hegemony in causing this shift as follows:

In the process of trying to reach the upper caste, you change your diet, and then you change your agriculture. And the government policies pushed hybrid seeds and chemical fertilizers and pesticides for rice production, as well as a minimum support price for rice. This has pushed millet out of production. And everyone is maximizing water from the ground for rice. Even the government only distributes rice and wheat for people in need of food.[42]

Representatives of the dominant upper castes thus praise Dalit communities and culture for contributing to ecological sustainability while at the same time ignoring these facts. Subaltern movements like the TWC critically challenge this attitude of ecological colonialism. They also demonstrate the various ways in which the Dalit resist such ecological colonialism.

Engaging Transformation: In this step, Harris addresses how eco-spirituality or earth-honoring faiths of Afro-American communities influence their spiritual activism for environmental justice. She points out that inherent in the spiritual life of Afro-American communities is the motivation to engage in activism to transform contemporary living conditions. For some, the spirituality may not be characterized merely from their African tradition, but also might be part of a fluid spirituality that encompasses both Christianity and the cultural veneration of the earth as sacred.[43]

The work of the TWC may have not focused on the religious framework of the Dalit communities for their activism. Nevertheless, it is acknowledged as a significant part of Dalit environmental work by many Dalit thinkers and activists. Kancha Ilaiah, a prominent Dalit scholar and historian, shows that Dalits' ecoknowledge is both spiritual and scientific. In contrast to the Brahmanical (upper-caste) Hindu belief that manual productive labor is lower than spiritual practices, Kancha Ilaiah explains that Dalit ecospirituality affirms that spirituality is reflected in daily work.

A spiritual ideology has to interact with scientific process, as spirituality and science are closely related. The Mala (a Dalit caste) mode of thought possesses this understanding of the relationship between science and spirituality—that is why the Malas spent their days working in the fields and making manure and went to the temples that they built near the village in the evenings. The Hindu temples, on the other hand, do not allow any productive community to set foot inside them.[44] The organic farming practices of the TWC bring out their eco-spirituality by propagating a vision of the peaceful co-existence of earth and future generations. This organic farming could sprout from their eco-spirituality. But more studies are needed to see how Dalit spirituality impacts environmental activism.

Sharing Knowledge through Dialogue: In this step, Harris affirms that protecting the earth is a concern for all religions. According to Harris: "Most religious traditions embody an Earth-oriented ethics that can guide an individual's faith."[45] Hence it is important for African and Afro-American communities to engage in knowledge sharing and learning through dialogue.

I see this aspect of knowledge sharing and learning from a missional perspective. Though many have criticized Western missionaries for imposing Western Christian thinking on India, many Dalits respect Christian missionaries for bringing education and mobility, which uplifted Dalits who were subjugated by upper-caste communities. In a casteist society that prevented Dalits from any avenues of knowledge, the missionary schools gave them new life by empowering them through education. The TWC is one among the many subaltern eco-missionaries today that share the eco-gospel through their alternative and organic agricultural method. They conduct several programs on agroecology and have encouraged many rural Dalit women to engage in community farming. This has empowered many women to affirm their agency and to live an independent life. Moreover, the TWC participates in dialogue on global and national efforts for agroecological, multi-functional approaches to agriculture.[46] They also provide opportunities for women to learn from the agro-wisdom of other grassroots movements in other parts of India and in South Asia by participating in national and international programs on sustainable agriculture.[47]

Take Action for Earth Justice: Teaching Ecowomanism: For Harris, this means linking social justice and earth justice. This process involves exposing the injustice to earth and earth communities and their causes, protesting the logic of domination and abuse in all of its forms, naming and resisting structural and individual forms of violence, and replacing them with *truth force* and *love*.[48]

Sheelu Francis of the TWC identifies the production of evil in the agrarian crisis of India as being rooted in the Green Revolution, colonialism, and the caste system. To resist this structural evil, the TWC proposes and practices agroecology. This agroecology is a prophetic re-imagination of agriculture that challenges and criticizes dominant profit-oriented capitalist practices. The TWC aims to employ this prophetic re-imagination in teaching students in schools and colleges about the need for agroecology as a way to fight climate change.[49]

The TWC's work is about resistance to the sickness that the earth and the earth community currently face. Sheelu Francis states that they started agroecology because they saw an increase of cancer among women and children in places that see intensive fertilizer use.[50] The TWC teaches that agroecology provides hope to Dalits, us, and the earth through subaltern resistance. The TWC's resistance, resurgence, and alternatives are where we envision the micro-eschatos today.[51]

CONCLUSION

The TWC, understood through an ecowomanist methodology, affirms that subaltern movements are eco-prophets and eco-missionaries. This challenges totalitarian regimes and proves that alternatives are possible. The ecowomanist methodology and the TWC are not triumphalist. Instead, they create a subversive space for creative dialogues to mediate praxeological solutions. Subaltern (Dalit and African-American) communities provide hope of a redeemed earth amidst their pain and pathos, and they are a site of divine revelation in today's world. They are the eco-prophets and eco-missionaries of today, inviting us to join God's mission to heal this world and all who belong to it.

NOTES

1. The term "subaltern" comes from the Italian Marxist Antonio Gramsci, who used it to define the subordinate situation of social groups and individuals who are repressed, neglected, and misinterpreted by oppressive hegemonic social forces. This term has been popularized by postcolonial theories.

2. James Massey, *Downtrodden: The Struggle of India's Dalits for Identity, Solidarity and Liberation* (Geneva: World Council of Churches Publications, 1997), 11.

3. The etymology of the term "Dalit" dates to the nineteenth-century Marathi social reformer and revolutionary Mahatma Jyotirao Phule, who used it to describe the "outcasts" and "untouchables" as the "oppressed and crushed victims of the Indian caste system." In the 1970s, the Dalit Panther Movement popularized the term "Dalit."

4. According to the 2011 Census of India. See "India: Official Dalit Population Exceeds 200 Million," International Dalit Solidarity Network, May 29, 2013, https://idsn.org/india-official-dalit-population-exceeds-200-million/.

5. Amita Bhaduri, *Impact of Climate Change on the Life and Livelihood of Dalits: An Exploratory Study from Disaster Risk Reduction Lens* (New Delhi: National Dalit Watch of National Campaign on Dalit Human Rights and Society for Promotion of Wastelands Development, 2013).

6. Mahima A. Jain, "Long Read: Landless Dalits Hit Hardest by Disasters Are Last to Get Relief," The London School of Economics and Political Science, November 1, 2019.

7. Ibid.

8. Bhaduri, *Impact of Climate Change on the Life and Livelihood of Dalits*, 33.

9. Ritwajit Das, "Caste and Climate Change: How Systemic Oppression, Exclusion and Caste-Based Discrimination Against Dalit Women of South Asia Will Further Push Them to the Margins in the Quagmire of Climate Emergency," *Youth4Nature*, September 23, 2021.

10. Ibid.

11. Mukul Sharma, *Caste and Nature: Dalits and Indian Environmental Politics* (New Delhi: Oxford University Press, 2017), xix.

12. Ibid., xiv.

13. Ibid., ix–xx.

14. Ibid., xxii.

15. Ibid., xxv.

16. Ibid., xxvi.

17. Ibid., 83.

18. Walter Brueggemann, *The Prophetic Imagination* (Minneapolis: Fortress Press, 2001), 3.

19. "A Dalit view on Climate Change," International Dalit Solidarity Network, December 17, 2009, https://idsn.org/a-dalit-view-on-climate-change/.

20. Shanthi Sudha Monica writes about Yerrangūntala Periah, a Dalit who converted to Christianity in 1866 and worked beside the Baptist missionary J. E. Clough for the upliftment of Dalit missionaries. One of the main aspects of Periah's life was helping the Dalit communities during the famine of 1876 in the Indian state of Andhra Pradesh. See Shanthi Sudha Monica, "Biographical Musings II—Yerranguntala

Periah," in *Frontiers of Dalit Theology*, ed. V. Devasahayam (Delhi: ISPCK/ GURUKUL, 1997), 236.

21. Jean Friedman-Rudovsky, "From Untouchable to Organic: Dalit Women Sow Change in India," *Al Jazeera*, June 14, 2014, http://america.aljazeera.com/features /2014/6/from-untouchabletoorganicdalitwomensowchangeinindia.html.

22. Tristan Quinn-Thibodeau, "This Woman's Collective Is Using Agroecology to Fight India's Green Revolution," *Alternet*, October 26, 2015, https://www.alternet .org/2015/10/womens-collective-using-agroecology-fight-indias-green-revolution/.

23. Karthikeyan Hemalatha, "Tamil Nadu Women's Collective Gets US Honours," *The Times of India*, August 15, 2013, https://timesofindia.indiatimes.com/city/ chennai/tamil-nadu-womens-collective-gets-us-honours/articleshow/21843396.cms.

24. Melanie L. Harris, *Ecowomanism: African American Women and Earth-Honoring Faiths* (Maryknoll: Orbis Books, 2017), 14.

25. Ibid., 10–16.

26. Ibid., 19.

27. Ibid., 19–20.

28. Ibid., 20–21.

29. Ibid., 28.

30. Ibid., 37.

31. Y.T. Vinayaraj, "Envisioning a Postmodern Method of Doing Dalit Theology," in *Dalit Theology in the Twenty-First Century*, ed. Sathianathan Clarke, Deenabandhu Manchala, and Philip Vinod Peacock (New Delhi: Oxford University Press, 2010), 97.

32. Shiney Varghese, *Women at the Center of Climate-friendly Approaches to Agriculture and Water Use* (Minneapolis: Institute for Agriculture and Trade Policy, 2011), 13.

33. "Women Farmers Leading the Way: The Tamil Nadu Women's Collective Raises Crops Awareness in India," *Reliefweb*, March 5, 2014, https://reliefweb.int /report/india/women-farmers-leading-way-tamil-nadu-womens-collective-raises-crops-awareness-india.

34. Harris, *Ecowomanism*, 40–41.

35. Friedman-Rudovsky, "From Untouchable to Organic."

36. Harris, *Ecowomanism*, 44.

37. Marcos Arruda, "Interview of Sheelu Francis, Tamil Nadu Women's Collective, Tamil Nadu – India," *Socioeco*, February 2004.

38. Friedman-Rudovsky, "From Untouchable to Organic."

39. Harris, *Ecowomanism*, 50.

40. The Green Revolution was introduced in post-independent India for addressing the food crisis of the 1960s. It represented an intensive chemical-based agriculture following the Western model. Though it solved the food crisis issue in the short term, it polluted land and environment.

41. Quinn-Thibodeau, "This Woman's Collective."

42. Ibid.

43. Harris, *Ecowomanism*, 56.

44. Kancha Ilaiah, *Post-Hindu India* (New Delhi: Sage Publications, 2006), 61.

45. Harris, *Ecowomanism*, 57.

46. Varghese, *Women at the Center of Climate-Friendly Approaches*, 14.

47. Ibid.

48. See Harris, *Ecowomanism*, 58.

49. Ibid.

50. Quinn-Thibodeau, "This Woman's Collective."

51. Baiju Markose, *Rhizomatic Reflections: Discourses on Religion and Theology* (Eugene, OR: Wipf and Stock Publishers, 2018), 57.

13

Ignoring the Protectors:
Slipping Soil and Relations in Village Resettlement Projects in the West Sikkim Himalayas

Kalzang Dorjee Bhutia

SIKKIM IS A STATE IN NORTHEAST INDIA where rain and mud are part of daily life for long periods of the year. Historically, they were associated with the monsoon months; but in the last few decades, the monsoon has become erratic and unpredictable, departing and arriving with no regularity. Many other changes have accompanied the shift in weather patterns and its impacts on the region's soil and water. One among them is an increase in cloudbursts and floods, which have resulted in landslides and damage to local infrastructure, and particularly the recently developed infrastructure of roads and concrete buildings that have appeared throughout the state since it became part of India in 1975.[1] Additionally, crop blights associated with changes in temperature have impacted agriculture, particularly the important cash crop cardamom.[2] Until two decades ago, agriculture was the primary source of livelihood for most Sikkimese people. The rise of Sikkim as a tourist destination has coincided with the marketization of local products and the concurrent movement of young Sikkimese people away from their family lands to seek work in the cities, which has made it harder for them to maintain cultural and linguistic ties to their traditions. In turn, we can also see radical changes in foodways and consumption patterns. And even when crops survive, they are increasingly attacked by wild boars and bears due to the growth of urban settlements displacing animals from their homes, which has led to an increase in conflict between species.[3] Finally, statistics have shown that changing water and air patterns have led to an increase in health conditions such as asthma and skin problems.[4] Some of these processes are clearly linked to climate change; others are connected, but also interlinked with other broader changes brought on by colonialism and globalization.

Soil and water have been a constant through these changes, but the quantity has changed, resulting in more frequent mudslides, landslides, and other natural disasters. On one autumn day in 2019, a cloudburst caused torrential rain, which led to flooding that severely damaged a village in West Sikkim.[5] One villager died, and the rest were left without homes. While the government compensated the villagers, it also encouraged them to move back to the area afterwards and has also resettled villagers in other parts of West Sikkim where there is no stable soil. While this cloudburst was just one of several that have caused immense destruction in the Himalayas in the last decade, the suffering was compounded by the awareness that the damage from this particular cloudburst could have been avoided and that, with some foresight and caution, damage from future cloudbursts could be as well. Local religious authorities from the Indigenous Lepcha, or as they call themselves, Rong community, and Buddhist communities from across different ethnic groups had long warned that the land was too steep and not stable enough for an expanded human settlement. Their warning was based on local knowledge and prophetic histories of the area that recognized it as the residence of a very powerful local deity, Pawo Hungri. Pawo Hungri's presence and the physical characteristics of the place meant that humans needed to be careful to remain ritually aware of other seen and unseen residents of the area, including those from other dimensions. State authorities ignored this warning and gave incentives to move people back to the village. The cloudburst was understood by ritual authorities from Rong and Buddhist communities as a signal that Pawo Hungri had not been respected.

In this chapter, I will consider the tension between state interests and state conceptions of land as fit for human habitation, on the one hand, and Buddhist and Indigenous knowledge of the complexity of multispecies environments in the Himalayas, on the other. I consider how local knowledge can be included in development and planning to ensure that all species living in the mountain ecosystem can flourish. I will first discuss Sikkim's sacred landscape and then discuss how state initiatives generally fail to consider the multileveled, interdimensional residents of the landscape. By ignoring the protector deities, shortsighted development initiatives can lead to suffering and challenges for rural communities in the state. In a time of shifting climates and all the associated issues that come with them, it is more important than ever that state and national initiatives consult with local communities to undertake development projects that are just and stable, in contrast with the myopic, one-dimensional planning that contributes further to slippery futures for vulnerable rural communities.

SIKKIM'S SACRED LANDSCAPE

In our tradition of Sikkimese Buddhism, we perceive the land of Sikkim as a sacred habitat, or in the Bhutia and Tibetan language, a *ne* (Classical Tibetan: *gnas*). In this chapter, I focus on Sikkimese Buddhist traditions; however, Sikkim is a diverse, multiethnic, and multireligious state, so this is only one perspective. Buddhism is overrepresented in academic and popular representations of Sikkimese society, and especially of related environmental issues.[6] Centering these traditions is not a way to valorize Buddhism over other religions or cosmologies in Sikkim, because many of these traditions are interconnected. The sacredness of Sikkim's space is also revered across multiple cultural and ethnic groups. Very early oral traditions from the Rong community, who are acknowledged as the Indigenous people of Sikkim, understood Sikkim to be Mayel Liang, a heavenly abode.[7] This paper is inspired by my research within my own Buddhist community, particularly in West Sikkim, where the demographically dominant ethnic groups are the Lepcha, Bhutia, and Subba. Not all of these communities are Buddhist, but many people who do not identify as Buddhist also participate in the ritual traditions outlined here. Here I will discuss how local cosmovisions of sacred landscape can provide inspirations for alternative, non-extractive human-environment relations across different ethnic, cultural, and religious groups.

According to the Buddhist cosmovision, the sacred habitat is home to human communities, but also many other unseen agents, including protector deities led by the mighty Kanchendzonga, who is venerated as the guardian deity of the state, and his retinue of spirits of the hills, lakes, valleys, and even kitchens of human residents. Within Sikkimese Buddhism, many communities have developed systems of care based within this cosmology that facilitate ritual communication between the different dimensions that these residents inhabit. When Sikkimese Buddhist ritual practitioners undertake ritual practices, who are they communicating with? Kanchendzonga is at the uppermost apex of a complex and rich set of interdimensional co-residents in Sikkim's landscape. Many of these co-residents are forces and spirits that predate Buddhism's entrance into the region. They became Buddhist protectors of the Dharma, known locally as the *yullha zhidak* (Classical Tibetan: *chos skyong yul lha gzhi bdag*), when Guru Rinpoche visited Sikkim in the eighth century CE, thereby setting in motion Sikkim's Buddhist history. At that time, he proclaimed that the region was a hidden land (Classical Tibetan: *sbas yul*) that would provide refuge to Buddhist communities in times of need, and his activities and interactions with local beings led the entire region to be considered a sacred habitat (Classical Tibetan: *gnas*), where many powers and beings, seen and unseen, resided. In Sikkimese Buddhism, there is a unique prayer known as the *Nesol*, or in English, "The Propitiation of the Sacred Habitat." In this prayer, the different multidimensional residents of Sikkim are acknowledged and propitiated for protection and prosperity. The ritual includes a listing of the many forms that these interdimensional co-residents take.[8] Since there are so many powerful resident beings in the landscape, human residents must be careful to acknowledge them and appease them when they commit infractions. Sikkim's animated sacred habitat is marked by diversity. In the mountains, forests, and fields, there are a variety of classes of beings and forces present.

"DEVELOPING" THE SACRED HABITAT

In recent years, Sikkim's sacred geography has made global news, as local communities, especially in western and northern Sikkim, have struggled with the state and global companies over hydroelectric dams that have been installed along the region's sacred rivers, which are integral to the life ways of Sikkimese people. For these communities, hydroelectricity projects pose an existential threat, because in local Indigenous, Buddhist, and Hindu cosmologies, the health of the water is intertwined with the health of the human and nonhuman communities who depend on that water for their wellbeing. This importance is underscored by the strength of the protest movements against the dams. While these movements are sometimes positioned as ethnic and/or political movements, they are all calling for sustainable futures in the region without rapacious development and environmental destruction, and they all acknowledge the significance of water for interspecies health.[9] Local communities are directly seeing the deleterious impacts of the dams on their daily lives, which are compounded by other environmental challenges that have arisen from climate change, deforestation, and poorly planned projects like the construction of tourist infrastructure. For Sikkimese elders, ecological change has been vividly apparent, as the landscape has been transformed through these processes. Their concerns about the changes they see before them are not tied to nostalgia or romanticism for the past, but instead to their own awareness of how things have changed so dramatically in their daily lives.

Complicating this awareness has been the contradictory messaging of state-led development initiatives. Both the Sikkim Democratic Front and Sikkim Krantikari Morcha governments who have ruled Sikkim over the past three decades have promoted themselves as environmentally friendly. The former chief minister of Sikkim won international awards for his green initiatives, which included tree planting drives, bans on plastic, and public waste and sanitation campaigns.[10] However, these same governments have presided over the hydroelectric projects and the installation of other forms of infrastructure that have had a variety of negative environmental impacts with consequences that have only been compounded by climate change.

The village destroyed by the cloudburst in 2019 was an example of a state development project that was undertaken hurriedly without appropriate planning or in-depth consultation. After the cloudburst, residents were moved back to the area. Local Rong and Buddhist authorities were concerned about this plan. They warned that Pawo Hungri would not be happy to have so many humans residing there, and that their behavior—including tilling the land, raising livestock, and engaging in the daily life processes of giving birth, defecating, having sexual relations, and dying—would all bring actual and spiritual pollution (Classical Tibetan: *sgrib*) to the area, which would make Pawo Hungri sick. These forms of pollution were also connected to concepts of moral decline that local Buddhists had argued were being fueled by modernity, as people were not attentive to the protector deities, and instead built, lived, and farmed as they pleased. The government did not heed this warning and encouraged resettlement there.

FINDING JUSTICE IN THE HIDDEN LAND

When the cloudburst occurred and villagers lost their homes, the government did compensate them with 50,000 rupees per family (the equivalent to about 650 US dollars at the time). However, this compensation did not begin to cover the long-term economic impact of the cloudburst. Many villagers were farmers who lost their cardamom crops, while others lost dairy animals. While the government has provided additional assistance since 2019, the cloudburst has demonstrated that the area is not stable enough for expanded human habitation.

In interviews and discussions at the time, I heard that some nearby Buddhist communities had commented that the villagers must have brought pollution into the area and not paid appropriate respect to Pawo Hungri. These comments represent something that Sikkimese geographer Mabel Gergan has noted in her important research on climate change and religion in North Sikkim. In her interviews, she found that some local people blamed problems with cardamom production on other vulnerable communities residing in the area, particularly people who had moved from elsewhere to participate in agriculture. She discussed how this attribution of blame was indicative of how religious lifeworlds could turn "rigid and insular." This rigidity and insularity was brought about in the context of the "fragile network of relationships" that became all the more fragile due to the losses of modernity. As she writes, even as researchers "support communities in the frontlines of this [climate] struggle, we must be wary of insular, restrictive narratives that are prone to assuage collective anxiety through scapegoating."[11] This is important to cultivate a "more just narrative where we look on our neighbors not as opponents but as fellow sojourners."[12] In Sikkim, these local forms of knowledge about interdimensional co-residents of the land can be productive for encouraging interdimensional awareness and empathy. They can also encourage people to act sustainably, with awareness of the environment. However, the attached narratives of moral decline—that people have contributed to the illness, angering, or departure of protective deities due to their behavior— can often shift blame for disasters onto local communities. This blame, however, fails to acknowledge that climate change is a much larger problem that extends beyond the agency of local people.

Another significant challenge is the state's instrumentalization of local knowledge for political and tourist purposes. As anthropologist Mona Chettri and sociologist Vibha Arora have noted in separate studies, Sikkim's landscape is frequently Buddha-cized in popular imagination, but this marginalizes diverse forms of local knowledge of human-nonhuman relations.[13] How can the aspirations of local communities, state development initiatives, and local knowledge come together to create a more just future for the eastern Himalayas? These are complicated issues. Recently, other Himalayan scholars such as Pasang Yangjee Sherpa, Ritodhi Chakraborty, and Mabel Gergan have worked with international teams of climate scientists to consider these questions.[14] Local experiences in Sikkim point towards how religious knowledge and lifeworlds can generate new opportunities.

In my research into village resettlement and what took place after the cloudburst of 2019, the senior Buddhist authorities whom I spoke to, including lamas and ritual specialists from different parts of West Sikkim, were more circumspect in tracing the blame for the destruction brought by the cloudburst. Instead of talking about the pollution caused by villagers, they said that the government's rush to create photo opportunities and good publicity opportunities left unconsidered the long-term repercussions of ignoring local warnings about the presence of protector deities. They questioned state-driven development narratives, while acknowledging humans' contribution to climate issues in Sikkim. Instead of scapegoating, Buddhist authorities that I spoke to discussed how the pursuit of contemporary conceptions of prosperity—the pursuit of money—was contributing to moral degradation. Scholars working in other parts of the Buddhist Himalayas such as Karine Gagne and Elizabeth Allison have noted how moral decline is often associated with the impacts of climate change.[15]

Buddhist authorities in West Sikkim prescribed ritual intervention and communication in response to cloudbursts, landslides, earthquakes, and other climate-related events. Historically, Buddhist rituals have not always been environmentally friendly. However, the lamas I spoke with believed that relations between humans, nonhuman animals, and other seen and unseen beings, including the deities, could be emphasized in rituals to promote more awareness of the land and its agents. They discussed how rituals bring together human communities and develop their awareness of their unseen co-residents. Especially effective rituals include:

- Enactments of the *Nesol*. In many monasteries and temples in Sikkim, this is undertaken twice a month according to the lunar calendar. The *Nesol* educates humans on the layout of the sacred habitat and acknowledges its many residents.[16]

- Undertaking *Sadaglunyen* before any major building to give offerings to the *sadag*, or landlord, of the place.[17]

- Burning *sang*, or smoke offerings, to purify the land and apologize for any infractions. The burned offerings are made from cuttings from local trees, which also function as a form of local forest management since people gathering the cuttings will prune off any dying or diseased sections of trees, leaving the rest of the branches to continue to grow.[18]

Buddhist authorities argue that these traditions encourage awareness as well as initiatives to clean up the landscape and prevent the waterways from being polluted.

However, even if these rituals work within local communities, how to encourage government and private development actors to take local traditions seriously is another matter. As Sikkim's population increases due to the arrival of migrants in search of work in the construction and service industries and previously unsettled areas are opened for housing these groups, as well as for tourist development and the building of resorts, how can people be encouraged to consider the broader impact of their actions? Education for different communities at different levels of the school curriculum and in state training initiatives—especially for the state and other development actors—in how to see and acknowledge the sacred habitat, might be a starting point. Scholars in conservation have already noted the effectiveness of locally driven initiatives based on Buddhist worldviews.[19] In the Sikkimese context, Kanchendzonga remains ever vigilant as he presides over the landscape, and his presence acts as a powerful reminder of the existential need for balance between all the different human and nonhuman co-residents of Sikkim's landscapes. Only this balance can bring a just future where all species can flourish in the sacred habitat.

CONCLUSION

My research on climate justice developed out of discussions I had with my father, who passed away at the age of ninety-five in 2020. In the years before he passed away, he often commented to me that he was deeply concerned that Kanchendzonga, the mountain deity that presides over our state, was looking black and blue as the glaciers were receding. He felt that this could not bode well for the future of all the different ethnic and cultural communities residing in our diverse state, since the health of the mountain is intertwined with the health of human and nonhuman communities whom Kanchendzonga presides over.

My father's sense of environmental connection was steeped in his education and lifelong contemplative practice as a Buddhist practitioner. In my continued research on what climate justice might look like in Sikkim, I consider what alternative paths might exist by drawing on my father's conception of interdimensional health and the significance of maintaining interspecies relations for it. When discussing environmental change, he said:

> The snow on the mountains, rain on time for the harvest, rich soil, clean, flowing rivers—these are all signs of hope. If these are in place, the world is in balance. We propitiate the mountains, rivers,

land, and waters as a way to care for the land of the Valley of Rice; in this way, we care for the world, and all sentient beings.

Here, my father explicitly tied the health of land to the wellbeing of all human communities in and beyond Sikkim. He considered ritual life to be one way to express care and concern for the wellbeing of all sentient beings, a reflection of Buddhist conceptions of communities and ethical obligations that go beyond the human. It is this vision that I take to heart as I reject narratives of ritual and tradition as lost or in decline or as mere nostalgia, and instead see them as resources to be mobilized in the making of hopeful just futures in the mountains for all human and nonhuman residents. Here, relations should not be left to slip away and the protector deities should not be ignored. Soil, water, and mud do not always have to lead to disaster, but instead can bring prosperity and happiness.

NOTES

1. Duncan McDuie-Ra and Mona Chettri, "Concreting the Frontier: Modernity and its Entanglements in Sikkim, India," *Political Geography* 76, no. 102089 (2020).

2. Mabel Gergan, "Loss and Recovery in the Himalayas: Climate Change Anxieties and the Case of Large Cardamom in North Sikkim," in *Understanding Climate Change through Religious Lifeworlds*, ed. David Haberman (Bloomington: Indiana University Press, 2021), 208–32; Kabita Gurung, Khashti Dasila, Anita Pandey, and Niladri Bag, "*Curvularia eragrostidis*, A New Threat to Large Cardamom (*Amomum subulatum* Roxb.) Causing Leaf Blight in Sikkim," *Journal of Biosciences* 45, no. 113 (2020): 1–8.

3. Nidhi Jamwal, "Climate Change Exacerbates Human-Wildlife Conflict in Sikkim," *The Third Pole*, August 23, 2018.

4. Sundeep Chettri, Sudha Kumari Jha, and D.R. Dahal, "An Analysis of Climate Induced Health Impacts in Sikkim Himalaya, India," *International Journal of Current Research and Modern Education* 3, no. 1 (2018): 499–503.

5. I have intentionally not named the village here to prevent political reprisal.

6. Mona Chettri, "Ethnic Environmentalism in the Eastern Himalaya," *Economic and Political Weekly* 52, no. 46 (2017): 34–40; Vibha Arora, "Framing the Image of Sikkim," *Visual Studies* 24 (2009): 54–64.

7. Charisma Lepcha, "Religion, Culture, and Identity: A Comparative Study on the Lepchas of Dzongu, Kalimpong and Ilam," PhD diss. (Meghalaya, India: Northeastern Hill University, 2014).

8. The text of the *Nesol* has been published as Lha btsun Nam mkha' 'jigs med., *'Bras ljongs gnas gsol* (Delhi, India: Chos spyod dpar khang, 2009). For more on Sikkim's Buddhist history, see Khenpo Lha Tsering, *Mkha' spyod 'Bras mo ljongs kyi gtsug nor sprul pa'i rnal 'byor mched bzhi brgyud 'dzin dang bcas pa'i byung ba brjod pa blo gsar gzhon nu'i dga ston—A Saga of Sikkim's Supremely Revered Four Pioneer Nyingmapa Reincarnates and Their Torchbearers* (Gangtok: Khenpo Lha Tsering, 2002). For an overview of the sacred landscape, see Kalzang Dorjee Bhutia, "Purifying Multispecies Relations in the Valley of Abundance: The *Riwo Sangchö* Ritual as Environmental History and Ethics in Sikkim," *MAVCOR Journal* 5, no. 2 (2021).

9. For more on the environmental destruction caused by hydroelectricity and local protests, see Mabel Gergan, "Living with Earthquakes and Angry Deities at the Himalayan Borderlands," *Annals of the American Association of Geographers* 107, no. 2 (2016): 490–98; Mabel Gergan, "Disastrous Hydropower, Uneven Regional Development, and Decolonization in India's Eastern Himalayan Borderlands," *Political Geography* 80 (2020): 102175; Kachyo Lepcha, "The Teesta Hydro Power Projects: A Historical Analysis of the Protect Movement in North Sikkim," PhD diss. (Gangtok, India: Sikkim University, 2020); Vibha Arora, "'They Are All Set to Dam(n) Our Future': Contested Development through Hydel Power in Democratic Sikkim," *Sociological Bulletin* 58, no. 1 (2009): 84–114; Anna Balikci, *Lamas, Shamans and Ancestors: Village Religion in Sikkim* (Leiden: Brill, 2008); and Chettri, "Ethnic Environmentalism in the Eastern Himalaya," 34–40.

10. For more on the representation of the former Chief Minister Pawan Chamling as environmentally friendly, see "The Lone Crusader," *Down to Earth*, February 15, 1999.

11. Gergan, "Loss and Recovery in the Himalayas," 225.

12. Ibid., 226.

13. Chettri, "Ethnic Environmentalism in the Eastern Himalaya," 34–40; Arora, "Framing the Image of Sikkim," 54–64.

14. Ritodhi Chakraborty, Mabel Gergan, Pasang Sherpa, and Contanza Rampini, "A Plural Climate Studies Framework for the Himalayas," *Current Opinion in Environmental Sustainability* 51 (2021): 42–54.

15. Karine Gagne, *Caring for Glaciers* (Seattle: University of Washington Press, 2018); Elizabeth Allison, "The Spiritual Significance of Glaciers in an Age of Climate Change," *WIREs Climate Change* 6, no. 5 (2015): 493–508.

16. Lha btsun Nam mkha' 'jigs med., *'Bras ljongs gnas gsol*.

17. Bhutia, "Purifying Multispecies Relations in the Valley of Abundance."

18. Ibid.

19. Palayanoor Sivaswamy Ramakrishnan, "Demojong: A Sacred Landscape within the Sikkimese Himalayan Landscape, India," in *Protected Landscapes and Cultural and Spiritual Values*, ed. Josep-Maria Mallarach (Heidelberg: IUCN, GTZ and Obra Social de Caixa Catalunya, 2008), 2:159–69.

14

Structural Environmental Racism through Public Welfare Policy in Indonesia

Hanry Harlen Tapotubun, Ismetyati Natalia Tuhuteru,
and Kritsno Saptenno

INDONESIA, A DEVELOPING COUNTRY, HAS SIGNIFICANT POSSIBILITIES in terms of national economic development. It has abundant natural and cultural resources, which the government can harness to strengthen its national economic resilience and improve social welfare. Largescale national development ascended during the New Order era (1966–1998) and still continues to this day. This has entailed the development of a national scale industry and the construction of public facilities such as airports, roads, ports, etc. To reach these targets and objectives, the formation of laws and regulations to guide development policies became a necessity.

However, these development efforts have proven to have negative effects for the country's population. In particular, massive development has caused serious damage to the environment, which has triggered natural disasters. For example, in Kinipan, located in Central Kalimantan, massive deforestation caused by the development of industrial agriculture needed for national food security created prime conditions for floods and forest fires.[1] Another example can be noted in the mass deforestation on the island of Sumatra to create palm oil plantations, the results of Indonesia's grand ambition to become the largest palm oil exporter in the world. This deforestation has led to fires that occur regularly every year in the provinces of Riau, Bengkulu, and Jambi.[2] Besides problems caused by the agricultural industry, the development of tourism has also led to many issues for Indonesia. According to some national news reports, the community on Komodo Island in East Nusa Tenggara is threatened by a relocation program known as the "Komodo Dragon Conservation" program. Ironically, the narrative of conservation is creating the opposite, as Komodo Island is being transformed into a premium tourism spot. This massive change negatively impacts the social, economic, and cultural lives of the Indigenous community on Komodo Island, who for hundreds of years have peacefully coexisted with the Komodo dragon as their neighbor.[3]

This chapter elucidates how development policy has been biased towards profit generation and has ignored the Indigenous communities and local knowledge of the places where it is carried out. The government's development policies have taken a narrow, shortsighted view on improving social welfare. As a result, their implementation has had negative impacts on the community. But the question is: what kind of paradigm causes environmental racism in the name of development by the Indonesian government to still occur even though the goal of the development is for social welfare? This chapter will unravel the roots of environmental racism against the Indigenous peoples of Indonesia. Environmental racism in Indonesia is a structural component of the state's economic development policies and practices.

To be able to understand the complex structural problems of environmental racism in economic development, several stages will be analyzed. First, we will explore what kinds of discourses contribute to the Indonesian government's understanding of "development" and "social welfare" by comparing these ideal concepts in state laws with how development is actually planned and executed. Second, through in-depth analysis of various discourses, we will draw a conclusion about the paradigm underlying the construction of developmental policies and why these policies generally lead to what is academically understood as environmental racism. Then, at the end of our chapter, we will provide an alternative, arguing that development policies should be based on equality and should consider the relationship between humans and nature in order to avoid perpetuating the structural environmental racism towards Indigenous peoples that has characterized the government's policies.

INDONESIAN LAW ON SOCIAL WELFARE AND ENVIRONMENTAL PROTECTION

Ideally, the development process in a democratic state should be based on the will, the needs, and the capabilities of the community. Because those living in the community know their locality best, their culture and ways of life should play a key role in the formulation of policy. In Indonesia, development policy is generally designed by legislative councils and then brought to and approved by the president. Development in Indonesia, from the process of policymaking to its execution, ideally proceeds by considering main principles written in state laws. These principles encompass: human development; economic development; infrastructure development; institutional development; and sustainable development. Thus, development projects must support the social welfare of the community as it comes from the people, by the people, and for the people even though it is driven by the government.

According to Indonesia National Law Number 32 of 2009, the government's development plans must prioritize the social welfare of the community. They must also consider environmental impact. In national economic development[4] and national sustainable development, the utilization of natural resources is guided by the Environmental Protection and Management Plan (or in Bahasa Indonesia, *Rencana Perlindungan dan Pengelolaan Lingkungan Hidup*—RPPLH). According to this legal regulation, national development policies must consider ecological biodiversity, human population, natural resources and their distribution, local wisdom, the people's aspirations, and climate change. The complex relations between diverse interested parties, including the government, Indigenous people, and scientists, necessitates strategic environmental analysis, geospatial instruments, environmental eligibility standards, environmental pollution limit criteria, Environmental Impact Analysis (EIA),[5] legal permits, ecological instruments, and all other kinds of legal regulations to protect nature.[6]

Among these instruments, attention generally focuses on the Environmental Impact Analysis (EIA), because the approval of every industrial activity undertaken in the name of national development requires deep EIA analysis. The public can also file an objection to the EIA document.[7] The EIA is conducted by multiple experts, such as environmental analysts, environmental organizations, community representatives, the representatives from the company or industry, and government agencies.[8] The EIA document is prepared by industrial representatives, the government, and the local community. The community involved must be supplied with complete information about the project's details and be notified before development activities start. Thus, the law requires that the voice of the community be heard and the environmental impacts be analyzed.

According to the law, the development process must be a grassroots endeavor where the local community plays an active role in formulating policies. The government is required to plan projects in line with the needs of the community, especially for those who live side-by-side with nature—for example, Indigenous people located in rural areas. Environmental protection becomes one of the important points that must be considered, in line with the needs and social welfare of the community because of the impact environmental conditions have on social welfare.

INDONESIAN STATE POLICY ON SOCIAL WELFARE AND ENVIRONMENTAL PROTECTION

The concept of development and social welfare in Indonesian law places great emphasis on the community as the subject of development. However, most Indonesian developmental policies deny these ideal concepts required by law. There are many cases that demonstrate that the development policies and their execution generally tend to destroy the community and their environment. Based on our online and direct observation, there are at least four major factors that demonstrate how the government denies aspects of community needs and environmental protection. They are: 1) the politicization of EIA by the government for industrial interests, 2) the manipulation of local community engagement in policy making, 3) the manipulation of environmental regulations while ignoring comprehensive expert studies, and

4) the unfair compensation by the government (unfair because the government just values land based on economic value) for those directly affected by the development projects.

First, the EIA, which should be the government's preventive measure to harmonize environmental sustainability with the national development program, has been politicized. For example, in the case of an iron sand mine of Malang Regency in East Java, the coastal area should have been protected due to the uniqueness of its ecological landscape. However, after the iron sand was discovered, the designation of the coastal area was changed to a limited-production forest in 2010. This legal change directly impacted the coastal area, initially turning it into a tourist spot and then later into the iron sand mine. The legal change from protected area to limited-production forest eliminated the requirement for an EIA report. The only required document became the UKL-UPL (*upaya kelayakan lingkungan—upaya penyelamatan lingkungan*),[9] which indicates the mining process in the area is considered harmless to the environment. Iron sand material was mined by heavy equipment and transported by massive trucks in large quantities. This mining activity directly changed the coastal landscape and its environment.[10]

Second is the politicization of EIA or AMDAL, where the role of the community in national developmental policies is often manipulated. Throughout 2015, statistics from the Ministry of the Environment demonstrated 256 cases of public complaints related to environmental damage due to natural resource management. Of these 256 cases, forty-four of them are in legal disputes.[11] One of those disputes occurred at Sukolilo village in the Pati Regency of Central Java. Some members of the community involved in the decision-making were bribed with money or employment in the mining company. The mining company, Sahabat Mulia Sakti, mines karsts in that area. Even worse, the elite in the village fill official posts or work with the company.[12] However, the majority, who generally live as farmers, are not involved because they tend to reject these projects, which will—in their opinion—destroy springs necessary for their rice fields. The Sukolilo village example shows that when fulfilling the requirements for local community participation, the government and investors can manipulate the voices of the people by only involving a few members who have similar interests with the mining industries.[13] Thus, those members of the community were used to legitimize the natural resource management plan that had already been agreed upon.

Third, the government and corporations manipulate regulations originally conceived to protect people and the environment. One example is the violation of the rules in the New Yogyakarta International Airport construction project in Kulon Progo Regency in Yogyakarta Province. The central and regional governments were ambitious when building the "Aetropolis"—a city whose spatial planning, infrastructure development, and economic growth revolves around the airport. However, this project violated many laws and regulations, including the issuance of environmental permits without an in-depth study from the EIA.[14] Another violation involved ignoring the legal status of the area, especially the agricultural zone[15] and cultural heritage protection zone,[16] as well as the disregard for disaster analysis in this area, especially along the coast.[17] The interests of development by the government, in the name of a "vital national project," were prioritized at the expense of other important factors—in this case, the social and cultural existence of the community as well as environmental sustainability.

Fourth is the issue of compensation paid to the community by the government, which mostly neglects the cultural and spiritual value of land by solely focusing on its economic value. The government and developer companies (both state-owned and private companies) tend to understand compensation as limited to the nominal price of the land. In contrast, for some, like Indigenous people who have a strong relationship to the land, the land symbolizes community existence and is thus more valuable than the nominal price. The land and everything on it (rivers, mountains, forests, etc.) often have a strong spiritual, cultural, socio-political, and even cosmic significance for the community. For example, revisiting the community affected by the New Yogyakarta International Airport project, the government and airport construction companies claimed to have "paid" for land compensation, but in fact, the reimbursement was only nominal. The destruction of the social, cultural, and spiritual features of the land was ignored.[18] The decision to sell the land was conducted unilaterally by the central government, local governments, and airport construction companies without community involvement.[19]

During her 2015 visit to the village of Oping in the northern coastal region of Seram Island in Maluku, one of the authors of this chapter witnessed a similar problem. A shrimp trading company that had been operating in this area for years negatively impacted the cultural way of life in the Oping village community. This was evident by the daily behavior of the community, especially women, who went from being gardeners to shrimp-packing workers. This meant that their role in supporting food production for the family was replaced by food traders from the city, forcing them to now buy food from the market with their wages. Soon, the identity of the community began to erode as the cultural memory of local cuisine slowly disappeared among newer generations. In addition, the ecological and health conditions in the area were worsened by the traffic of heavy vehicles and the pollution of the sea, an effect of the exporting of frozen shrimp from their coastal port. This resulted in the destruction of marine ecosystems. Over a seven-week period during our 2015 observations, we noticed a strong fishy stench along the coastal area because the company, at times, would dump their waste into the river and beach. We also noticed an increase in respiratory disorders and skin diseases. While conducting interviews with women of the village, we noticed that many who were employed at the company had skin diseases, even when they wore gloves—gloves that were too thin and tore easily. They said the skin diseases started soon after they began their employment.

Unfortunately, the cultural, environmental, and health problems caused by the existence of the company were not taken seriously by the government, which only promised to "give compensation" by constructing a steam power plant in the area, an effort to "prosperize the Oping people." These examples demonstrate that the government, when formulating developmental policies, often ignores the socio-cultural aspects, local wisdom, beliefs, and health conditions (both physical and mental) of the community. The government's interpretation of "welfare" is rooted in economic considerations, in this case manifested as money, wealth, and physical infrastructure.

STRUCTURAL ENVIRONMENTAL RACISM: BETWEEN THE MODERNISM PARADIGM AND CAPITALIST WORLDVIEW

Robert Bullard defines environmental racism as an environmental injustice, in the form of practice and policy, perpetrated by certain dominant races or ethnicities upon those who are racially or ethnically minoritized. This makes environmental racism an institutionalized form of discrimination.[20] A more concrete definition is offered by Shari Collins-Chobanian and Kai Wong. They argue that environmental racism is the intentional disposal of hazardous waste, garbage, and industrial pollution in places inhabited by minority groups and/or poor communities.[21] Thus, environmental racism means discrimination in the form of environmentally unjust practices and policies committed by a majority or powerful racial or ethnic group against other minoritized groups (racial, ethnic, as well as political and economic minorities).[22] Building on these definitions, we understand that environmental racism is not only a matter of practice, but is also rooted in a colonialist worldview believed by a group of people. Frantz Fanon, in his criticism of colonialism, explains that racism is not only about "what white people do to the people of color," but also "what makes people of color feel inferior compared to white people." Fanon explains this as an inferiority complex, where people of color feel inferior to Western people and in response attempt to adopt Western ways of thinking, attitudes, and behavior in order to get recognition. In other words, this inferiority slowly develops into a kind of standard where everything that comes and is shaped by the Western society is something that must be necessarily followed by everyone.[23]

This mode of environmental racism exists in Indonesia in the form of adaptation to Western-style industrial development based on the paradigm of modernism. This, of course, is a consequence of colonialism, aiming to "civilize society" by continuously echoing the narrative of social welfare. Because the paradigm of modernism is considered to be the only way to achieve social welfare, massive industrialization continues to be pursued without considering the traditional ways of life of Indigenous people. As a result, in the name of social welfare, the traditions and culture of Indigenous peoples who are considered "primitive" are slowly being suppressed, either persuasively or repressively. This structural environmental racism occurs when state actors unilaterally impose their worldview on development and social welfare (which are adapted from the West) and are applied without considering the paradigms and practices significant for local Indigenous peoples.

Environmental racism exists in the formation of development policies and practices in Indonesia, which affects and impacts Indigenous people. Generally, the Indonesian government operates from a modernizing perspective based on capitalist principles. Industrialization is assumed to be a tool able to achieve social welfare for the Indonesian people. The resulting conception of "social welfare" is rooted in the scientific paradigm in which society is classified as either traditional (based on agriculture) or as modern (based on industry and markets).[24] This view was adopted and further developed by Walt Whitman Rostow, who explained that progress in society could be measured by how quickly it is moving from a traditional to a modern society.[25] These two understandings of society underpin a concept of modernization as industry-based and market-oriented. Thus, the promise of prosperity can only be achieved through industrial-based national economic development.[26]

Indigenous peoples have a different way of understanding social welfare. Some key values include resilience and harmony between human life and nature. Social welfare for Indigenous peoples means they can live alongside and grow healthy with nature. The problem is that this understanding is no longer considered relevant in a world of industry and capitalism. Hence, the roots of environmental racism begin to emerge as government, with an adapted Western worldview, slowly dominates and hegemonizes the local understandings of social welfare existing among Indigenous peoples.

Heavily influenced by the colonial legacy to "civilize" and "humanize" society, the Indonesian government considers Indigenous people incapable of realizing social welfare. This is because those who are Indigenous peoples are not and have not been considered fully human. Hence, the Indonesian government is obliged to "civilize" Indigenous peoples through a concept of social welfare based on capitalist modernism and industrialization. Unequal power relations ultimately lead to structural violence, where social and political forms of violence (i.e., discrimination, political persecution, or cultural impoverishment) are institutionalized so that it appears natural and legitimate. This is no way to promote social welfare.

In conclusion, we believe that Indonesia's economic development policies are defined by environmental racism because of the different definitions of social welfare existing between the government and the Indigenous society. Consequently, because the government has power and authority, the Indigenous people or community are forced to accept the national development and policies based on the government's capitalist worldview, which does not consider the needs of local people nor the impact of policies on nature. As a result, environmental degradation has led some to become refugees, while others remain living in an unhealthy environment, contributing to the creation of underclasses and cultural impoverishment, both of which are detrimental to Indigenous people and nature.

WHAT'S NEXT?

This chapter may not have a significant impact on the struggle against structural injustice, because structural environmental racism continues to become more dangerous. We, the authors of this chapter, want to shine light on how economic development, generally considered a positive, is one of the main drivers of environmental racism. While promoting social welfare is in itself good, its realization in Indonesia is biased, because welfare is complex and cannot be reduced to material things. Development to establish prosperity must consider many aspects, specifically humans, nature, and the socio-ecological bonds between humans and nature. We interpret Bruno Latour's words, "we (humans) have never been modern,"[27] to mean that the modernism which tends to separate humans and nature should never happen. As this chapter demonstrated, the separation between humans and nature in the project of modernity sees nature as an object to be exploited and managed for the benefit of humanity. Contrary to this modernism, the Indigenous worldview—knowing we are responsible for our actions—understands that when someone takes something from nature, they must reciprocate by giving back, thus creating a strong bond. Humans and nature are intertwined and run together, so separating the bonds between humans and nature will only lead to disaster, and the most affected are Indigenous communities who do not have political and economic access and privileges.

NOTES

1. See *Kinipan*, uploaded May 1, 2021, YouTube video, https://www.youtube.com /watch?v=3LnT4_8Titc&t=4666s.

2. *Asimetris*, uploaded April 28, 2018, YouTube video, https://www.youtube.com /watch?v=2OhaxAalJdk.

3. Rachmawati, "Polemik Suku Komodo di Pulau Komodo, Dianggap Penduduk Liar hingga Wacana Relokasi," *Kompas*, December 8, 2019, https://regional.kompas .com/read/2019/08/12/10271591/polemik-suku-komodo-di-pulau-komodo-diang-gap-penduduk-liar-hingga-wacana?page=all.

4. According to Indonesia National Law Number 32 of 2009 concerning Environmental Management and Protection: sustainable development considers environmental, social, and economic factors in the development strategies to save life for future generations.

5. In Bahasa Indonesia, the Environmental Impact Analysis (EIA) is translated as "*analisis mengenai dampak lingkungan*" or AMDAL.

6. Indonesia National Law Number 32 of 2009, 15.

7. Ibid., 22.

8. Ibid., 24.

9. This document is similar to the EIA but has a lower legal standing.

10. Genta Mahardhika Rozalinna and Lutfi Amiruddin, "Politisasi lingkungan oleh aktor PERHUTANI dalam kasus koperasi tambang Indonesia III (Tiga) di kabupaten Malang-Jawa Timur," *Kawistra* 8, no. 2 (August 22, 2018): 118–19.

11. Indonesian Ministry of Environment and Forestry, *Statistik Kementerian Lingkungan Hidup dan Kehutanan Tahun 2015* (Jakarta: KLHK, 2015), 223.

12. Sunarko, "Karst: ditambang atau dilestarikan konflik sosial rencana pemban-gunan pabrik semen di Kabupaten Pati, Jawa Tengah," *Jurnal Ilmu Sosial dan Ilmu Politik* 17, no. 2 (November 2013): 163–79.

13. Wahyu Krisnanto, Martika Dini Syahputri, "Objektivasi Proses Uji Kelayakan Lingkungan dalam Pemberian Izin Lingkungan," *Jejaring Administrasi Publik* 9, no. 1 (January–June 2017), 1006.

14. Muhammad Imam Fitriantoro, "Drivers of Conflict in Urban Infrastructure: Case Study of the New Yogyakarta Airport," *Jurnal Politik* 6, no.1 (August 2020): 112.

15. According to Local Government Regulation of Yogyakarta Province Number 2 of 2010 concerning the Provincial-level Spatial Plan of Yogyakarta Province 2009–2029 section 51, point G, the Bantul Regency, Kulon Progo Regency, and Gunung Kidul Regency are determined to be areas prone to tsunami wave disasters.

16. Some cultural heritage sites related to local communities' beliefs, such as Stupa Glagah, Arca Perunggu Amoghasiddhi dan Vairapani, Lumpang Batu, Makam Mbah Drajat, Situs Petilasan Gunung Lanang, and Gunung Putri are in danger of

being destroyed because they are in the airport construction area. These legal sites have been protected by the Governor Regulation of Yogyakarta Province number 62 of 2013, which deals with cultural heritage preservation.

17. Presidential Decree number 28 of 2012 determined Kulon Progo as an area prone to geological natural disasters. In a study by the Indonesian Institute of Sciences geotechnology research team, it was found that there were tsunami deposits around the NYIA location. See also Fitriantoro, "Drivers of Conflict in Urban Infrastructure," 112.

18. Most people of Kulon Progo, who are farmers, rejected the New Yogyakarta International Airport development project and thus refused to sell their land for thousands of millions of rupiah. This refusal was based on the people's belief that land is the most important asset for food production and has been preserved as an important inheritance from their ancestor. Thus, land is not a property to simply be disposed of. See Fitriantoro, "Drivers of Conflict in Urban Infrastructure," 111–12.

19. According to Presidential Decree number 71 of 2012, consignment is a form of land acquisition. However, in the case of New Yogyakarta International Airport, the consignment was invalid because the community that disagreed with selling their land was forced to calculate its value. See Fitriantoro, "Drivers of Conflict in Urban Infrastructure," 107–108.

20. Robert D. Bullard, "Environmental Justice in the 21st Century," *People of Color Environmental Groups: 2000 Directory* (Atlanta: Environmental Justice Resource Center, Clark Atlanta University, 2000), 1–21; and Robert D. Bullard, "Confronting Environmental Racism in the Twenty-First Century," *Global Dialogue* 4, no. 1 (Winter 2002): 34.

21. Shari Collins-Chobanian and Kai Wong, "Environmental Racism, and Monitored Retrievable Storage Sites for Radioactive Waste," in *Applied Ethics: A Multicultural Approach*, 4th ed. (Upper Saddle River: Pearson, 2006).

22. Christina Dhillon and Michael G. Young, "Environmental Racism and First Nations: A Call for Socially Just Public Policy Development," *Canadian Journal of Humanities and Social Sciences* 1, no. 1 (2010): 24.

23. Frantz Fanon, *Black Skin, White Masks*, trans. Richard Philcox (New York: Grove Press, 2008 [1952]), 73.

24. Henry Bernstein, "Modernization Theory and the Sociological Study of Development," *The Journal of Development Studies* 7, no. 2 (1971): 144.

25. Walt Whitman Rostow, "The Stages of Economic Growth," in *Sociological Worlds: Comparative and Historical Readings on Society*, ed. Stephen K. Sanderson (Los Angeles: Roxbury Publishing Company, 2000), 130–34.

26. Steven Cohen, *Understanding Environmental Policy* (New York: Columbia University Press, 2014), 84.

27. Bruno Latour, *We Have Never Been Modern*, trans. Catherine Porter (Cambridge, MA: Harvard University Press, 1993), 78.

15

The Necropolitics of the Armed Lifeboat

George M. Schmidt

SINCE 1947, generally considered the first year of the Cold War, the members of the Bulletin of the Atomic Scientists have maintained a symbolic clock that represents the probability of global catastrophe due to a nuclear exchange between the Soviet Union and the United States. "The stroke of midnight" figuratively represented a real global catastrophe, and at worst, total biological annihilation on a planetary scale. The clock was set originally at seven minutes to midnight and has fluctuated ever since, with the furthest from midnight being 17 minutes in 1991 with the signing of the Strategic Arms Reduction Treaty, or START I, which was a bilateral treaty between the US and USSR to scale back and limit strategic offensive arms. Since its founding by former members of the Manhattan Project, the Bulletin of the Atomic Scientists has been very aware of the link between militarization and ecological devastation.[1] However, the Doomsday Clock dramatically, and perhaps myopically, focuses on an event to come that is an explicit expression of military power. And yet, while the arms race of the Cold War threatened global habitability, its research and advancement generated sites of death where life would be unable to flourish for generations, even without a formal nuclear exchange. Hiroshima and Nagasaki are atrocities all their own, but public discourse generally makes little mention of the Marshall Islands, where between 1946 and 1958, a nation of twenty-nine atolls was turned into a laboratory and power display for the United States' testing of sixty-seven nuclear and thermonuclear weapons. The Marshallese people still suffer to this day from the radiological contamination of their homes, a clear example of what Winona LaDuke and Ward Churchill call "radioactive colonialism."[2]

Rather than the Doomsday Clock, with its threat of the event to come, any examination of militaries, militarization, and militarism should be framed in terms of the legacy of the Marshall Islands. It is not merely the military's death-dealing capacities that render places uninhabitable, which they in fact do, but the very nature of the petro-military industrial complex that engenders ecological devastation. As Andrew Jorgenson, Brett Clark, and Jeffrey Givens put it, "even in the absence of armed conflict, military institutions and their activities consume vast amounts of nonrenewable energy and other resources for research and development, maintenance, and operation of the overall infrastructure."[3] In this sense, warfighting itself is not the sole means with which the military contributes to climate change. Maintenance and preparation for war, as exemplified in the Marshall Islands, result in devastating environmental impacts. In fact, emerging research is slowly revealing the link between environmental degradation and US military activity, both explicitly operational and non-operational.[4] In this sense, the petro-military industrial complex simultaneously intensifies fossil capitalism while exacerbating the lethality of the climate catastrophe.

It is important to note the difficulty in precisely measuring the Department of Defense's contribution to climate change, particularly in the form of raw CO_2 emissions. While estimates always point to colossal consumption of oil, exact numbers simply cannot be determined. "Due to the culture of militarism in the United States," writes Ronald Kramer, "the DOD is often treated as a 'sacred cow' and is not subjected to the same level of scrutiny and oversight that is common for other federal agencies."[5] It is important to note here that neither independent researchers *nor the*

Pentagon are able to say exactly how much oil the DOD consumes.[6] Despite complications in determining precise measurements, researchers have still been able to offer representative figures with stark conclusions.

Perhaps most dramatic is the evidence gathered by the Union of Concerned Scientists that certifies the US military as the largest institutional consumer of oil in the world.[7] They estimate that the military uses 100 million gallons of fuel every year. In terms of emissions, Neta Crawford of the Watson Institute at Brown University presents her conservative data, which I quote in full:

> The best estimate of total US military greenhouse gas emissions (including installations and operations) from 2001 when the wars began with the US invasion of Afghanistan, through FY2018, is 1,267 million metric tons of greenhouse gases (measured in CO2equivalent, or CO2e). The Overseas Contingency Operations (war-related) greenhouse gas emissions portion of those emissions—including for the major war zones of Afghanistan, Pakistan, Iraq and Syria—is estimated to be more than 440 Million Metric Tons of CO2e for the period of FY2001–2018....[8]

To be sure, such consumption is difficult to grasp because the Pentagon uses, in the words of Barry Sanders, "inconceivable amounts of gasoline."[9] In hopes of illustrating these numbers, the Pentagon's total greenhouse gas emissions most years is greater than entire industrialized countries.[10] In one year, the Pentagon uses enough oil to run the entire US transit system for the next fourteen to twenty-two years.[11]

Here, it is important to note that thirty percent of the DOD's greenhouse-gas emissions come from infrastructure, while the remaining seventy percent comes from operational energy, which is defined by the DOD as "energy required for training, moving, and sustaining military forces and weapons platforms for military operations" as well as "energy used by tactical power systems, generators and weapons platforms."[12] By its own estimates, in fiscal year 2017, the DOD consumed over eighty-five million barrels of fuel for non-operational purposes.[13] To reiterate, without any war or military action taking place, US militarism generates massive greenhouse-gas emissions as a mere baseline for potential operational energy expenditures. Over the past ten years, the Pentagon, along with each branch of the military, have had multiple projects underway intended to reduce installation energy consumption. Even though the expressed reason for such efforts is militarily pragmatic in nature, there is the benefit of mitigating production of CO_2 and other greenhouse gases.[14]

To this point, there are two central issues that pervade climate change literature: mitigation and adaptation. On the one hand, mitigation speaks to the drastic necessity to reduce CO_2 and other greenhouse gas emissions while moving toward supposedly cleaner energy sources. Adaptation, on the other hand, refers to the planning and implementing of technologies and political solutions necessary to live with the effects of climate change. For, to be sure, we are living in what Courtney White calls "the Age of Consequences."[15] While mitigation efforts, as meager as they are, seem to be pointed in somewhat the right direction, adaptation to the effects of climate change are increasingly violent and authoritarian. Generally speaking, adaptation is understood as an effort to reduce vulnerability of human and environmental systems to the impacts of climate change. For the most part, adaptation takes one of two approaches. The first is progressive and demands a radical redistribution of economic, social, and political resources with the core of the aid going to those in the Global South who are most affected by climate change. This first path might be considered "climate socialism," which would be a politics of adaptation based on cooperation and protection of the most vulnerable. The second path, which Christian Parenti calls "climate fascism," is a politics "based on exclusion, segregation, and repression."[16] On its most basic level, this is a militarized adaptation that prioritizes ambiguously long-term containment of failed and/or failing states and their desperate populations, which Parenti describes as "counterinsurgency forever."[17]

Indeed, the Pentagon is redesigning itself to better operate in a world reshaped by climate change, and the world they see is dangerous. In its 2014 Quadrennial Defense Review, a review process initiated by Congress in 1996 to analyze objectives and threats after the end of the Cold War, the Pentagon referred to climate change as a "threat multiplier" that will "aggravate stressors abroad such as poverty, environmental degradation, political instability, and social tensions—conditions that can enable terrorist activity and other forms of violence."[18] That is to say, the effects of climate change (such as water scarcity, forest fires, and extreme weather) exacerbate preexisting regional conflicts. The Pentagon-connected think tank CAN Corporation described the situation in this way: "Unlike most conventional security threats that involve a single entity acting in specific ways at different points in time, climate change has the potential to result in multiple chronic conditions, occurring globally within the same time frame."[19] In this way, prior antagonisms are escalated and enflamed by climate change. With such a situation coming closer on the horizon, the DOD is shaping US adaptation to a world that climate devastation has remade. "You could even say," writes Parenti, "the Pentagon is planning for Armageddon."[20]

Ultimately, this is a reframing of climate change from an environmental and social justice issue into one of security and war. Recall Parenti's description of "climate fascism," a politics of adaptation that is based in exclusion and repression. He furthers this point through the illustrative imagery of what he calls "the armed lifeboat," which is a way of "responding to climate change by arming, excluding, forgetting, repressing, policing, and killing."[21] This is a new form of authoritarianism perpetuated by the Global North. Ronald Kramer writes:

> But the impacts of global climate disruption in less developed countries will extend well beyond the boundaries of devastated areas in the Global South. Insofar as human populations typically do not accept their demise passively, we can anticipate substantial climate-induced migration from these areas as the effects of global climate change deepens.[22]

As climate-induced migration escalates, in the absence of a genuinely cooperative model of adaptation, we can expect that militarized adaptation will be the response of the Global North. In this sense, the "politics of the armed lifeboat" imagines many nations in the Global North as fortress-states that offer a relative amount of stability in a collapsing world. Ironically, those permitted to pass the fortress gates are often themselves consumed by the very machines that generate the conditions from which they are fleeing: an average of 8,000 immigrants (almost exclusively from the "Global South") enlist in the US military each year.[23] The Migration

Policy Institute estimates that 530,000 veterans were born outside of the United States and that almost 1.9 million veterans are the US-born children of immigrants.[24] Here the explicit promise of citizenship through enlistment obfuscates the implicit politics that subjugates bodily autonomy to the sovereignty of military demands. In this way, the US military worsens climate change while offering climate security in the form of the armed lifeboat. In this case, however, those defending the lifeboat are not those who sank the ship.[25]

All this brings to a head my contention that the politics of the armed lifeboat requires further theoretical elaboration. Parenti's description primarily offers tools for understanding the movement from the military-industrial complex to the security-industrial complex. The politics of the armed lifeboat primarily gives an account of operations and policies within the boundaries of a nation-state or supranational network. It conceives of the militarized adaptation to climate change in terms of interiority versus exteriority, or put differently, "counterinsurgency forever." This would be an exercise of sovereignty that deploys itself primarily on the borders while conducting surveillance within. Militarism is not merely a death-dealing apparatus. Rather, by its very nature, particularly regarding its ecological effects, it generates "zones of exception" whose borders must be patrolled and maintained.[26] For this reason, the death-dealing capacities of this militarism are focused on the border and borderlands. However, building on Parenti's initial concept of the armed lifeboat, we might begin to think of the effects that this politics exerts outside of the lifeboat. Achille Mbembé's conception of necropolitics can offer a further level of complexity and understanding for these reflections.

As an extension, and perhaps radicalization, of Foucault's biopolitics, Mbembé conceives of necropolitics as a form of governmentality that controls populations through their exposure to death. Foucault, as the progenitor of the concept, noticed how "calculated management of life" was a "power to expose a whole population to death."[27] Drawing on the nuclear annihilations of Hiroshima and Nagasaki, Foucault noted how human populations are eliminated in the name of protecting civilization. Mbembé draws on this conception of control and Frantz Fanon's postcolonial theory in order to study the making of spaces and subjectivities in and in-between life and death. In Mbembé's words, necropolitics is the "subjugation of life to the power of death" and therefore the "notion of biopower is insufficient to account for contemporary forms of subjugation of life to the power of death."[28] This subjugation is expressed through various means of maximizing the devastation of human life and broader ecological systems, thereby creating what he calls *"death-worlds."*[29] To be clear, however, death-worlds are coterminous to *life-worlds*. That is to say, the armed lifeboat generates death-worlds, and fear of the living dead produces the armed lifeboat.

The armed lifeboat, indeed, is the biopolitical that simultaneously generates the necropolitical. There are now migrant populations that no longer need to be managed, in a biopolitical sense, but must be exposed to death. For Mbembé, this necropolitics can be found in the confinement of those deemed surplus humanity in particular spaces, such as the refugee camp, the prison camp, the colony, or the plantation. These "death-worlds" enclose unwanted populations into highly militarized and precarious spaces in order to not only control them, but more importantly, expose them to mass death. Building on this concept of the "death-world" as a confined space, the politics of the armed lifeboat spatially inverts Mbembé's paradigm by confining the means to maintain life rather than generating spaces that necessitate death. In short, necropower remakes the world itself into a site of death. To this last point, necropower not only sequesters the vast majority of the earth's population to a death-world, but by increasing fossil fuel consumption, it engenders this world. Therefore, what I call the necropolitics of the armed lifeboat involves the "natural" elimination of mass populations. Starvation, terminal dehydration, exposure—all will be cast in the form of unavoidable death.[30]

All this brings to mind a deep necrotic truth about the military-industrial complex: oil consumption is necro-consumption. Materially speaking, the military-industrial complex's burning of fossil fuels further creates "zones of death" by a return of the long dead, which is to say: hydrocarbons formed underground from the dead remains of past life on the planet. As it was spoken at Standing Rock: "Water is life; oil is death." In other words, the military subjugates living bodies by consuming the bodies of the fossilized dead. Petro-politics is necro-politics. Necro-consumption, therefore, drives US military power as it produces populations fleeing embryonic zones of death.

In the words of the environmental sociologist Kenneth Gould, "Militarization is the single most ecologically destructive human endeavor."[31] This militarized consumption of the long dead and migrating bodies comprises polymorphous material assemblages of necrochemical infrastructures. Following Deleuze and Guattari, Mbembé refers to these assemblages as war machines. "A war machine," as Mbembé puts it, "combines a plurality of functions. It has the features of a political organization and a mercantile company. It operates through capture and depredations and can even coin its own money."[32] For Parenti, the armed lifeboat is primarily conducted by states. Mbembé's work adds to the analysis by shining light on the ways in which the arming of the lifeboat is far more non-traditional and dynamically adaptive than merely the operation of traditional armies on the border. As militarized forms of adaptation to climate disruption advance, they will become increasingly delinked from state formations and become more autonomous and incorporated.

As an illustration of one of these necrochemical configurations, rollback neoliberalism is transforming the way the United States exerts its military power abroad. It increasingly depends on private-sector military contractors to supplement and, at times, entirely conduct military operations. The general attitude seems to be that war is far too serious a matter to be entrusted to the state. In the words of Aaron Ettinger: "In the early twenty-first century, it is much too profitable."[33] The market for military contractors is only growing in size and operational diversity. Consequently, militarized forms of necro-adaptation to climate disruption tend toward privatization and their operation is not only pointed externally but increasingly internally. The ultimate conclusion is that we are all on our way to failing states.

For this reason, those who think they will be sheltered from climate catastrophe, perhaps because they live in or are a citizen in the Global North, are the most naïve. The necropolitics of the armed lifeboat is always and already on its way to collapsing and centralizing its limited capacities. The privatization of militarism will abound, and the monopoly of violence once held by the state will vanish. Ultimately, we will all find ourselves outside looking in. Parenti generously offers up brutal honesty on this point:

The struggling states of the Global South cannot collapse without eventually taking wealthy economies down with them. If climate change is allowed to destroy whole economies and nations, no amounts of walls, guns, barbed wire, armed aerial drones, or permanently deployed mercenaries will be able to save one half of the planet from the other.[34]

Borders surrounding nation-states like the United States are merely the first wall of Constantinople. It is the first line of defense for the ruling class. Capital, unfortunately, will hold out until the very end, the king of a smoking trash heap.

NOTES

1. As of March 16, 2022, the clock was set to "100 seconds to midnight." See Bulletin of the Atomic Scientists, "At Doom's Doorstep: It Is 100 Seconds to Midnight," https://thebulletin.org/doomsday-clock/current-time/.

2. Winona LaDuke and Ward Churchill, "Native America: The Political Economy of Radioactive Colonialism," *The Journal of Ethnic Studies* 13, no. 3 (1985): 107–33.

3. Andrew K. Jorgenson, Brett Clark, and Jeffrey Kentor, "Militarization and the Environment: A Panel Study of Carbon Dioxide Emissions and the Ecological Footprints of Nations, 1970–2000," *Global Environmental Politics* 10 (2010): 10.

4. Gregory Hooks and Chad L. Smith, "The Treadmill of Destruction: National Sacrifice Areas and Native Americans," *American Sociological Review* 69, no. 4 (August 1, 2004): 558–75.

5. Ronald C. Kramer, *Carbon Criminals, Climate Crimes* (New Brunswick, NJ: Rutgers University Press, 2020), 175.

6. Ibid.

7. "The US Military and Oil," Union of Concerned Scientists, June 1, 2014, https://www.ucsusa.org/resources/us-military-and-oil.

8. Neta C. Crawford, "Pentagon Fuel Use, Climate Change, and the Costs of War" (Providence: Watson Institute of International & Public Affairs, Brown University, 2019), 2.

9. Barry Sanders, *The Green Zone: The Environmental Costs of Militarism* (Oakland: AK Press, 2009), 50.

10. Crawford, "Pentagon Fuel Use," 2.

11. Sanders, *The Green Zone*, 50.

12. Crawford, "Pentagon Fuel Use," 6; "Operational Energy," Office of the Assistant Secretary of Defense for Sustainment, https://www.acq.osd.mil/eie/OE /OE_index.html.

13. "Operational Energy."

14. Crawford, "Pentagon Fuel Use," 7.

15. Courtney White, *The Age of Consequences: A Chronicle of Concern and Hope* (Berkeley: Counterpoint, 2016).

16. Christian Parenti, *Tropic of Chaos: Climate Change and The New Geography of Violence* (New York: Nation Books, 2011), 11.

17. Parenti, *Tropic of Chaos*, 11.

18. Chuck Hagel, *Quadrennial Defense Review, 2014* (Washington, DC: Department of Defense, 2014), 8.

19. CNA Corporation, *National Security and the Threat of Climate Change* (Alexandria, VA: CNA Corporation, 2007), 44.

20. Parenti, *Tropic of Chaos*, 13.

21. Ibid., 11.

22. Kramer, *Carbon Criminals*, 180.

23. "Military Naturalization Statistics," United States Citizenship and Immigration Service, March 3, 2021, https://www.uscis.gov/military/military-naturalization-statistics.

24. Jie Zong and Jeanne Batalova, "Immigrant Veterans in the United States," *Migration Policy Institute*, May 16, 2019, https://www.migrationpolicy.org/article /immigrant-veterans-united-states-2018.

25. The Transnational Institute released a report that found the world's greatest emitters of greenhouse gases are spending as much as fifteen times more on arming their borders as they are on "climate finance." Todd Miller, Nick Buxton, and Mark Akkerman, *Global Climate Wall: How the World's Wealthiest Nations Priorities Borders over Climate Action* (Amsterdam: Transnational Institute, 2021), 12.

26. Joseph-Achille Mbembé, "Necropolitics," *Public Culture* 15, no. 1 (2003): 34.

27. Michel Foucault, *The History of Sexuality, Volume 1: An Introduction*, trans. Robert Hurley (New York: Vintage Books, 1990), 137, 140.

28. Mbembé, "Necropolitics," 39–40.

29. Ibid, 40.

30. Justin McBrien makes a somewhat similar point by radicalizing the notion of Capitalocene as he posits the neologism: "Necrocene." In his provocative essay, he writes, "The Necrocene reframes the history of capitalism's expansion through the process of becoming extinction." Justin McBrien, "Accumulating Extinction: Planetary Catastrophism in the Necrocene," in *Anthropocene or Capitalocene? Nature, History, and the Crisis of Capitalism*, ed. Jason W. Moore (Oakland: PM Press, 2016), 116.

31. Kenneth Gould, "The Ecological Costs of Militarization," *Peace Review: A Journal of Social Justice* 19 (2007): 331.

32. Mbembé, "Necropolitics," 32.

33. Aaron Ettinger, "Neoliberalism and the Rise of the Private Military Industry," *International Journal* 66, no. 3 (2011): 743.

34. Parenti, *Tropic of Chaos*, 11.

List of Contributors

Faafetai Aiava, a Congregational pastor from Samoa, currently serves as head of the Department for Theology and Ethics at the Pacific Theological College in Fiji—the region's first tertiary institution to offer higher education and internationally accepted degrees. A member of the editorial board for the *Pacific Journal of Theology*, he has authored numerous articles and books, presented at global forums, and continues to teach on the intersections of ecojustice, theology, and Indigenous hermeneutics.

Luke Amadi is a distinguished international scholar who has presented papers at over one hundred international conferences across the world. He holds a PhD in development studies from the University of Port Harcourt. He has published over fifty articles in scholarly journals and has contributed over thirty book chapters. His most recent edited volume is *Decolonizing Colonial Development Models: A New Postcolonial Critique* (with Fidelis Allen). His research interests intersect ecological justice, political economy, sustainable development studies, African politics, and political ecology.

Emily Askew is Associate Professor of Theology at Lexington Theological Seminary in Lexington, Kentucky. Her research and publication interests include climate migration, LGBTQIA migration into the European Union and the United States, and theology and domestic violence.

César "CJ" Baldelomar is a doctoral student at Boston College. He holds two law degrees from St. Thomas University School of Law: a master's of laws (LL.M) in intercultural human rights and a juris doctor. He also holds a master's of theological studies (MTS) in religion, ethics, and politics from the Harvard Divinity School and a master of education (EdM) in learning and teaching from the Harvard Graduate School of Education.

Kalzang Dorjee Bhutia is a visiting scholar at the University of California, Riverside. He is originally from West Sikkim, India, and completed his PhD in Buddhist studies at Delhi University. His research has been supported by an ACLS/Robert H.N. Ho Research Fellowship in Buddhist studies and a Dalai Lama Studies Fellowship from the Foundation for Universal Responsibility. He is currently completing a monograph on the environmental history of Sikkimese Buddhism.

Abeer M. Butmeh is an environmental engineer based out of Palestine and coordinator of PENGON-Friends of the Earth Palestine. She has over ten years of experience in campaigning, coordination, communication, facilitation, research, and public relations. Abeer is a trainer on water management and environmental issues and an active member of various social movements and environmental networks both locally and internationally. She has written and published on multiple platforms to raise awareness on the climate justice issue in Palestine.

Emma Crow-Willard is an environmental filmmaker and managing producer at Climate Now. She is also a scientist and founder of Roots of Unity Media, formed to combat media stereotypes of women, people of color, and science through film and education. She holds a master's degree in environmental management from Yale and directed the Yale Environmental Film Festival in 2017–18.

Miguel A. De La Torre, an internationally recognized scholar, is professor of social ethics and Latinx studies at the Iliff School of Theology in Denver. The American Academy of Religion bestowed on him the 2020 Excellence in Teaching Award. He has published forty-one books (five of which won national awards). A Fulbright scholar, he served as the 2012 President of the Society of Christian Ethics and was the co-founder/first executive director of the Society of Race, Ethnicity, and Religion. He also wrote the screenplay for the documentary *Trails of Hope and Terror* (www.trailsofhopeandterrorthemovie.com/).

Tanaya Dutta Gupta is a doctoral student in the department of sociology at UC Davis. Tanaya has conducted research in Dhaka and the Sundarbans region in Bangladesh at the crossroads of migration, borders, gender and intersectionality, and migrant justice.

Ikani L. Fakasiieiki is an ordained elder of the Free Wesleyan Church of Tonga, a member of Liberty Park UMC. He is a community health worker, working with homeless families through Catholic Charities of Eastern Washington. He studied at Sia'atoutai Theological College in Tonga (BD), Pacific Theological College in Suva, Fiji (MTh), and Pacific School of Religion/Graduate Theological Union (MABL). He received his PhD from the Graduate Theological Union in Berkeley, California. He taught at Sia'atoutai Theological College and lectured at Eastern Washington University in Cheney, WA and Gonzaga University in Spokane, WA. His research interests include the Hebrew Bible, postcolonial/colonial discourse analysis, Oceanic/Pacific Islander perspectives, and climate change and the Pacific.

Saumaun Heiat worked in Bangladesh for the International Organization for Migration in 2017, where he supported Rohingya refugees in Cox's Bazaar and internal migrants in the capital city Dhaka. A graduate of the Elliott School of International Affairs at George Washington University, Heiat is now a program administrator at Chemonics, working to implement sustainability projects in Syria, Iraq, Yemen, and Afghanistan.

Rebecca M. David Hensley is a student in the Iliff School of Theology/University of Denver Joint Doctoral Program in the Study of Religion and an ordained deacon in the United Methodist Church. Her primary research interests involve intersectional feminist and liberative theologies, critical race and critical whiteness studies, and faith-based community organizing. She has a background in leading churches in multi-faith and multi-race organizing, and her most recent publication is a chapter in *Preaching in/and the Borderlands*.

Memona Hossain is a mother, community-based collaborator based out of the Treaty Lands of and Territory of the Mississaugas of the Credit on Turtle Island. She is a PhD candidate in applied ecopsychology who teaches community-based courses in ecopsychology through various universities and nature reserves. She holds a master's of education from the University of Toronto. She is involved in climate change discourse as it pertains to marginalized communities. Memona has also served on the board of directors for the Muslim Association of Canada.

Jennifer S. Leath is a Queen's National Scholar and assistant professor of Black Religion at Queen's University (Kingston, Ontario). Dr. Leath's research is at the intersections of African Diaspora and religion, ethics, gender, and sexuality. Her first monograph, *Black to Quare and Then (to) Where: Theories of Justice & Black Sexual Ethics*, is forthcoming with Duke University Press.

Kristina Lizardy-Hajbi is assistant professor of leadership and formation and director of the Office of Professional Formation at the Iliff School of Theology in Denver. She is a biracial Puerto Rican-Italian and a first-generation college graduate, having earned a BA and PhD from the University of Colorado and an MDiv from the Iliff School of Theology. Kristina teaches in the areas of contextual education, leadership theory and praxis, congregational and community formation and change, and applied research methods. She is an ordained minister in the United Church of Christ and has served in undergraduate student affairs, hospital chaplaincy, youth and young adult ministry, and denominational leadership.

Kritsno Saptenno serves as an assistant researcher at the Research and Development Department of the Protestant Church in the Moluccas. He finished his bachelor of theology at the Christian University of

Indonesia in the Moluccas focusing on postcolonial studies and the New Testament. His master of theology is from Duta Wacana University with an emphasis on theology of religions. He focuses on the involvement of Indigenous religion in interreligious dialogue.

George M. Schmidt is the father of Frida Romero-Schmidt, the husband of Rev. Larissa Romero, and the son of Judy and Steve Schmidt. He was born along the banks of the Ohio River in Indiana and received his MDiv under James Cone. In 2015, he was ordained and has served as a chaplain in the prison, military, and hospice setting. He is currently working toward his PhD at Vanderbilt University under Joerg Rieger and is a graduate research fellow with the Wendland-Cook Program in Religion and Justice.

Tina Shull is an assistant professor of history at UNC Charlotte and a public historian of race, empire, immigration enforcement, and climate migration in the modern United States and world. Her forthcoming book with UNC Press, *Detention Empire*, explores the rise of migrant detention in the 1980s as a form of counterinsurgency.

Hanry Harlen Tapotubun works as a part-time lecturer-researcher at a Christian state institution in Ambon, Indonesia and is a full-time scholar of religious studies, Indigenous studies, and conflict resolution. In 2019, he finished his graduate degree from the center for religion and cross-cultural studies at Gadjah Mada University in Yogyakarta with a graduate thesis about the narrative of conflict among youth in Ambon, Indonesia. He has a paper on Christianity and racism in post-colonial Ambonese society forthcoming from the UP Asian Center in the Philippines.

tink tinker is a citizen of the Osage Nation (wazhazhe) and emeritus professor of American Indian studies at Iliff School of Theology. As an Indian academic, tinker is committed to a scholarly endeavor that takes seriously both the liberation of Indian peoples from their historic oppression as colonized communities and the liberation of eurochristian americans, the historic colonizers and oppressors of

Indian peoples, whose own history of violence has been largely suppressed. A scholar/activist, tinker has worked closely with both Four Winds American Indian Council in Denver and the American Indian Movement of Colorado. He has written several books and dozens of chapters and journal articles.

Ismetyati Natalia Tuhuteru focused on gender and justice for her bachelor of theology at the Christian University of Indonesia in the Moluccas and focused on disability and ecclesiology for her master's degree from Duta Wacana Christian University in Yogyakarta. She was a participant of World Council of Churches Eco-School in Asia Region (2019) which included eleven countries. A teacher at Moluccas Green School, she also works as an intern at the World Communion of Reformed Churches representing the Protestant Church in the Moluccas.

Vinod Wesley is currently working on his PhD at Lutheran School of Theology at Chicago (LSTC), specializing in Christian theology and ethics. He completed his STM at Union Theological Seminary, New York. He has served as faculty at the Gurukul Lutheran Theological College and Research Institute, Chennai in the department of theology and ethics. His research focuses on climate change and subaltern communities, especially Dalit communities in India.

Christine Wheatley is a sociologist and scholar of global migration. She is the executive director of New-Age Environmental Development of Africa (NED Africa). She has worked with local crews in Ghana to collect and share stories of displaced and return migrants along Ghana's coast.

Index

subaltern movement, 157–58, 163–65, 167, 169–71, 171n1, 216
Summers, Lawrence, 104

Tamil Nadu Woman's Collective (TWC), 158, 164–71
Tanuro, Daniel, 125
Tenneco Oil, 120
theological education, 28, 50, 74, 82–83, 90, 143–45, 152, 165, 170
tornado, 87–88, 92–93
transatlantic slave trade, 99, 100, 103, 106, 118
Trump, Donald, 6, 64, 76
tsunami, 66, 132, 137, 197n15, 198n17
Turtle Island, 21, 28, 107–8, 214

unemployment, 13, 32
unhoused, 15, 89, 132, 213
Union of Concerned Scientists, 201
United Nations: Climate Conference, 163; Secretary General, 32; Environment Programme, 121–22; Refugee Convention of 1951, 65; University, 105
United States: Border Control, 19, 83; borderlands, 3, 5, 19, 65, 74, 76–83, 89–91, 96, 207; Congress, 202; Democratic Party, 107; Department of Defense, 200–3; exceptionalism, 52; Fair Housing Act, 93; immigration jail, 5, 205; Jones-Shafroth Act, 61; Manifest Destiny, 67; National Forest System, 11; Puerto Rico, 3, 7, 11–12, 61–70, 214; Puerto Rico

Oversight, Management and Economic Stability Act (PROMESA), 64, 70

Vaai, Upolu, 146, 151
Vaha'a ngatae, 131, 133–38, 141–42
Varghese, Shiney, 166
Vinayaraj, Y.T, 164, 166

Warren, Calvin, 48, 52
wastewater, 33–34, 75, 104, 193
water: as commodity, 28, 30n16; conservation of, 166, 182, 184; denied, 31–33, 39, 80, 159; human relation with, 21–23, 27–28, 38, 62, 100, 161, 179, 205; increase salinity, 7–8, 10, 34, 132; industrial contamination, 23, 79, 109, 120, 123; military contamination, 31, 33–35; respect for, 27–28; rising level, 3, 7–8, 11–17, 56, 88, 91, 107, 123, 131–32, 134, 137, 147; scarcity of fresh, 24, 33–34, 68, 73, 75, 77, 79, 92, 159–60, 167, 191, 203; *see also* drought, ground water, flood, wastewater
Westphalia, 1648 peace of, 54
wetlands, 24, 123
White, Courtney, 202
white supremacy, 52, 74–75, 82, 89–90, 100–2
Wilderson III, Frank, 49
Wilson, Woodrow, 61
World Bank, 78, 104, 120–21
World Council of Churches, 145, 216
World War, *see* military conflicts